True Stories of Law & Order

TRUE STORIES OF
LAW & ORDER

The Real Crimes
Behind the Best Episodes
of the Hit TV Show

KEVIN DWYER
AND JURÉ FIORILLO

BERKLEY BOULEVARD BOOKS, NEW YORK

THE BERKLEY PUBLISHING GROUP
Published by the Penguin Group
Penguin Group (USA) Inc.
375 Hudson Street, New York, New York 10014, USA
Penguin Group (Canada), 90 Eglinton Avenue East, Suite 700, Toronto, Ontario M4P 2Y3, Canada
(a division of Pearson Penguin Canada Inc.)
Penguin Books Ltd., 80 Strand, London WC2R 0RL, England
Penguin Group Ireland, 25 St. Stephen's Green, Dublin 2, Ireland (a division of Penguin Books Ltd.)
Penguin Group (Australia), 250 Camberwell Road, Camberwell, Victoria 3124, Australia
(a division of Pearson Australia Group Pty. Ltd.)
Penguin Books India Pvt. Ltd., 11 Community Centre, Panchsheel Park, New Delhi—110 017, India
Penguin Group (NZ), Cnr. Airborne and Rosedale Roads, Albany, Auckland 1310, New Zealand
(a division of Pearson New Zealand Ltd.)
Penguin Books (South Africa) (Pty.) Ltd., 24 Sturdee Avenue, Rosebank, Johannesburg 2196,
South Africa

Penguin Books Ltd., Registered Offices: 80 Strand, London WC2R 0RL, England

This book was not authorized, prepared, approved, licensed, or endorsed by any entity involved in creating or producing the *Law & Order* television series.

While the author has made every effort to provide accurate telephone numbers and Internet addresses at the time of publication, neither the publisher nor the author assumes any responsibility for errors, or for changes that occur after publication. Further, the publisher does not have any control over and does not assume any responsibility for author or third-party websites or their content.

PRINTING HISTORY
Berkley Boulevard trade paperback edition / November 2006

Library of Congress Cataloging-in-Publication Data

Dwyer, Kevin.
    True stories of Law & order / by Kevin Dwyer & Juré Fiorillo.
        p. cm.
    ISBN 0-425-21190-8
        1. Crime—United States—Case studies. 2. Criminal investigation—United States—Case studies.
3. Trials—United States—Case studies. 4. Crime on television. 5. Law & order (Television program).
I. Fiorillo, Juré. II. Law & order (Television program). III. Title. IV. Title: True stories of Law and order.

HV6791.D98 2006
364.10973—dc22   2006045744

PRINTED IN THE UNITED STATES OF AMERICA

10 9 8 7 6 5 4 3 2 1

CONTENTS

ACKNOWLEDGMENTS

We would like to thank the following people, without whose help this book could not have been completed:

Many thanks to our intrepid photo researcher Lori Andrews, whose hard work and enthusiasm we not only appreciated but admired. We are indebted to the families of the victims who were kind and brave enough to share their stories with us. Thanks to Elizabeth Cassidy and Jim McCormack for sharing their family remembrances of Kathie McCormack; Ed Gallardo, for recounting his time on the road with Richard Adan; Jim and Ann Fowler for opening their hearts and lives to us; and Theresa Navarro for helping us gain a better understanding of her beloved brother, Jeremy Giordano.

Thanks also to photographer Steve Spak for allowing us to use his compelling photos of the Happy Land Social Club fire, and Sam Alberti for providing an insider's view of the law enforcement system. Thanks to our agent, Barry Neville; our editor, Samantha Mandor; and to Tom Donnarumma and Jeanmarie Dwyer for all their support and encouragement during the writing of this book.

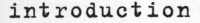

introduction

Law & Order is one of the most successful shows in television history. Millions of people watch the hour-long crime drama every week. Viewers identify with TV programs that are true to life, and no crime show does a better job of it than *Law & Order*. The writers and producers have remained loyal to the original formula—thirty minutes investigating, thirty minutes prosecuting. When it comes down to it, *Law & Order* is largely about legal and investigative procedure. Who would have thought procedure could be so dramatic?

The show's creators have remained faithful to another item: the marketing slogan "Ripped from the Headlines." Each *Law & Order* story revolves around a single theme—a legal loophole, an outrageous judgment, a creative prosecution tactic, or sometimes a perp we just love to hate. For sixteen years, the show's writers have found much of this material from the incredible facts of real-life crimes.

That's where this book comes in. After scrutinizing numerous episodes of *Law & Order* that suspiciously resemble true crimes, we've chosen to take a look at the twenty-five most compelling and varied in theme. Here you'll learn the details of famous stories—such as the

Subway Vigilante (Bernie Goetz) and the Unicorn Killer (Ira Einhorn)—and true-crime stories with which you might not be familiar, like that of Joyce Gilchrist, a forensic chemist who reportedly doctored evidence for the prosecution, and Anthony Riggs, who was welcomed home from the Gulf War by a hit man hired by his wife.

Just like the television show, *True Stories of Law & Order* reveals crimes that are so brutal they defy imagination; cases so groundbreaking they spurred new legislation; defense attorneys so sleazy you want to throttle them; and exasperating travesties of justice, as well as just deserts. We've also included sidebars throughout explaining real investigative and legal procedures, documenting where the show holds true to life and where it takes liberties.

After researching and writing about these twenty-five remarkable cases, we learned that art truly does imitate life. Or, as Detective Briscoe might say, you couldn't make this stuff up.

one

LAW & ORDER: An eccentric cross-dresser is accused of murdering three people, one of whom was his wife.

TRUE STORY: Acquitted of murdering a neighbor, transvestite billionaire Robert Durst remains a suspect in his wife's disappearance.

The security guards noticed the man right away. Not only was he acting strangely, skulking about the store, but he looked strange too. He was clearly wearing a wig and as it turned out, a fake mustache. They watched him pocket a single Band-Aid and a sandwich. Before leaving the supermarket, he also swiped a newspaper. Security guards summoned the police. The officers didn't know it yet, but the odd, haggard, seemingly homeless shoplifter with no eyebrows was actually billionaire and fugitive Robert Durst. His pockets were full, stuffed with the stolen sandwich and $500. Another $37,000 was found in the trunk of his rented car.

It was a story so bizarre, it defied belief. Wanted for the grisly murder of a cranky drifter and suspected in the mob-style execution of a Hollywood writer, the heir to one of Manhattan's most powerful families was caught shoplifting a six-dollar sandwich—chicken salad—from a Pennsylvania supermarket. He was miles away from the rundown Texas town where he'd been living incognito for the last few months, passing himself off as a mute woman. And if that wasn't enough, his beautiful blonde wife mysteriously disappeared in 1982 right after filing for divorce. Sometimes truth really is stranger than fiction.

Kathie McCormack had style and grace. She always looked like a million bucks, even when she was just scraping by. The youngest child in a close-knit middle-class Irish Catholic family, Kathie was a pretty, popular girl with hair the color of honey and a big, bright white smile. People noticed her and she liked the attention. As a teenager, Kathie was a sight to behold, tooling around Long Island in her '67 Chevy, her hair flowing through the open car window. She wasn't stuck-up, she just exuded a quiet self-confidence.

At nineteen, Kathie McCormack moved to Manhattan, renting a small apartment in one of the many buildings owned by the Durst Organization. A dental hygienist at the time, she met Robert Durst when he came around to collect the rent. The wealthy scion of the Durst family was immediately taken with the elegant blonde woman. And Kathie was smitten with Robert. Nearly a decade older than Kathie, Robert wasn't great looking, but he was dark and mysterious and well connected. He had been a regular at the legendary Studio 54 disco and he knew many celebrities. A few dates later, the couple decided to move to Vermont where they opened up a health food store. They were happy and things were going well until Seymour Durst pressured his son to return to New York and to the family business. Kathie and Robert moved back to the city. They got married and embarked on a cross-country trek for their honeymoon, taking the dog along with them. Robert was odd and had his quirks but Kathie loved him and she was both patient and accepting of his shortcomings. At first, explained Kathie's brother, Jim McCormack, "It was as though Cinderella had married Prince Charming. He had the resources to do the things she dreamed of doing."[1] Unfortunately, the happy couple didn't stay happy very long. Robert was secretive and frequently took off by himself for days at a time. Around Kathie's friends and family he was laconic to the point of being rude. Kathie realized she needed a career of her own and enrolled in medical school.

Kathie McCormack moved to New York City at the age of nineteen, where she met and married Robert Durst. Her family and friends soon noticed that the marriage was fraught with problems.
The McCormack Family

On paper, of course, Kathie's life looked fabulous—a millionaire husband, a house in Westchester, two apartments in New York City, glamorous parties, and just three months away from becoming a doctor. In reality, Kathie was in the midst of a life crisis. Her marriage was falling apart. She loved Robert but his behavior had become increasingly bizarre and he was abusive. To top it off, Durst was carrying on with Prudence Farrow, actress Mia Farrow's sister, and the inspiration for the Beatles' song "Dear Prudence." Prudence was pressuring Durst to leave his wife and was not shy about her relationship with him.

Durst, a man worth billions, was now refusing to pay for Kathie's medical school tuition. Robert was notoriously stingy and Kathie often had to borrow money from her friends just to pay for gas and tolls. She was broke and depressed. The prospect of becoming a doctor was the one thing that kept Kathie from completely falling apart. She wanted to work in the emergency room. Working in the ER was really the essence of being a doctor, she told her brother Jim. "You get to give people who are truly hurt both emotional and physical care." Kathie found the experience very rewarding.

In early January, Kathie had an occasion to visit the emergency room, not as a doctor but as a patient. Her face was bruised and she had a minor head injury. She admitted that her husband had been violent with her but refused to press charges against him. The couple began to avoid each other as much as possible, which wasn't difficult considering they owned homes on Manhattan's East and West sides, and in Westchester County. When Kathie was in the city, Bob was in the country. A social butterfly who drank and partied occasionally, Kathie began to get high to deal with her problems. She was missing classes and her grades started to plummet. She tried desperately to salvage her marriage but it was clearly too late. Friends advised her to file for divorce. Kathie knew Durst would refuse to pay her alimony, which she felt she deserved. Reluctantly, she consulted a divorce attorney.

On Sunday, January 31, 1982, Gilberte Najamy was hosting a dinner party at her home when Kathie Durst arrived unexpectedly. Najamy was startled to see her normally well-dressed friend wearing sweatpants and looking disheveled. Kathie was distressed and over the next few hours drank a considerable amount of wine. Robert Durst called around 7 p.m. After handing the phone to Kathie, Najamy could hear Robert screaming at his wife on the other end. Kathie hung up the phone and got her coat. "I have to leave," she said. "Bobby wants me home. He's really upset."[2] Najamy saw Kathie to the door. The two women made plans to meet for dinner the next day. "If anything happens to me, check out Bobby," Kathie told Najamy.[3]

When Kathie failed to show up for their dinner date on Monday, Najamy began to worry. She called Kathie but got no answer. Najamy says she had a "gut feeling" that something terrible had happened to her friend.[4] By Thursday, Najamy was convinced Kathie was dead. She went to the police.

Five days after Kathie disappeared, Robert Durst filed his own missing persons report in Manhattan. He sauntered into the police station with his dog and nonchalantly told detectives that he wanted to report his wife, Kathie, missing. He'd last seen her on Sunday. She'd arrived at their South Salem home drunk and angry, he said. The couple argued and then Durst drove her to the Katonah train station in time to catch

A family photo of Kathie and Robert during happier days. "If anything happens to me, check out Bobby," she once told a friend after a fight with her husband. She was never seen again.
The McCormack Family

Robert Durst, arrested in Pennsylvania for the theft of a chicken sandwich and a Band-Aid (pictured here under his nose). When police learned who he was, Durst was put on trial for the murder of Morris Black.
Colonial Regional Police Department

the 9:15 train to New York City. Police were not able to confirm whether Kathie ever reached Manhattan. When asked why he waited so long to report his wife missing, Durst explained that the couple often spent days apart without any communication. The detectives were struck by how blasé he was about the situation. Durst said he suspected Kathie had a boyfriend, a drug dealer who may have murdered her. He was disparaging, telling them that Kathie was a coke fiend.

Durst said he had drinks with neighbors after dropping Kathie off at the station. Later, when the neighbors denied seeing him, Durst changed his story. He said he'd stopped and had a meal at a café. He claimed to have called and spoken to Kathie in Manhattan—proof that she had indeed made it into the city. The detectives told him that they could check phone records, and Durst said he was mistaken; he hadn't

Kathie was described by everyone who knew her as sympathetic and always ready to help those in need, so it was no surprise to her family and friends that she wanted to be a doctor. She was about to graduate from medical school when she disappeared.
The McCormack Family

called Kathie from the house after all, but from a pay phone. The closest phone booth was across the lake, three miles from the Dursts' stone cottage.

Determined to find out what had happened to Kathie, Gilberte Najamy conducted her own investigation. She rode the train Kathie allegedly took the night she went missing and interviewed the passengers. "The same group of people rode that train every Sunday night," she told a reporter. "I talked to all of them. Kathie was not on that train."[5] Najamy, not content to wait for police to find Kathie, broke into the Dursts' South Salem cottage. There, she found the clothes Robert claimed Kathie was wearing when she left for the city Sunday night. She also found Kathie's unopened mail in a garbage pail.

Robert Durst offered a $100,000 reward for information about his wife's disappearance. However, he was elusive with detectives and stopped cooperating with their investigation. He also hired a criminal defense attorney. Soon after Kathie went missing, the superintendent of the couple's Riverside Drive apartment claimed he saw Durst disposing of Kathie's belongings. Rumor had it that Durst was already looking to sublet the apartment.

The Durst family had money and power and if they had asked for help in finding Kathie, the city would have responded pronto. Mayor Koch had even called Seymour Durst to offer his help. His offer was declined. Robert Durst was more reticent than ever, and the McCormack family was left in the dark. Kathie's powerful in-laws hadn't bothered to contact them at all. Jim McCormack, who had assumed the role of patriarch after Kathie's father died, was beside himself. Finally, out of desperation, he arranged a meeting with Seymour Durst. They wanted his help, answers, anything. Seymour was cold, officious, and offered nothing; no help, no guidance, not even a glass of water. Seymour's son Tom Durst arrived home and kicked Kathie's family out. "Meeting's over, you'll have to leave," he said rudely. "Wait a second," Jim said. "We're talking to your father. We need his help!" Tom was unmoved. "I said the meeting is over," he told the McCormacks before unceremoniously ushering them out of the posh apartment.[6]

Robert Durst cut off all contact with Kathie's family. His longtime confidante Susan Berman acted as his spokesperson, fielding questions from the press and trying her best to deflect attention away from Robert. Berman, the daughter of mobster Davie Berman, who had been an associate of Bugsy Seigel and Meyer Lansky, did her job well. Despite efforts by her friends and family, Kathie's disappearance remained a mystery. "We are convinced that Kathie didn't just walk away. We believe that [Durst] had something to do with her disappearance," Jim McCormack said.[7] If Robert Durst knew where Kathie was, he certainly wasn't talking.

In 2000, police received a tip that led them to reopen the investigation into Kathie Durst's disappearance. A Westchester man arrested for exposing himself wanted to barter with the DA—leniency in exchange for information he claimed to have about Kathie Durst. He told police that he had heard from friends that Kathie was dead and buried in Westchester County. The flasher's tips didn't pan out but they did reenergize the search for Kathie. "Over the last few months, there have been a few developments that I am not at liberty to disclose," Westchester District Attorney Jeanine Pirro said.[8]

Detectives began contacting the key players in the case. On the eve of her scheduled interview with police, Susan Berman was murdered in her Hollywood home, shot in the back of the head. As of this writing,

Kathie and Robert Durst's stone cottage in South Salem. Investigators believe this is where Kathie was murdered. Shortly after she went missing, Robert had the kichen floor ripped up and replaced. *The McCormack Family*

Berman's murder remains unsolved. Some speculate that Berman, who was down on her luck, had been blackmailing her friend Robert Durst. Berman had reportedly confided to a friend that she had information about Kathie's disappearance. Shortly before her death, she received $50,000 from him, much more than the $7,000 she had asked to borrow.

Unbeknownst to the McCormacks, Robert Durst had divorced Kathie in 1990 and married Debrah Lee Charantan, a wealthy Realtor whom he had been secretly dating for ten years, in 2001. Durst severed ties with his own family after his youngest brother was appointed head of the Durst Organization. He kept a low profile and seemed to have fallen off the radar. In reality, he was living in Galveston, Texas. Durst had lavish homes around the country but for reasons known only to him, he took up residence in a $300-a-month apartment in a neighborhood populated by drifters and people down on their luck. He dressed in drag and lived as Dorothy Ciner, a mute and rather homely woman. Ciner had a frequent visitor, a man who introduced himself to people as

Robert Durst. In fact, it was Durst who had rented the apartment for "Ciner." Tenants thought it odd that they never saw Dorothy and Robert at the same time.

A man named Morris Black lived across the hall from Robert Durst/Dorothy Ciner. A former seaman, the seventy-one-year-old Black was cantankerous and prone to fly off the handle. Black and Durst became friends and they often got together to watch television and get drunk. It's unclear whether Black knew that Ciner and Durst were one and the same. At some point, the two men had a falling-out. Later, in court Durst claimed that he returned home one day to find Black in his apartment, armed with a gun. They struggled and the gun went off, accidentally shooting Black in the head. Fearing no one would believe his account of the crime, Durst dismembered Black's body and disposed of the parts in the bay.

A few days later, a human torso was found floating in Galveston Bay. The torso had been stuffed into a trash bag. Matching bags found ashore nearby contained more grisly surprises. The body, or rather, what was left of it, was identified as Morris Black. His head was nowhere in sight.

Robert Durst was arrested after police found a receipt bearing his name in one of the trash bags. Furthermore, a neighbor had witnessed Durst loading trash bags into the trunk of his car—the night he and Morris fought.

Durst was charged with Black's murder. Not realizing that the suspect was filthy rich, the judge set bail at $300,000, which Durst quickly raised. "We arrested a haggard-looking man who drove an old car and lived in a $300-a-month apartment with no telephone. He didn't look or act anything like a millionaire," Galveston police lieutenant Mike Putnal said.[9] Durst jumped bail and fled the jurisdiction. For six weeks, he was a fugitive, moving constantly and using aliases to avoid detection. He managed to elude police until he was caught shoplifting at a Wegman's supermarket in Bethlehem, Pennsylvania. In the end, the elusive fugitive was done in by a chicken salad sandwich. Durst had $500 on him. Another $37,000 in cash was found in the trunk of his rented car alongside a handgun, some marijuana, and Morris Black's driver's license.

Robert Durst was tried in Texas for the murder of Morris Black. He pleaded not guilty by reason of self-defense or accident. High-powered attorney Dick Guerin headed up Durst's legal team. The defense contended that Black had attacked Durst and that his death had been an unfortunate accident. Durst took the stand and told jurors that Black had entered his apartment while he was out. He said he came home to find his neighbor watching TV and holding the gun Durst kept hidden in a kitchen cabinet. They fought and then Black began waving the gun at him, he claimed. "I was concerned that Morris was going to shoot the gun, most likely at my face," he said. According to Durst, Black "died struggling for the gun," in a tragic accident. Afterward, in a panic, Durst said he cut up Black's body. "I did not kill my best friend," he said. "I did dismember him."

The prosecution argued that Durst had ambushed Black from behind, shooting him in the head. But, since Black's head had not been recovered, the prosecution was unable to disprove Durst's version of the event. In a risky move, the prosecution had decided to charge Durst only with murder. The jury was not given the option to convict the defendant on lesser included charges, such as manslaughter in the first or second degrees. It was all or nothing. The gamble paid off—for the defense. Robert Durst was acquitted of Morris Black's murder. "After three days of poring through all of the physical evidence, including testimony from witnesses, there was nothing to support the prosecution's claim that it was not self-defense," juror Chris Lovell told Court TV.[10] Kathie McCormack's friends and family were shocked and dismayed by the not-guilty verdict. Even Durst seemed to be stunned by the jury's decision.

Durst beat the murder rap but he wasn't in the clear. Prosecutors charged him with bail jumping and evidence tampering, both felonies. He pleaded guilty and served five months in prison before being released on parole. Five months later, Durst was back in jail for violating his parole. To this day, Westchester DA Jeanine Pirro is anxious to speak with him about his first wife's disappearance but Durst remains tight-lipped. Pirro vows to "get to the bottom of what happened to Kathie Durst, one way or another."[11]

Kathleen McCormack has never been found. She was declared legally dead in 2001. The McCormacks have long since come to terms with the fact that Kathie is most likely dead. Still, they long for closure, and a proper burial. Jim McCormack still remembers the first time he held his baby sister. Kathie was just days old and so full of life and promise. He remains in close contact with the detectives investigating her disappearance and works with the press to keep Kathie from being forgotten. "It's like leaving the porch light on," he said of his ongoing efforts. "I'm hoping Kathie will see the light and know that we haven't stopped searching for her."

two

LAW & ORDER: The wife of a war veteran hires a hit man to kill her husband.

TRUE STORY: Weeks after returning from combat duty in the Gulf War, Anthony Riggs was killed in a life-insurance scheme hatched by his wife and brother-in-law.

In early March 1991, American troops were mopping up after their outrageously successful drubbing of the Iraq military and looking forward to their victory parade in the States. Saddam Hussein, the Butcher of Baghdad, had rolled over Kuwait, his tiny and powerless neighbor to the south, about seven months before. In response, the United States built an international coalition, mobilized record numbers of troops and weapons in record time, and ran the Iraqi army out of Kuwait, slaughtering hundreds of thousands of them, including the much-vaunted Republican Guard, in mere weeks. A peace treaty was signed, Hussein promised to behave, and the troops started boarding planes home.

Within a couple of weeks, some U.S. newspapers were covering Hussein's merciless suppression of Kurdish rebels who, hoping in vain for American support, had risen against him in Northern Iraq. But, by and large, the American press was off the war and on to other matters—legislative battles in Congress, school lunch programs, Hollywood gossip. The hottest story of the day was the LAPD's videotaped beating of a black man named Rodney King, viewed by every American who wasn't blind, brain-dead, or living on the moon.

A few front pages contained small pieces about a Gulf War veteran, home on leave, who had been murdered on a street in northeast Detroit. Anthony Riggs had been outside the home of a relative when, suddenly, everyone inside the house heard gunshots. They ran out to find the war veteran dead on the street, apparently shot by someone stealing his 1989 Nissan Sentra.

But there was more to the story. Way more.

Specialist Anthony Riggs had manned a Patriot missile battery in Iraq and saw plenty of action. He hated the Middle East and wanted nothing more than to come home, even though his marriage was on the outs; while he was serving overseas, his wife, Toni Cato-Riggs, he learned, had emptied the savings account, crashed the car, and contracted VD—a trifecta guaranteed to strain any marriage. Bad as things were between the couple, Riggs was probably still surprised at his "homecoming." Toni and her nineteen-year-old brother, Michael Cato, greeted Anthony on the tarmac at his base in Texas with a hello and three requests: Toni wanted a divorce, the Sentra, and alimony. Some homecoming.

Determined to salvage the marriage, Riggs convinced his wife to give it another shot. He traveled with Toni and Michael to Detroit, where Toni had been living at her aunt's house. There they would retrieve Toni's belongings and move into an apartment together in Warren, Michigan, about twenty minutes away from Toni's family home.

At about 2:00 a.m. on March 18, Anthony was packing up a moving van in front of the Cato residence. The morning was misty with rain, and Toni stayed inside. As Toni went to turn the outside lights on for Anthony, she heard five gunshots. She and her relatives ran out of the house screaming. Anthony was lying in the street, shot point-blank in the back of the head. "He was gasping for air. Then he coughed a couple times and that was it," said a neighbor who had also come outside after hearing the shots and screeching tires.[1]

In grim irony, one of Anthony's letters from Saudie Arabia arrived in the States hours after he died. "There's no way I'm going to die in this rotten country," Riggs had written to his family. "With the Lord's grace and his guidance, I'll walk American soil once again."

Anthony would be missed by everyone. In an interview with the *Detroit Free-Press* Toni's aunt, Marjorie Cato, recalled his great sense of humor. The day before he was killed, she said, he had made her laugh so hard her side hurt. And when he was in the Gulf, he had sent a care package of strangely shaped Arabic chocolate bars for everyone in the family; she still had hers stored in the freezer. In the same article, a member of Anthony's Army unit said that Anthony had wanted nothing more than to come home and see his wife and stepdaughter.* A family man to the core, he constantly looked at the pictures he kept of them in his wallet and locker.[2]

Detroit in the early nineties wasn't exactly Shangri-la. Known for its crack dens and street shootings, it was among the most violent cities in America. But for Riggs, it beat war any day. "I just got back from where they were firing missiles at my head. Those bullets aren't really going to frighten me now," the twenty-two-year-old told his mother, Lessie Riggs. Numerically speaking, though, Detroit was more dangerous than the battlefields of Kuwait, especially for a young black male such as Riggs. According to a study conducted by the Heritage Foundation, a fifteen-year-old black male in Detroit stood a 7.2 percent chance of being murdered before the age of forty-five—the third highest rate in the nation.[3] Though it's not a valid *direct* comparison, the less than one-tenth of one percent combat casualty rate of the Gulf War shows that the inner city of Detroit was extraordinarily dangerous.

The irony of a soldier surviving war only to be murdered for his car two weeks after coming home wasn't lost on the press. The murder

---

*Toni Cato had entered into the marriage with a daughter, Ambere; it turned out that Toni was never officially divorced from her previous husband, technically rendering her marriage to Anthony invalid.

quickly became a cause célèbre for activists. The streets were filled with drug dealers and killers, they said. Why fight a war overseas when a generation of black youths was being gunned down at random in its own neighborhood? The real war was *here*, not in the Middle East. Jesse Jackson was among the notables to attend Anthony Riggs's funeral, where Toni Cato, dressed in black and crying, said good-bye to her husband with a kiss to his cheek before he was lowered into the ground.

Though concerns about America's inner cities were valid—random violence was indeed cause for alarm—Detroit detectives weren't assuming anything; they quietly went about their business of investigating the Riggs murder, following clues wherever they led. Police soon located the car and found a gun in the garbage near the murder scene. Then they learned about the Riggs's rocky marriage and Anthony's "substantial" life insurance policy. The dots were being discovered and connected simultaneously. Police weren't dealing with criminal masterminds here. A friend of Anthony Riggs, Sgt. Gary Welliver, told newspapers that once he and other friends of Riggs heard about the murder, their antennas went up. "There was a lot of speculation about it," Welliver said. "For anyone who knew what was actually going on with them, the speculation ran even deeper."[4]

"He was set up," said another. They all knew Toni's story, and they didn't like her or trust her. She had once considered joining the army with her husband, but couldn't pass the physical. Then she moved in with Anthony's mother in Las Vegas and did nothing but sit around, eat, watch TV, and talk about the expensive clothes and cars she thought she was entitled to.[5]

Police picked up Michael Cato, and he sang like a bird. Twice he confessed to pulling the trigger, and in one confession he told police that his sister masterminded the whole operation. On March 26, the scheming siblings were charged with first-degree murder. Michael's attorney James O'Connell told the court that his client talked only after thirteen straight hours of questioning; the confession had clearly been coerced and should be dropped. "My guess is after thirteen hours, he would have implicated Abraham Lincoln," O'Connell said, adding that police didn't allow Michael access to a telephone or lawyer.[6] Judge Vesta Svenson didn't agree, and the nineteen-year-old Michael was sent to jail without bond.

Toni, however, was another story. The judge ruled that Michael's confession couldn't be used against his sister. With little else to connect Toni to her husband's slaying, the prosecution had to set her free. Toni gave her brother a hug before she left the courtroom, and began planning her new life: that of a widow with $175,000 in her pocket—life insurance money Anthony had purchased for her in case the worst happened in Kuwait. Toni Cato was single, rich, and off the hook, but, as subsequent events would prove, not a whit smarter.

Michael Cato languished in jail until the following fall, when he stood trial for first-degree murder. Building their case that the Riggs killing was a murder for hire, prosecutors focused largely on Toni and Anthony's marital problems. It took the jury just over three hours to decide on a guilty verdict. Michael was put away for life.

But everyone involved knew that the story was only half over. Police still had their sights set on Toni, and made no bones about it. Prosecutors and cops publicly stated that eventually they would gather enough evidence to ensure that *both* Catos would spend their lives behind bars.

One would guess that Toni would maintain a low profile, given the amount of publicity focused on her; and one would *certainly* think she'd go out of her way to keep her nose clean, at least until the heat died down. But Toni had ants in her pants. Her behavior thus far was that of a woman completely devoid of patience—and a close call with the law wasn't about to change that. Plus, she desperately needed more cash. As it turned out, her brother wasn't the only person involved in murdering her husband. Supposedly, a third party involved in the deed was now blackmailing her: "Pay up, or I squawk." Further, she had blown a good chunk of the insurance money on defense lawyers. So Toni Cato decided to establish herself in the Detroit drug trade—taking one step closer to that sticky web she started weaving in March 1991.

· · ·

In February 1993, undercover operatives of the U.S. Drug Enforcement Agency (DEA) posing as high-level drug dealers sat down with a woman arguing her case that she was an ideal candidate to smuggle drugs over the borders from South America. She offered a plan: she would fill up balloons with narcotics, swallow them, and hop a flight to the United States. Simple as that. The agents heard her out. They were in the middle of a major sting, hitting the big drug-trafficking spots across the entire country.[7]

The woman in the "job interview" was, of course, Toni Cato, and the agents were more than happy to sit and listen to her pour her criminal intentions out on their laps. The best part was that they never sought her out; she had come to *them*! It would actually be funny if the circumstances weren't so tragic.

Toni Cato had unwittingly entered the DEA's snare through a colleague named Rosita de la Paz, who was attempting to traffic large quantities of cocaine from Texas to Detroit. When de la Paz was caught with over twenty pounds of the drug in her car trunk in April 1992, she complained to police that she wasn't supposed to have been the one moving the coke; it was that damn Toni Cato who should have been doing it, but she had backed out at the last minute to take a final exam for a class she had enrolled in.[8] Toni Cato? *The* Toni Cato?! Yup. The agents immediately contacted Detroit homicide and went to work.

The DEA agents met with Cato periodically over the next few months—armed with wires and hidden video cameras. It was a turkey shoot; Cato blabbed one incriminating tale after another—all beautifully captured on tape.

First, she told the agents all about how she masterminded her husband's murder so she could cash in on the insurance money. Perhaps she was trying to prove she had the guts to play with the big boys, or perhaps she was just plain bragging—but she revealed every bloody detail, on multiple occasions. One day her brother had approached her with an offer to kill Anthony and collect on the insurance. "I need some money. You need some money. We can both help each other out," said Michael, according to Toni. She informed him that if he were serious, there was no getting cold feet. "He ain't my husband, so it's no matter to me," her brother reportedly responded.[9]

Toni Cato-Riggs, arrested after unwittingly informing undercover agents about how she masterminded the murder of her husband, Gulf War veteran Anthony Riggs. *Detroit Police Department*

"So I was like, fine, whatever," Toni said. Her demeanor was a far cry from the sobbing wife she portrayed at her husband's funeral; she often laughed as she told the details.[10]

In another meeting, she talked about the blackmail situation. A friend of her brother named Antonio Shelby had given Michael the gun used to kill Anthony Riggs, she said. Now he was threatening to rat her out if she didn't pay up.*

In one more incredible misstep, Toni tried to pay the agents to kill Shelby. She said that this bone in her throat wouldn't go away. The agents asked her what she wanted. "Him eliminated—period," she was captured on video saying. "No coming back. No nothing."[11]

Toni Cato was arrested in November of 1993 on drug charges; she was later arrested for the murder of her husband, after which she provided a confession ten pages long. The confession, though, couldn't be used against her. Although the police sergeant to whom she confessed

---

*Shelby had been an important witness for the prosecution in the Michael Cato trial. He testified that he had supplied Michael with the murder weapon, but convincingly argued that he had had no idea what it would be used for.

testified that he informed Cato of her Miranda rights, and that she signed or initialed her confession in twenty-five places, the judge sided with Cato, who claimed she had been denied counsel. Yet *another* confession that couldn't be used against her.

However, the tapes would be admitted because they were made during an unrelated investigation—and they were more than enough for the prosecution. Toni Cato would face four charges: first-degree murder, conspiracy to commit murder, solicitation to commit murder, and use of a firearm while committing a felony.

The trial began in May 1994. Lessie Riggs, Anthony's mother, was the first to testify. She read a letter Anthony had sent from the Middle East, expressing his desire to work things out with Toni. "I want our marriage to last. I would put my neck through a hot-sauce bottle to please her," Anthony wrote. Lessie fought back tears while she read, and cried when she finished.

Various other witnesses helped finger Toni, including the insurance agent who sold the couple the life insurance policy. When he met with them, he said, Toni wanted a much higher policy than Anthony thought she needed. Antonio Shelby also testified. But the audio- and videotapes were the clincher. There she was, telling the world about her cold-blooded crimes right on the TV screen.

LUDs

Hardly a *Law & Order* episode goes by without detectives pulling someone's LUDs, which more often than not lead to a breakthrough in the investigation. The acronym stands for "local usage details," which is a list of a person's incoming and outgoing phone calls over a specified period of time. While LUDs are relatively easy to obtain for police, they're not readily available at a cop's whim. Phone records are treated as private information, so investigators must prove to a judge that the "search" is warranted, in which case, the judge will grant a court order for the phone company to provide a suspect's LUDs.

Her defense consisted of various motions to suppress evidence; claims that she was the target of a police conspiracy (her attorney repeatedly called head investigator Sgt. William Rice "Slick Willie"); suggestions of doctored evidence and intimidation by the DEA agents; and arguments of entrapment—a claim that outraged even the judge.

The attempt to cast even the slightest doubt about Toni Cato's guilt failed miserably. The jury only took three and a half hours to decide on a guilty verdict. The convict was cuffed and led out of the courtroom to begin her sentence of life without parole. "We were all very conclusive," the forewoman said. "There was nothing to explain."[12]

Cato's lawyer wasn't even mildly taken aback by the verdict. "I'm surprised the jury stayed out that long," she said.[13]

three

LAW & ORDER: A well-meaning but misguided priest comes to the aid of a poor college student accused of murdering his wealthy girlfriend.

TRUE STORY: Bonnie Garland, a student at Yale University, was murdered in her Scarsdale home by fellow student and ex-boyfriend Richard Herrin; the Catholic church spoke out in Herrin's defense.

The temperature hovered in the low eighties but the weather report was predicting rain. It was July 6, 1977, and New York City had already recuperated from the party it held for Independence Day. Just two days earlier, one hundred ships and sailboats had gathered in the East River to participate in the Harbor Festival. A spectacular fireworks display lit up the skyline, delighting old and young alike. The scent of gunpowder and charred paper had lingered in the air for hours afterward. Now, the scent, like the colorful sails that had populated the harbor, was gone. No matter. Neither Bonnie Garland nor Richard Herrin felt much like celebrating as they made the half-hour trip back to Scarsdale.

Bonnie had just registered for the summer session at Columbia University; classes were scheduled to begin in less than a week. Richard was glum. With Bonnie taking classes—and surely meeting new people at Columbia—she would have no time for him.

Of course, she had already made it clear that she wanted to break up. Richard was trying his hardest to change her mind. Bonnie was only twenty and longed to be free. Richard, twenty-three, had other plans. He wanted to get married.

They had spent the previous two months apart; he attended graduate school in Texas, she toured Europe with the Yale Glee Club. Bonnie had fallen out of love with Richard. During their time apart, she'd been able to evaluate her life, reorder her priorities. She wanted to end their relationship. Bonnie returned from Europe in high spirits. She had a slight cold, and a new love interest. Hoping to change her mind, Richard flew to New York, showing up at her parents' house, unannounced and uninvited. In Scarsdale, Richard learned that Bonnie was out sailing with her father and her new beau. Joan Garland, Bonnie's mother, felt sorry for Richard. She served him lunch and sent him on his way. The next day, he returned. Bonnie had persuaded Joan to let Richard stay at the house. She was worried about him and wanted to make the breakup as painless as possible. Joan agreed but insisted that Richard leave in two days.

Richard had come to Scarsdale determined to win his girlfriend back. Yet, after one day together, it was clear he was losing the battle. Bonnie was resolute, gently but firmly telling him she no longer wanted to be in a serious relationship with him. They spent hours discussing their relationship—hours filled with explanations, bitter recriminations, apologies, tears, and hope. It had been an emotional day—an emotional year, really. Bonnie was exhausted; by 10 p.m. she could barely keep her eyes open. She undressed and slipped into bed. Richard was too wired to sleep. He sat on a couch in her room flipping through the pages of a *Sports Illustrated* magazine.

Bonnie's family was asleep; the house was so very quiet. His childhood home had never been so quiet. At night, the Los Angeles barrio where his mother still lived came alive, and not in a good way. There was always something going on outside—shouting, laughing, music blaring from cars and boom boxes, an occasional gunshot in the distance. Here, in Scarsdale, it was peaceful. No noises now except for the faint rustling of the pages beneath his fingers, and the sound of Bonnie's breathing, a soft, even sound with a slight rasp to it, a remnant of the cold she caught in Europe.

Richard watched her as she slept, her face turned toward the wall, her beautiful red hair splayed across the pillowcase. He decided to kill her.

. . .

Born to affluent, well-educated parents, Bonnie Garland was encouraged to shine from an early age. She was a smart, sunny girl with brilliant red hair and a beautiful singing voice. Her father, Paul, was a successful attorney; her mother, Joan, had a master's degree in human genetics and was pursuing a second degree in social work at Columbia University. When Bonnie was a child, the family lived in Brazil, where Paul opened a successful law firm. The Garlands returned to the States in time for a teenaged Bonnie to attend the exclusive Madeira School in Virginia. By then, Bonnie had two brothers and a younger sister. The family moved into a stately, handsome, Tudor-style home in New York's Westchester County.

Paul Garland was thrilled when his eldest daughter decided to attend Yale University, his alma mater. A gifted soprano, Bonnie majored in music and joined the glee club. For a time, it seemed that fortune had favored Bonnie Garland. All that was about to change. Bonnie didn't know it yet but her luck and her life were about to run out.

Richard Herrin was born in a Los Angeles barrio to a Mexican mother and an Irish father. From the start, life was less than idyllic for the dark-haired little boy. His parents had never married and when Richard was three, his father abandoned the family. The boy's mother struggled to make ends meet. Money was tight and dinner often consisted of little more than rice and beans. Despite his home life, young Richard grew up to be, in the words of his high school principal Peter Martinez, "the kind of son everybody would like to have."[1]

A good-looking young man, Richard was a devout Catholic who attended Mass often and worked at his stepfather's store. He managed to stay out of trouble—not an easy feat in his neighborhood. With a strong work ethic and an IQ of 150—above average—Richard excelled academically. In high school he played football and baseball and was valedictorian of his class of 415. His stellar high school record caught the attention of Yale University. Looking to recruit more minority students, Yale offered Richard a full scholarship. It was a sweet deal. Richard moved east, leaving the barrio behind for the Ivy League.

Bonnie Garland was seventeen, a new freshman on the Yale campus, when she met Richard Herrin in the fall of 1974. He was twenty, a senior, who had never fully adjusted to college life. The poor-boy-made-good from the barrio had been left to fend for himself socially at Yale. Although he made friends, including members of the Catholic Club, he had difficulty fitting in at the vaunted school. Bonnie was a rich girl who didn't make him feel like a poor boy. Money didn't matter to her and she didn't judge him. Their backgrounds were so very different but the two clicked right away. Soon they were spending all their time together. They were in love.

Richard was Bonnie's first boyfriend, and she his first serious girlfriend. In the beginning, the couple was ecstatic. But the happy, carefree honeymoon phase was short-lived. Theirs was a toxic love—passionate and destructive. Rather than inspire each other, they seemed to sap the life from each other. It wasn't long before the couple was cutting classes to spend days together sleeping, watching television, and eating junk food. Bonnie's weight ballooned as her grades plummeted. They made plans for a future together, all the while sabotaging the present. Richard barely graduated, taking summer classes in order to complete his degree.

Sullen and sulky, Richard often sat silent when he and Bonnie were with her friends and family. Paul and Joan Garland didn't care for Richard and he made little effort to endear himself to his girlfriend's parents. The Garlands believed he was a negative influence on their daughter; since meeting Herrin, Bonnie had changed dramatically. The once sunny, joyful young woman had become moody, distracted, and uninspired. She was also flunking out of Yale. The Garlands were relieved when the young lovers parted during the summer of 1977. Richard was off to graduate school and Bonnie left for an extended tour of Europe with the Yale Glee Club. Her parents hoped the separation would help Bonnie come to her senses.

For Bonnie, the trip was liberating. With her boyfriend across the ocean, she felt free to be her own person—just Bonnie, not Richard's Bonnie. Yes, he was crazy about her, but Richard was also controlling, demanding. Sometimes Bonnie felt as if she were suffocating. At home, he called constantly and wanted her to check in with him, update him with her schedule. After dating sporadically for two and a half years, Bonnie wanted to end the relationship for good but lacked the courage to tell Richard. She also worried that a breakup would distract him from finishing his thesis, so she put off the inevitable. She still loved him, she just wasn't *in love* with him. And there was someone else, a fellow member of the glee club with whom she had become infatuated.

In Texas, Richard was floundering, skipping classes and neglecting his thesis. Lonely and depressed, he spent whole days obsessing over Bonnie and writing her letters that went unanswered. He had not heard from her in weeks. It didn't make sense. The couple hadn't broken up—in fact, earlier that day they had talked about getting married as soon as Bonnie graduated. The last time she toured with the glee club, Bonnie sent him a letter nearly every day. Alone in his spartan apartment, Richard spent hours staring out the window trying to solve what had become an increasingly painful mystery. He wrote her again and again. Still no reply. Richard lay awake at night wondering what had happened, his mind searching for the reason behind Bonnie's silence. *She was sick and unable to write . . . her letters had gotten lost in the mail . . . she had amnesia.* After a while, reason gave way to fantasy—dark, violent fantasies that always ended in death.

And then, at last, a letter from Bonnie!

Dear Rick,

I know this has been an unforgivable crime not to have written you all this time, but I have been trying to postpone action on something very important which has come up. . . . I have spent almost all my time on this tour in the company of one specific man, someone I saw off and on during the semester. To make things short, he has fallen in love with me. I am in a state of total confusion, because I know I still love you as much, but I feel an infatuation at least with him. I did not want to tell you, because I thought it would all be over when the tour ended. But now I am not so sure. It makes me sick to write this letter, I couldn't lie and I didn't want to tell the truth. So I just haven't written. You remember those conversations we have had about being constrained and feeling like I hadn't had a social life—well in a way, I think that the elastic finally broke into this. . . . I hate this letter and this mess, but please be patient and I'm sure things will work out because I still love you and I need your love as much as ever—please don't desert me. I'll be back soon, and we can talk. I've missed you a great deal.

Love, Bonnie[2]

Richard didn't know what to think. He left Texas for New York, intent on winning Bonnie back, "reclaiming" her. Two days had passed without much success.

The stairs creaked ever so slightly as he made his way down to the first floor. Barefoot and shirtless, Richard moved through the darkened house, looking for a weapon. He found one in the basement—a claw hammer. He wrapped it in a towel and carried it back up the stairs to Bonnie's bedroom. There, he struck his sleeping girlfriend in the head with the claw hammer. He struck her again and again until, as he would later explain, "Her head split open like a watermelon."

While Bonnie lay dying, Richard fled the house in the Garland's Impala, driving until the car ran out of gas in Coxsackie. He thought about committing suicide but decided against it. Instead, he took a short nap. Then, he went to church. Father Petraglia had just unlocked the door when the stranger entered, shirtless, shoeless, and covered in blood. The priest was startled by the young man's appearance, more so by what he said: "I just killed my girlfriend."

Persuaded by Father Petraglia, Richard turned himself in to the

Coxsackie Police Department. He was calm, and seemed almost relaxed as he gave them a full confession. "Knowing I couldn't have her exclusively, knowing I didn't want to live without her, I entertained the thought of killing her while she slept," he told police.

"I took the hammer and struck her on the head at least three times. I may have struck her in the chest, may have tried strangling her but I was too weak."

The police phoned their counterparts in Scarsdale who immediately drove out to the Garland's house. Joan Garland awoke to find detectives at her door asking about Bonnie's whereabouts. Confused, Joan raced upstairs to find her oldest daughter covered in blood on the floor, gasping for air.

Bonnie's larynx was crushed and her brain was bleeding. She was taken to the hospital where surgeons worked frantically to save her life. It was too late. She died at 10:38 p.m. that evening.

The brutal murder of twenty-year-old Bonnie Garland shocked the community at Yale. However, it was the events that followed that left many shaking their heads in disbelief. There was no doubt as to who killed Bonnie; Richard had given a full confession to the police. Yet many Yalies rallied around Richard. While Bonnie was being laid to rest, a group led by the clergy of Yale's Thomas More Catholic Church launched a campaign to get her killer released on bail. "We were involved in being *horrified* with him, not *judging* him," explained Sister Ramona Pena, one of Richard's staunchest defenders. There was nothing they could do for Bonnie, she said. "The girl is dead."[3] This attitude was shared by the rest of Richard's fans who, in a letter to the judge requesting bail, explained, "While we are left only to mourn Bonnie's tragic death, it is important that having lost one life, we do what we can to salvage another."[4]

The judge was impressed by the outpouring of support for Richard and the credentials of those championing his cause. Thirty-five days after bludgeoning his college sweetheart to death, Richard was free. Released into the care of the Christian Brothers in Albany, he attended classes at the State University of New York at Albany under an assumed name and was free to come and go as he wished.

The Garlands were aghast. Fellow Catholics—Paul had even been an altar boy—they felt that the sympathy was misplaced. As grieving family members, they believed that the church should have been intent on comforting them, not getting their daughter's killer released on bail. The family viewed the tremendous outpouring of support for Richard as "the second assault."[5]

In the spring of 1978, Richard Herrin stood trial for the murder of Bonnie Garland. Represented by Jack Litman, he pleaded not guilty by reason of temporary insanity. The defense conceded that Richard killed Bonnie, but argued that he had been under the influence of extreme emotional disturbance at the time—an important distinction. Under New York law "homicide committed under the influence of extreme emotional disturbance constitutes a mitigating circumstance reducing the charge of murder to manslaughter in the first degree." A plea of temporary insanity is a way for the defense to hedge its bets. The ultimate goal is an acquittal, of course, but barring that, the plea allows the jury to convict the defendant of manslaughter rather than murder, which carries a much heavier prison term.

Confident that he'd get a murder conviction, prosecutor William Fredreck rejected the defense's request for a plea bargain. With solid forensic evidence and the defendant's confession, Fredreck believed he had a slam-dunk case. Jack Litman was unfazed by the mountain of evidence against his client. A brilliant lawyer with an impressive record, Litman understood that emotions can be just as convincing as facts in a jury trial. He worked hard to make Richard appear sympathetic to the jury. If that meant tarnishing Bonnie's image, so be it.

The defense attorney painted Richard as a poor, soulful, guileless Mexican boy who had his heart broken by a globe-trotting, spoiled rich girl. The insinuation was that the victim was partly to blame for her own death. Though distasteful and highly controversial, Litman's methods were effective. He would employ this same "blame the victim" strategy a decade later in his representation of "Preppie Killer" Robert Chambers (see chapter 12). Litman told the jury that Bonnie was sleeping around, a remark the judge ordered stricken from the record. The jury, however, was not apt to forget such a salacious detail.

The trial lasted twelve days and featured testimony from twenty-nine witnesses, a half dozen of whom were psychiatrists called to offer expert opinions on the defendant's sanity—or lack thereof. The prosecution's experts declared Richard sane and devoid of mental defect. Not suprisingly, the defense's hired guns disagreed with this assessment. Instead, they described Richard as a "borderline personality" who had deep-rooted abandonment issues stemming from childhood. Bonnie, one defense expert testified, was Richard's "link to people and reality." When she broke up with him, Richard lost his bearings—and his sanity. Richard *had* to be insane at the time of the murder, Litman insisted. How else to explain how "a highly moral, gentle, religious, sensitive young man performs an act that is so totally foreign to his character, to the way he has acted for the first twenty-three years of his life?"

Prosecutor Fredreck was unimpressed. "The defendant had the oldest motive in the world: jealousy," he told the jury. "This insanity plea is an insult to your intelligence. He's suffering from instant insanity, the chief ingredient of which is fear of conviction. This is a concoction to avoid responsibility and punishment for a planned, cold, calculated killing of a young girl in her sleep." A conviction for manslaughter would be a "cop-out," Fredreck said.

After four days of deliberations, the jury reached a unanimous verdict. Believing that Richard had, in fact, been suffering from "extreme emotional disturbance" at the time of the murder, they found him guilty of first-degree manslaughter. The deliberation process had been difficult and stressful and the jurors agonized over their decision. They deeply resented the prosecutor's "cop-out" remark.

At sentencing, Richard made a plea for leniency, telling the judge, "Bonnie Garland meant everything to me. She was my whole life. I wish to dedicate my life to serving others in Bonnie's memory. I am truly sorry for the suffering and the grief the Garlands had to go through."

The judge was not easily swayed by sentiment. "To hammer Bonnie Garland to death while she lay sleeping in bed was a needless, heartless, cruel, and brutal act. I'm convinced that the only just sentence is the maximum possible allowed under state law," he said, before sending Richard away for 8⅓ to 25 years.

Bonnie's family felt he had gotten off easy; had he been convicted of murder, Richard would have received a life sentence. With good behavior, it was possible he would be released in less than ten years. "If you have a thirty-thousand-dollar defense fund, a Yale connection, and a clergy connection, you are entitled to one free hammer murder," an understandably bitter Joan Garland told reporters.

Richard, on the other hand, didn't view his sentence as lenient. Less than two years into his incarceration, he told reporter Peter Meyer, "In my own view, I think I have served enough time to compensate . . . I am not going to punish myself for what happened. I am not going to live my life to repay all of society for Bonnie's loss. I have suffered enough because of it, and I have felt the loss perhaps more than anyone else."

The parole board disagreed and denied his requests for early release. Richard Herrin was paroled in 1995, after serving eighteen years in prison.

four

LAW & ORDER: Sports Rage is offered up as a defense in the murder of a hockey coach.

TRUE STORY: Hockey dad Thomas Junta beat Michael Costin to death after their kids' practice game in Massachusetts.

You've probably seen it before. A kid goes down on a called strike in a Little League baseball game, and his father screams at the umpire: "Get a pair of glasses, jerk!" Or, even worse, he curses out his own kid. Parents mouthing off in the stands has always been a problem in the world of youth activities, but more and more parents are backing up their words with fists. Referees, coaches, and fellow parents often have to keep one eye on the game and another on the angry ex-jock living vicariously through his child. The combination of an overly competitive spirit with a fiercely controlling personality is a volatile mixture indeed, and sporting events all too often work as catalysts that set off an explosion.

Fortunately, the worst thing these skirmishes usually produce are grass stains on golf shirts, maybe a bloody nose and, one can only hope, a lot of embarrassment. But a growing number of incidents in which parents act more like children than the little ones running around the field have inspired op-ed pieces, TV news commentary, and even "assault insurance" available to coaches through the National

Association of Sports Officials. The worst and most publicized incident occurred in 2000 in a Reading, Massachusetts, ice rink.

At about two o'clock on the afternoon of July 5, 2000, Thomas Junta got off work early from his job driving a delivery truck for U.S. Food Service, a national food supplier of restaurants and cafeterias. The forty-two-year-old father of two was a big guy, standing six feet tall and weighing 275 pounds. He had a receding hairline, strong jaw, thick neck, and wore a serious expression on his face. People who saw Junta might compare him to Tony Soprano.

He got a call from his wife asking him to pick up their ten-year-old son, Quinlan, and his two friends Travis and Garrett from Burbank Ice Arena in Reading. In the Boston area, they take hockey deadly serious and it's a year-round sport. The three boys had spent the day at the arena's public "stick practice" session, during which kids come to skate, practice their hockey skills, and often take part in a pickup game with other kids. With stick practice over, the kids wanted to go swimming— the perfect ending to a perfect summer day.

Junta pulled up to the rink and parked his pickup truck. The summer air was still and warm as he walked toward the front doors. When he entered, it was replaced by the frosty air of the rink, the peacefulness obviated by the sounds of hockey—skates scraping ice, sticks hitting pucks, shouts of players and coaches. Junta spotted Quinlan and his friends playing in a pickup game, and he walked toward the ice.

The scrimmage was being refereed by Michael Costin, a forty-year-old carpenter and single father of four children, three of whom were on the ice. Everyone was in full hockey gear, including Costin. Junta noticed that some of the kids were playing a little too roughly for a simple scrimmage. They were cross-checking, tripping, giving cheap shots to the face, and Quinlan was on the receiving end. At one point a fight broke out and Costin did nothing to prevent it. Junta was pissed. As he ran down to the ice, he saw one kid swing his stick at another. "None of that cheap-shot bullshit," Junta yelled. "This is supposed to be fun hockey!"[1]

Costin looked up and said dismissively, "That's hockey." He separated the two boys who were brawling, and the game resumed. One player skated up to Junta's son and hit him in the face. Quinlan, holding his neck and face in pain, started crying. The scrimmage ended, and Junta was furious. Costin and his three sons skated off the ice and headed toward one of the locker rooms to change. Junta followed them. He approached Costin and told him what he thought of his refereeing. The profanities began to fly, then the fists. Though the two men were about the same height, Junta was burlier than Costin, who weighed only 156 pounds. But Costin was scrappy. He threw punches and kicked at him with his razor-sharp hockey skates. The fight was quickly broken up by some bystanders, and each man retired to separate locker rooms in which their kids were changing.

Junta was in a hurry to leave the rink and told Quinlan, Travis, and Garrett to get dressed fast. The rink's assistant manager approached and asked him to leave the building immediately. Junta went outside to wait for the kids, but he reentered a few moments later—shoving aside an employee who had tried to block him. The employee, Nancy Blanchard, phoned the police.

Junta was heading straight to the locker rooms just as Costin was walking toward a nearby soda machine, still wearing his skates. Costin saw Junta coming toward him. He didn't wait to find out what the big guy wanted. Costin threw the first punch, and the two fathers went at it again—and this time it was more vicious. The 270-pound Junta threw Costin to the floor and kneeled on his chest, pinning him to the ground. As Costin vainly swung his arms, kicked his legs, and tried to squirm free, Junta exploited his advantage in size and leverage to pummel him. With the kids gathered around screaming at him to stop, Junta dealt one blow after another with his fists and powerful arms. As an older hockey player attempted to pull the big truck driver off his victim, Junta administered the coup de grace, smashing Costin's head into the floor twice. Costin stopped fighting, and Junta stood up. One of Costin's sons was crying, pleading with his father, "Dad, get up."

His rage extinguished, Junta walked outside. He heard police sirens in the distance and knew he'd have to answer for the grisly scene inside:

Costin's broken body sprawled on the floor, inert, his neck bruised and swollen, face bloodied, nose flattened, and eyes wide open—and his thirteen-year-old son Brendan, in a state of shock, sitting on the floor with his father's head on his lap.

The first cop on the scene moved the group of horrified children away from Costin's body and performed CPR. Costin didn't respond; there was no pulse. EMTs arrived and applied a defibrillator to shock his heart into beating again. Still no response.

As doctors frantically tried to revive Michael Costin in the hospital, Thomas Junta was being grilled by the police at the local precinct. He spent a half hour giving his version of the events to a Reading detective and a Massachusetts state trooper, who recorded the session. When asked at the end of the interview if there were any final statements he would like to make, Junta said, "Other than I wish it never happened, no. And I hope the guy's fine." He was charged with assault.

Michael Costin never woke up. He died in the hospital the next day. Junta's blows had inflicted severe damage to an artery in Costin's neck, which prevented oxygen from reaching his brain.[2] His children were heartbroken. Tara, his nine-year-old daughter, was so distraught at the wake that she tried to climb into the casket.

The charge against Junta was now stepped up from assault to manslaughter. Junta protested that he had simply defended himself. No one argued his point that Costin had thrown the first punch in the second altercation, but prosecutors said Junta had gone way too far during the fight—certainly beyond simply defending himself. The trial of Thomas Junta would focus largely on two questions: Why did Junta come back to the rink after he had been ordered to leave? And how many punches did he throw as he kneeled atop Costin? The answers would determine who really started the fight (no matter who actually threw the first punch), and whether Junta crossed the line that separates self-defense from outright aggression.

Junta was clearly no gentle giant. But was he a violent brute? According to his wife, Michelle, he was—or at least used to be. Nine years before her husband killed Michael Costin, she requested and received a restraining order against him based on her claims that Junta beat her (although she never pressed charges and Junta wasn't arrested), and he had to spend one year away from the family. This information, however, surfaced after his trial and the jury never heard it. The following year, Junta was arrested for assault and battery (he punched a Boston cop), but charges were never filed; instead, he had to pay the police officer $250 for a gold chain he had torn from his neck. He had also been arrested and found innocent of willful destruction of property.[3]

No one would accuse Junta of being a choirboy, but his record had only the occasional blemish. Michael Costin's was a train wreck. Costin clearly had a fierce temper and wouldn't back down from a fight for any reason. He had a history of violence, criminal activity, and heavy drinking. Between 1983 and 1995, he had served a total of seven prison terms for crimes ranging from assault to weapons possession.[4]

But if a man is ever deserving of sympathy—no matter what his criminal record looks like—Costin fit the bill. Costin's upbringing was horrible. At the age of thirteen, he witnessed his father stab his seventeen-year-old brother to death, for which his father was convicted of manslaughter and incarcerated.* Now, ironically, Costin himself was the victim of manslaughter, with his own children forever cursed for having witnessed the crime.

What made the situation even more tragic was the fact that Costin was turning his life around. He was beating his drinking problem and had won a custody battle against his ex-wife. By all accounts he was a devoted father who didn't let his personal problems get in the way of loving his children.

The trial began in January 2001. Nine women and three men were chosen for the jury, and all eyes in America were on them. The Junta case wasn't just a manslaughter case; it was the newest "rage." Suburban

---

*After Junta's conviction, Costin's father, Augustine Costin, actually appealed to the judge for leniency on behalf of his son's killer.

America had long ago begun to experience sudden and unexplained "rage" violence—give someone a dirty look in traffic and risk becoming a victim of "road rage," refuse to serve an airline passenger his fifth vodka and experience "airplane rage"—but this was the latest and strangest rage of all: sports rage.

The jury heard the entire recording of Junta's interview with the police following the incident at the ice rink. They heard him patiently and politely explain his side of the story—how the kids were "cheap shotting," how Costin obnoxiously dismissed his complaints, how his son got an elbow in the face and was crying, and how Costin got him so worked up, he was physically shaking with anger. He described how Costin kicked at him with his skates during the first altercation, and how he willingly stopped fighting and left the rink. He claimed that he came back into the ice rink only after he realized that Quinlan was in there with Costin and his kids. He was worried about his son's safety. When police asked if he remembered shoving Blanchard out of his path, he said he didn't recall.

Costin, Junta said, threw the first punch. "He came out looking for me. You could tell he came out looking for me." And he added that when he and Costin saw each other "[i]t was like a switch on . . . It was just like a stupid guy thing." Junta repeatedly claimed to have punched Costin only two or three times.

The jury members had their job cut out for them. Basically, they heard two completely different stories and had to decide who was telling the truth—or at least whose version was closest to the truth. They faced major discrepancies in the experts' opinions. Stanley Kessler, forensic pathologist for the prosecution, testified that Costin's injuries could have come only from a vicious attack. "This is a substantial force injury," he said. "It takes a lot of trauma to tear ligaments and the ligaments at the back of [Costin's] neck were torn." He showed the jury close-up photos of Costin's horrific injuries. But the pathologist of the Connecticut Medical Examiner's Office, Ira Kanfer, testifying for the defense, said that the torn artery Costin suffered could just as easily have resulted from one blow as from multiple blows.

Then the eyewitnesses took the stand. One witness, Virginia Brings, who was at the rink to pick up her grandson, testified that Junta pounded Costin over and over and over. "He went on and on, and I kept hollering and saying 'Stop' and I was thinking the whole time he's either going to kill this man or he was going to have brain damage," she testified.[5] Yet a twenty-one-year-old hockey player named Ryan Carr, who helped pull Junta off Costin in the first skirmish, said that Junta stopped after only three punches during the second fight, verifying the story Junta told police.

Everyone had a different story to tell, and the jury members had to decide who they believed. After thirteen hours, they made their decision. They took the middle ground, convicting Junta of involuntary manslaughter. Though Junta had failed in his claim of self-defense, he had escaped the highest charge, voluntary manslaughter, which carried a maximum twenty-year penalty.

THE GRAND JURY

We rarely see the grand jury on *Law & Order*, possibly because the proceedings aren't usually very dramatic (or, more likely, because a half-hour is barely enough time to hold a courtroom trial to begin with). In the rare instance that a grand jury is depicted on the show, the ADA reigns supreme. This *is* the case in real life. Grand jury proceedings are secret, and the defendant isn't even present unless he or she is testifying—which a defendant must do if called to the stand (unlike a trial). The defendant isn't represented by a lawyer during grand jury proceedings and can't call witnesses. Grand juries send the vast majority of defendants to trial. (New York State judge Sol Wachtler famously once said that a grand jury would "indict a ham sandwich.")

For these reasons, the system is subjected to an enormous amount of criticism, and numerous jurisdictions have done away with it, opting instead for hearings before a judge. New York City, however, still uses grand juries.

If Junta was hoping for leniency from the judge when it came to the sentencing, he was sorely disappointed. Costin's children were allowed to make statements at the hearing. "I realized I had just witnessed my dad literally getting beat to death," Brendan Costin said, after describing how he had held his father's bleeding head in his hands.[6]

"He is just not there anymore," said Michael Costin Jr., the other son who had witnessed his father's death. "Even now, not ten minutes go by that I don't think of him. I talk to him at church and before I go to bed at night, but it's just not the same."[7]

All Junta could do in his defense was muster up a short and quiet apology to the family. His lawyer said that Junta was just an average guy who got caught up in a bad situation. People fight and bad things sometimes happen. It's tragic, but it's life. He asked the judge to suspend the sentence.

The judge was insulted. If Junta was your typical family man, America had a lot to worry about. No, Junta was far from ordinary, and he would go to jail for the maximum six years.

In 2003, Junta hired a new attorney and appealed his conviction, contending that the prosecution had withheld information that might have helped the defense discredit the testimony of pathologist Kessler. At a medical conference prior to the trial, Junta's attorney argued, Kessler in a presentation said Costin's injury could have been inflicted by something as minor as a chiropractic gaffe—the exact opposite of what he had said at Junta's trial.[8]

The appeals judges reviewed Kessler's testimony and abstract from his medical conference presentation. They decided Kessler's courtroom testimony wasn't inconsistent with his presentation. Request denied.

five

LAW & ORDER: The murder of a taxi driver is linked to a famous author and the brilliant ex-con he has taken under his wing.

TRUE STORY: Pulitzer Prize–winning author Norman Mailer helped get Jack Abbott, a convict with literary promise, paroled. Six weeks later, Abbott killed a man and was sent back to prison.

New York summers can be brutal—temperatures and tempers soar as people look for ways to keep cool in a city of steel, concrete, and glass. If the heat doesn't get to you, the murderous humidity and city stench will. In the early morning of Saturday, July 18, 1981, temperatures were already well into the eighties—and rising fast. New Yorkers were hot under the collar over the baseball strike, now going into its second month. While disgruntled sports fans gathered in pubs to gripe over beers, scores of other locals flocked to the movie theater to catch the latest Steven Spielberg blockbuster, *Raiders of the Lost Ark*, and enjoy the frosty air-conditioning. The few who could afford it trekked out to Long Island beach houses to swim in the ocean and sip cool drinks.

Richard Adan was too happy to sweat the heat. Besides, he'd been born in Cuba; he could handle it. An aspiring actor and playwright, the twenty-two-year-old had plenty to celebrate. He had just returned from Spain where he had starred in the touring production of a play called *Simpson Street*. He'd been a big hit with audiences, especially the ladies, who waited after the show with their phone numbers ready. The newly married actor was flattered but uninterested. He was deeply in love with his wife, Ricci. Adan had just learned that the producers at the famed experimental theater LaMama wanted to stage one of his plays. He couldn't hide his excitement. Handsome and personable, he was a favorite with the patrons at Binibon, an all-night East Village eatery, where he worked part-time as a manager and waiter.

It was well past midnight, and Adan was all smiles as he chatted with his customers. He had no way of knowing he'd be dead before sunrise—stabbed to death in a spat over a toilet.

The Binibon was located just a stone's throw away from the Salvation Army halfway house that thirty-seven-year-old Jack Henry Abbott currently called home. Abbott, the son of a GI and a Chinese prostitute, despised his apartment. But it was better than the alternative: prison, which had been Abbott's home the majority of his life.

Life had dealt Abbott a lousy hand. A fairly attractive man with a slight Asian cast to his face and the letters J-A-C-K tattooed on the fingers of his left hand, he had spent his childhood shuffling among foster homes, until he was sent to reform school at the age of nine. At eighteen, he graduated to federal prison, convicted for passing forged checks. In 1966, while serving his sentence in Utah State Penitentiary, he stabbed and killed a fellow inmate. His claim of self-defense didn't fly, so he tried insanity—offering a demonstration by hurling a pitcher of water at the presiding judge. Court officials were unimpressed, and Abbott was sentenced to fourteen more years. He escaped in 1971, robbed a Denver bank, was promptly caught, and once again made his home inside a federal penitentiary.

Psycho that he was, though, Abbott was clearly no idiot. He discovered the prison library and, despite his sixth-grade education, immersed himself in the works of Marx and Engels, Nietzsche, Russell, and Hobbes. Then he came across a *Time* magazine article about Norman Mailer. The Pulitzer Prize–winning author was writing a book about Gary Gilmore, the double-murderer who had made the news by asking to receive the death penalty. (After much ado, Gilmore got his wish: he was shot to death by firing squad.) In the *Time* article, Mailer expressed his dismay over the fact that he had never had the chance to meet Gilmore.

Abbott saw his chance. Armed with this new information, he advanced to more subtle means of gaining his freedom than submitting lame pleas and playing the loon. He wrote to the author offering his expertise on prison life; Mailer was intrigued. Harvard-educated and a favored member of the literary elite, Mailer had made a name for himself (and a pretty penny) with his bestselling novel *The Naked and the Dead*. Despite his pedigree—or perhaps because of it—he was easy prey for Abbott. A gifted con, Abbott, like many inmates, was always looking for an edge, an out, a way to beat the system. He hit pay dirt with his new pen pal.

Abbott and Mailer corresponded for three years. In his letters, Abbott bemoaned his bleak existence, chronicled his days behind bars, championed Karl Marx, bragged about what a badass he was, and chastised Mailer for romanticizing the life of a criminal. In one letter, he described how it felt to stab someone and feel his life drain away. Mailer was deeply impressed by Abbott's prison posturing and stark prose, and believed he had discovered a literary genius, an underdog whose talent was wasted behind bars—not to mention a perfect specimen for his own fascination with blood and death.

Having friends in high places definitely pays off. Mailer used his influence and connections to convince the prestigious *New York Review of Books* to publish some of Abbott's letters in 1980. A book deal with Random House soon followed, for which the convict was paid an advance of twelve thousand dollars. Mailer contacted the parole board arguing that they were incarcerating an "important American writer."[1] He promised that if Abbott were released, he would hire him as a researcher. Scouts honor. Random House editor Errol McDonald offered his professional opinion that Abbott could easily make a lucrative career authoring books instead of robbing banks.

Even though prison psychiatrists strongly objected to parole, due to Abbott's history of violence (the inmate even described himself as a "violent man"), Abbott was nevertheless set free on parole. He quickly became the toast of the town—feted and fawned over by the New York literati. The paroled killer was profiled in *People* and *Rolling Stone*, and even made an appearance on the *Today* show. He regularly hobnobbed with the likes of novelist Jerzy Kosinski, actress Susan Sarandon, and, of course, his mentor Norman Mailer. Conveniently, Abbott's release from prison coincided perfectly with the release of his book, *In the Belly of the Beast.*

Those in the know—convicts—saw the book, a collection of Abbott's letters to Mailer, as "proof of how easily conned people in the free world were."[2] It was the "kind of stuff somebody on the inside writes somebody on the outside who doesn't know jack-shit about the penitentiary and never will," an inmate said. Bruce Jackson, editor of the *Buffalo Report* commented, "With Abbott, Norman Mailer had his own pet convict. It was like those people who get a big animal you're not supposed to have and show it to you on a leash with a jewel-encrusted collar. You don't know if you're supposed to admire the animal or them for having it on the leash with the jewel-encrusted collar. Well, yes. You do know."[3]

As the buzz about his book was building, Abbott was working on a fine buzz of his own, knocking back cocktails and talking trash with two young ladies in a bar downtown on that steamy Saturday in July. After a few rounds, the trio decided to head out to the Binibon for an early breakfast. It was a little cooler at this hour, but still hot and muggy for 5 a.m. The tiny restaurant was crowded with night owls and club hoppers stopping in for a bite to eat before going home to bed. Richard Adan was doing double duty as manager and waiter. He was tired but upbeat as he waited on Abbott and the two women.

Adan was handing a breakfast order to the cook when Abbott approached, looking for a restroom. For insurance reasons, the Binibon didn't have a bathroom for customers, only one for employees, Adan explained apologetically. Abbott insisted on using the employee restroom and the two men began to argue. Adan led Abbott outside to show him where he could relieve himself. Enraged by what he perceived as a personal affront, Abbott pulled a knife from his pocket and plunged it into Adan's chest with such force the blade pierced his heart. It was a

Richard Adan was a well-liked actor living in New York City. Before his chance run-in with Jack Henry Abbott, his career was just taking off.
Photo by Edward Gallardo © 2006

Adan was working in a late-night diner when he was murdered by Abbott, simply because he wouldn't let the paroled killer use the employee bathroom.
Photo by Edward Gallardo © 2006

---

brutal act, chillingly similar to a moment described in the ex-con's book: "You have sunk the knife to its hilt. Into the middle of his chest. Slowly he begins to struggle for his life . . . You can feel his life trembling through the knife in your hand."[4]

Fatally wounded, Adan clutched his chest and cried out in pain. Abbott fled the scene.

Abbott returned to the halfway house he so despised and collected his few belongings, along with two hundred dollars he had squirreled away. The Sunday papers were just hitting the stands. The early edition of the *New York Times* featured a glowing review of *In the Belly of the Beast*. Reviewer Terrence Des Pres labeled the book "awesome, brilliant, perversely ingenuous."[5] He also thanked Normal Mailer "for getting these letters into publishing form and, a job more difficult, for helping to get Abbott out on parole."[6] Ironically, hours later, the headlines screamed for Abbott's head. "Society will be a lot safer when Jack Henry Abbott is locked up for the rest of his life," the *Daily News* said about the New York literati's golden boy.

By then, Abbott was gone. At 6:30 a.m., he had reached the Port Authority and hopped a bus to Philadelphia. He was going nowhere in particular, just getting out of New York. In Philadelphia, he got on a bus to Chicago. En route, he left a phone message at Mailer's Provincetown, Massachusetts, summer home that he would be in touch soon. Mailer didn't hear from his new friend again. Abbott then hitched a ride on a tractor-trailer going south and reached Laredo, Texas, in a few days. He was headed for the border.

Richard Adan's murder was the nation's story of the week. In the newspapers, the gifted, multitalented, hardworking young man was referred to repeatedly as "the waiter." Sometimes, his name was omitted altogether. It was an affront to everyone who knew Adan, especially his lovely new wife. *Simpson Street* playwright Edward Gallardo had become fast friends with Richard in Spain. He'd seen the effect Adan had on the audience. Gallardo, an accomplished actor and writer, is convinced that Richard Adan would have made it big in Hollywood, had he lived. Adan, he says, had so much to offer the world and it's a shame he never got a chance to really shine.

While media commentators expressed outrage about Adan's murder, Abbott's pals were dumbfounded. "[Abbott] was a very gentle, quiet-spoken person," said his literary agent, Scott Meredith, "the opposite of what he is accused of."[7] U.S. marshals tracked Abbott for several weeks, relying on tips from people who had seen the murderer in Philadelphia and Chicago. Abbott's personalized prison tattoo was a dead giveaway to anyone who read the papers.

Despite the publicity of his crime and the army of law enforcement officials on his tail, Abbott made it to the Mexican border and bribed a guard to let him cross. From there, he traveled south, looking for a place to "lay down and think and write,"[8] as Abbott later told an interviewer. The tiny huts available for rent didn't suit the needs of the newly famous author. And the flies bothered him, too. So he kept going—all the way to the border of Guatemala. This didn't pan out, either. Abbott was broke and job prospects were scarce for English-speaking prison-literature visionaries. After a failed attempt to board a Cuba-bound ship, Abbott decided to head back north.

Federal and local law enforcement trackers were scouring the southwest for their quarry as Abbott crossed back over the border. Living under the alias Jack Eastman, Abbott began moving from town to town working in the oil fields of Louisiana, always one short step ahead of his hunters. In his first-ever day job, Jack Henry Abbott toiled sixteen hours a day, earned less than minimum wage, and had to pay his employer a third of his wages to sleep in on-site quarters no more comfortable than his New York City rat hole or those fly-ridden Mexican shanties. In the meantime, his book had become a bestseller.

Cops soon learned about "Jack Eastman" and his tattooed fingers. After a number of unsuccessful raids on itinerant worker camps, they found their man. Undercover cops posing as laborers arrested Abbott in an oil field in St. Mary's Parish, Louisiana.

Abbott's trial for murder in the second degree began on January 3, 1982. Unrepentant and belligerent, Abbott once again resorted to a bogus self-defense claim, insisting that Adan was about to attack him. At one point, the victim's father-in-law was removed from the courtroom for standing up and shouting, "You intended to do it, you scum!" He had to spend the rest of the trial sitting on a bench outside the courtroom.

The testimony of witness Wayne Larson, one of the Binibon night owls who saw the murder occur, sunk any hopes Abbott might have been clinging to concerning his self-defense motive. Larson described the scene firsthand, illustrating in detail the sight and sound of Abbott's knife ramming into Richard Adan's chest.

The jury, though, was moved by the details of Abbott's hard life. They listened, riveted, as the killer testified about living in foster homes,

suffering abuse by guards, and being abandoned by a society he believed was responsible for his crimes. In the galley, Mailer, Sarandon,
Kosinski, and actor Christopher Walken gathered to lend their support.* Swayed by the defendant's sob story, a sympathetic jury found
him guilty of manslaughter in the first degree. It was a lenient verdict;
murder in the second mandated life without parole. The judge sentenced Abbott to fifteen to life. "I would just like an apology of some
sort. A little consideration. Just a small recognition by society of the in-
justice that has been done to me," Abbott said after the trial.[9] (Richard
Adan's family also wanted an apology. It never came. In fact, during the
civil suit Adan's widow, Ricci, filed against Abbott, the murderer told
her that her husband's life "wasn't worth a dime." The court disagreed
and awarded Mrs. Adan $7.5 million in damages.)

After all this, Norman Mailer remained as unfazed about his pro-
tégé's actions as the murderer himself. Throughout the trial, the writer
steadfastly pleaded leniency for the so-called genius. "Culture is worth
a little risk," he had lectured the judge. Even after the relatively light
verdict was passed, Mailer complained that by the time Abbott was
released from jail he would be an old man. It might as well be a life
sentence, he groused.

This time around, the court had learned its lesson. Turning a deaf
ear to Mailer, it sent Abbott back to his old stomping ground, the Utah
State Penitentiary, to serve out the eight years still remaining on his original murder sentence. After that, he was shuttled off to New York for
the fifteen-year manslaughter conviction. This time, there were no celebrities awaiting his arrival, no champagne, no caviar. Unsurprisingly, Abbott's second book received dismal reviews.

In June 2001, Abbott appeared before the New York State Parole
Board. The parole commissioners were dumbfounded by how little
Abbott had changed after nearly two decades languishing behind bars.
The killer showed no regret, remorse, or sympathy for the family of his
victim. In one instance, he even griped that one of the questioners ad-

---

*Soon after the trial, Susan Sarandon and actor Tim Robbins had a son and named him Jack Henry.

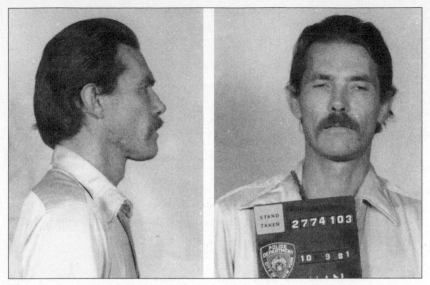

Jack Henry Abbott, two-time murderer and pride of the New York and Hollywood glitterati. *New York State Department of Correctional Services*

dressed him in a disrespectful tone. On behalf of all those people who don't want Jack Henry Abbott stabbing them for no good reason, the board denied the parole.

Cause célèbre, radical polemicist, con man, and two-time murderer Jack Henry Abbott hanged himself in his prison cell in February 2002. He was fifty-eight years old. Abbott's last work was a suicide note, the contents of which, ironically, have been kept from the public's eye.

six

LAW & ORDER: Neighbors look on as a woman is viciously attacked on the street. Years later, the woman must relive her ordeal when new questions surface about the guilt of her rapist.

TRUE STORY: Kitty Genovese was repeatedly stabbed on a street in a Queens, New York, neighborhood. No one called the police until after she had been killed.

As Winston Moseley plunged his knife into Kitty Genovese's back on a Queens, New York, sidewalk, he heard someone shout "Leave that girl alone!" from the apartment building across the street. It was then that Moseley noticed something: He had parked his car in a spot where nearby residents could see it. Moseley curtailed his attack long enough to back his car up a one-way street and park it out of view. As he did so, Geneovese limped, bleeding and terrified, to the back of the building in which she lived. Moseley sat in his car until he was confident that no one was going to come to Genovese's aid.

Catherine Genovese—whom family and friends endearingly called Kitty—was a bright, energetic twenty-nine-year-old woman, an individual in the purest sense of the word. Raised in Brooklyn, Kitty was the oldest of five siblings. She stood five foot, one, and weighed all of 105 pounds. About the time that Kitty graduated from high school, her mother, Rachel, witnessed a shooting in the neighborhood, and the family decided that the city was no longer safe enough in which to raise a family.* The Genoveses packed up and moved to Connecticut. Despite her family's wishes, though, Kitty remained behind.[1]

It was natural for such a curious young woman, who loved to be around people, to make a life for herself in New York City, with its cultural diversity, high level of energy, and constant hustle and bustle. Kitty was full of energy. She enjoyed dancing, learning, debating politics, and going out with her friends. Suburban Connecticut just wasn't for her, and her family accepted this—although they did worry about her. Genovese moved to Kew Gardens in the spring of 1963 and landed a job as a barmaid at Ev's 11th Hour in Hollis, a Queens neighborhood about five miles east of Kew Gardens. The commute from Kew Gardens to Hollis by subway or train was not only inconvenient, but not very safe considering the hours Genovese worked. She purchased a car for the commute, a small red Fiat.[2]

In a neighborhood like Kew Gardens, where many families own at least one car, parking was tight; finding a spot in front of your apartment was like hitting the jackpot. By the time Genovese normally got home from work, all the spots on the street were taken, so she would park her Fiat in the Long Island Railroad parking lot next to her building.

On March 13, 1964, Winston Moseley decided he would kill a woman. Any woman. He got in his car at 1:30 a.m. to search for a lone female driving a car. At 3:15, he spotted Genovese and followed her. As she pulled into the LIRR parking lot, he pulled up to the side of the road. Unseen by Genovese, he got out of his car and ran into the parking lot, pulled out his knife, and hid in the shadows.

---

*In 1954, when Rachel Genovese witnessed the shooting, crime in New York City was still relatively low. Her decision might have been viewed by some as rash, but Rachel had seen the writing on the wall. Homicides in New York (and the entire country, for that matter) would soon spike, and the city would become notorious for its alarmingly high murder rate.

As she got out of her car, Kitty spotted Moseley, wearing a stocking cap and holding the knife out. She began to run up Austin Street—either toward the Old Bailey Bar up the block or to the police call box on the corner. She didn't reach either. Moseley quickly caught up to Genovese. "I ran after her and stabbed her twice in the back," Moseley bluntly stated in his confession.* It was then that the neighbor yelled out the window and scared Moseley off . . . temporarily.

As he was backing up his 1960 Chevy Corvair, Moseley watched Genovese get up and limp around the corner of the building. He put a black fedora on his head to disguise himself, got out of the car, and headed to the train station looking for his victim. Genovese wasn't there, so he went to the back of the building next to the parking lot—the two-story building in front of which he had first attacked Genovese. She had made it inside a door in the rear of the building, and Moseley had found her.

Genovese started screaming when she saw him. He stabbed her again, in the chest, stomach, and throat. He then raped her and stole her keys, makeup, a bottle of medicine, and forty-nine dollars. During the attack, Moseley heard an apartment door open directly up the stairs from him, along with some muffled voices but, again, somehow knew the people wouldn't interfere. He was right. Moseley left Genovese's bleeding body on the vestibule floor and walked the far way around the building, making eye contact with a milkman making an early-hour delivery to a deli. Moseley didn't think too much of it. He got in his car and drove off. The tenant upstairs finally decided to call the police. Kitty Genovese died before she got to the hospital.

NYPD detectives investigated but couldn't find a lead of any sort. They canvassed the neighborhood, but many people said they didn't see anything. Those who did could offer only vague descriptions. They had never seen him in the neighborhood.

---

*Even if Genovese had reached the bar, it would have done no good. Because of the neighbors' recent complaints about boisterous patrons leaving the saloon after closing hours, the manager had closed up early that night. Had there been patrons inside the bar and heard her first screams, Genovese might have been saved.

Six days later, though, the NYPD caught a break. A man who was arrested for breaking into a home and stealing a television fit the description furnished by the milkman who had seen the killer. The police didn't have to prod too hard to get a full confession out of Moseley; he cracked like an egg, quickly admitted to murdering Kitty Genovese . . . in addition to two other women before that: Barbara Kralik, a fifteen-year-old from Springfield Gardens, Queens, and twenty-four-year-old Annie Mae Johnson from South Ozone Park. He also confessed to multiple rapes and robberies. Moseley, an introverted father of two, was twenty-nine years old and worked a perfectly respectable job as a machine operator in Westchester County, north of the city. Little did his family know he had a secret history of robbery, rape, and murder.

As the details of Genovese's murder unfolded, Kew Gardens locals were astonished. Kew Gardens, situated closer to the Long Island suburbs than to Manhattan, was (and still is) a neighborhood of peaceful, tree-lined streets, middle-class apartments and homes, and Tudor-style buildings. Walking down the main drag, Austin Street, on a sunny spring day, a person used to the noise and pollution of Manhattan would note the smell of the trees, sounds of the birds, and general tranquility in the air. The neighborhood, in fact, was named after the English town of Kew, world renown for its botanical gardens. People moved to outer-borough neighborhoods like Kew Gardens to *escape* the city. Vicious murders on the street just didn't happen here.

The rest of the country was astonished, too, but for different reasons. The slaying was horrible, to be sure, but what particularly outraged people was the neighborhood's seeming lack of concern as it happened. Exactly two weeks after the killing, the *New York Times* chronicled the attack in an article titled "Thirty-seven Who Saw Murder Didn't Call the Police." The lead sentence read: "For more than half an hour thirty-eight respectable, law-abiding citizens in Queens watched a killer stalk and stab a woman in three separate attacks in Kew Gardens."[3]

Millions of readers nationwide came away with the perception that the last moments of Kitty Genovese's life were some sort of public theater, viewed live by people who were at best horrified but too afraid to get involved; at worst, entertained.

Everyone from sociologists and mental health experts to politicians to average joes quickly formed opinions about the fact that residents stood mute as one of their own was stabbed to death in front of their eyes. One psychiatrist blamed the witnesses' apathy on the effects of a relatively new commercial phenomenon—televisions in every home. People who watched too much TV (which accounted for pretty much everyone) were unable to discern between fact and fiction.[4] One woman wrote a letter to the *Times* blaming feminism: Men of the sixties had become so emasculated that the chivalric act of coming to a woman's rescue would be an abomination.

U.S. Representative John Lindsay even took advantage of the outrage, stumping at the very site of the murder in his bid for mayor. After marching in the Columbus Day Parade in 1965 and buying a round of drinks for patrons of a bar in the Bronx, he headed down to Kew Gardens. Facing Mowbray Apartments, he dramatically called for a more unified citizenship. He railed against apathy and championed the value of "people-to-people responsibility." Then he made his campaign promise to install bright lights on every street and in every park. Lindsay won the mayoral election.[5]

Some police were just plain confused; others were disgusted. Why would people be afraid to call the cops from the safety of their own homes? For time immemorial, people have remained tight-lipped when approached by a cop asking, "What did you see?" for reasons ranging from distrust of police to fear of criminal retribution.

But how could thirty-eight people sit and watch a murder happen without at least dialing 911? One reason is that the centralized 911 system wasn't invented at the time. To contact the police in an emergency, a person had to call his or her local precinct directly. The 911 system wasn't fully in place until 1969. And, in fact, at least one person did call the police—far too late and only after phoning a friend and asking for advice on what to do. (*Call the police!* was the friend's reply.) Over the years, some have argued that several people did actually call the cops, but couldn't get through or didn't want to provide the personal information police usually requested when taking an emergency call; others said they opted against picking up the phone because NYPD dispatchers had a reputation for rudeness.

For those who were, and still are, outraged at the neighborhood, this argument doesn't exactly absolve the community of Kew Gardens. Thirty-eight eyewitnesses should have done something to help the poor woman. It's not uncommon for a person—victim or witness—to "freeze" during a crime, as his brain attempts to adjust to the new "reality" he's been thrust into. But the people of Austin Street had a full thirty minutes to sort out the reality of events occurring before their eyes.

Problem is, for most of the witnesses the crime likely didn't take place before their eyes. The *New York Times* used the word "eyewitness" loosely. The majority of witnesses lived in the seven-story-tall Mowbray Apartments across the street from the first assault. And most residents probably couldn't see clearly, if at all, due to certain vantage points, trees, and the dim light on the street. The inability to correctly interpret what they were actually seeing or hearing was, by most accounts, the most common problem.[6]

The Old Bailey Bar, located just a few steps away from the first attack, was occasionally the source of late-night noise on Austin Street, drinkers bringing their barroom antics out to the street. Some Mowbray tenants awoken by the screams assumed it was just a few carousers spilling out of the Old Bailey. Slightly annoyed, they rolled over and went back to sleep.[7]

Many who *did* see the attack occur claim they didn't see a weapon. Some assumed it was a couple having a fight. One woman testified in court that she witnessed "a girl laying down on the pavement and the man was bending over her and beating her." Police said that if they had received a call after the first attack, Kitty Genovese would likely have survived.

As those who have dissected the scene point out, Genovese was attacked once on Austin Street, before Moseley was frightened away by the voice from Mowbray Apartments. Those who saw Moseley run away, climbed back into bed and went to sleep; the ones who saw Genovese stagger around the corner of the building across the street said they assumed that the whole incident, whatever it was, was over. Since the second attack occurred in the vestibule at the back of the building across the street, Mowbray tenants wouldn't have seen, and probably wouldn't have heard, anything.[8] But the tenant directly up the stairs, who was home at the time, did hear his neighbor being attacked and screaming for help; he didn't call the police initially, he said, because he was drunk and didn't want any problems.

It's certainly understandable that a tenant, with his windows shut and awoken from a deep slumber, would be unable to discern the words of a person screaming on the street below. More often than not, loud voices on a city street turn out to be nothing more than two people joking around or arguing. By almost every account of the story, though, Kitty Genovese screamed, "Oh my God, he stabbed me! Help! Help!" Did no one make out her words? Did everyone who heard them assume it was a prank? Did people really call the police but fail to get through? If so, how many? We'll never know the full truth.

The murder made headline news around the country, prompting a nationwide process of a little soul-searching and a lot of city-bashing. The constant hustle, noise, and tension of life in the big city, many believed, had finally turned average citizens into uncaring monsters. Cities had become nothing more than corrupt, crime-ridden cesspools inhabited by ultra-individualists.

Academics saw a more complex problem at work, which they termed the Bystander Effect, or Genovese Syndrome. The fewer the number of witnesses, sociologists maintained, the better off a victim of a violent crime is. In an emergency, people have a tendency to look for answers from others; if no one takes charge, or even seems worried, the assumption is that nothing is really amiss, and the more people present during a crime, the more responsibility each individual can hand off to others.*

---

*In 1974, Sandra Zahler, a model, was beaten to death in her Mowbray apartment on Christmas at 3:20 a.m. Her next-door neighbor heard the entire thing and reported what she heard in extraordinary detail: Zahler entering her apartment with a man, Zahler's screams of "No! No! No!" five minutes later, the sound of slapping, and a loud crash. Why didn't she call the police? The superintendent lived on the floor, and she assumed he would. (Robert McFadden, *New York Times*, "A Model's Dying Screams Are Ignored at the Site of Kitty Genovese's Murder," December 27, 1974.)

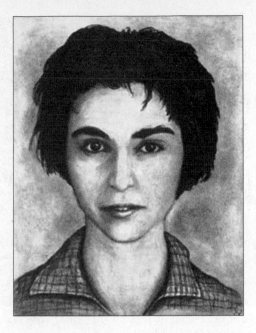

Catherine "Kitty" Genovese was coming home from her late shift as a barmaid when she was murdered by Winston Moseley. Some neighbors witnessed the attack but did little to stop it.
Illustration by Bill Rose

The trial of Winston Moseley was fairly cut-and-dried. Moseley never contested that he committed the murder. Diagnosed as a catatonic schizophrenic, he pleaded innocent by reason of insanity. On the stand at his trial he was chillingly candid about why he wandered the streets of Queens looking for a female victim: "What I had was just an idea that would come into my mind and it would override any other idea I had and I just had to sort of complete that idea." His parents and wife portrayed him as a quiet introvert, a neat freak who was fond of dogs and "always thinking." But his ex-wife painted a different portrait of Moseley, explaining how he pointed a rifle at her one day and expounded upon how easy it is to pull a trigger. One thing is for sure: No one really knew Winston Moseley.

When the jury convicted Moseley and suggested the death penalty, the crowd in Queens Court went crazy, applauding and cheering as if the Mets had just won the pennant. The judge, who opposed the death penalty on principle, couldn't control himself. He lashed out at Moseley when the verdict came in, expressing his desire to pull the switch himself.

Kitty Genovese's life was put to an end on March 13, 1964, but Winston Moseley's was far from over. He escaped the death penalty on

A contemporary view of the LIRR parking lot in which Kitty Genovese parked her Fiat. Winston Moseley waited for her on the right side of the lot.

appeal, on the grounds that the court had neglected to take into consideration certain testimony pertaining to Moseley's mental condition. His new sentence was life in prison.

Mosely had dodged the executioner's axe. And he wasn't finished with his life of crime. The thief, rapist, and murderer would go on to flout the system, commit more violent crimes against innocent people, and torment the Genovese family in his attempts at gaining parole.

In the spring of 1968, four years after slaying Kitty Genovese, Winston Moseley, then thirty-three years old, escaped from Meyer Memorial Hospital in Buffalo, New York. He had been transferred to the hospital from Attica Prison to receive treatment for a self-inflicted injury. He overpowered a guard, stole his gun, and disappeared into the city of Buffalo, finding a vacant house to bide his time in. The house was owned by a young couple by the name of Kulaga who had not yet moved in. When they stopped by one day, they ran straight into their worst nightmare. Winston Moseley, armed with the guard's gun, tied the husband

The alley down which Kitty Genovese fled after the first attack. Her apartment entrance was through a door under one of the small awnings to the right.

up with a length of clothesline he had found. Then he took the wife into another room and raped her. Dressed in the husband's clothes he stole the couple's car and headed back to New York—only he went the wrong way and ended up in a small town northwest of Buffalo.[9]

Realizing his mistake, Moseley again resorted to violence. He rang the doorbell of a woman named Mary Kay Patmos, who was home taking care of her five-month-old daughter, and overpowered her. Not long after, a friend of Patmos happened to stop by. Moseley informed her that he would kill Patmos if she didn't bring him a car. Shaken, the friend left. She called her husband, and he contacted the FBI.[10]

As dozens of federal and local law enforcement agents descended on the neighborhood, Patmos's friend drove up in a car. She got out and put the keys on the roof, signaling for Moseley to come out and take the car. Moseley wasn't buying it; he knew it was a trap. (Had he come out of the house and tried to start the car, he would have had a rude awakening: the keys were fakes.) The FBI's ruse had failed.[11]

Neil J. Welch, an FBI special agent, called Moseley on the phone and convinced him to talk. With a gun hidden in his coat pocket, Welch

Winston Moseley left his home on the night of March 3, 1964, with the specific intent of randomly killing a woman. Convicted for the murder of Kitty Genovese, he briefly escaped and raped a woman in Buffalo, New York.

entered the home and sat down with Moseley. They talked for almost an hour about Moseley's life in Attica, his future, and even his favorite TV shows. During the conversation, Patmos and her child escaped out a back window. Moseley knew he had nowhere to go and eventually handed the gun to Welch. His adventure was over.[12]

Back in Attica, Moseley became one of the first convicts in New York State to earn a college degree. He chose sociology as his major. Perhaps he had a serious interest in the subject or, more likely, it was a stunt to minimize his prison time. From there on in, Moseley abandoned such straightforward tactics as fighting guards and taking hostages and resorted to more subtle means of getting himself an early trip out of prison.

In 1977, he wrote a letter to the *New York Times* gracefully chronicling the changes he had undergone in recent years. The *Times* printed the letter in full. In it Moseley explained how the combination of his studies and the now-famous Attica prisoner revolt of '71 changed him as a man. Strangely, the prisoner uprising taught him the value of life,

Moseley said in the article. He then proceeded to describe, in pseudo-religious language that sounds like it was lifted from a cheap greeting card, how one of his professors guided him to his final transformation into a different man, a man who wanted to contribute to society, not rape and kill helpless women.[13]

It was a valiant attempt, but subsequent events would prove that the only thing that had changed about Moseley was the tactics he employed for his self-serving purposes.

Over subsequent years, Moseley's appearances before the parole board were colored by fantastic tales meant to prove that he was a changed man. Once, he claimed to have written a letter to the Genovese family explaining how sorry he was for the "inconvenience" he had caused them. (Not one member of the family said they received such a letter.) Moseley explained to the parole board that, the way he saw it, a crime is sometimes worse for the perpetrator than the victim. The victim, especially a murder victim, suffers for only a few moments; the murderer, locked up away from society, suffers for years.[14]

Finding nary a sympathetic ear, Moseley came up with a new one. In 1979, he told reporters that he had been justified in killing Kitty Genovese. While he was driving around just minding his own business at 3:00 a.m. on March 13, 1964, Moseley said, Genovese pulled out of Ev's 11th Hour and cut him off. He tailed her only to convey what he thought about her poor driving skills. When she saw him in the LIRR parking lot, she called him a "nigger." He was so angry that he pulled out the knife he happened to be carrying and killed her.

Once again, Moseley found no takers. Then, in 1995, he thought he had hit pay dirt. He learned that his defense attorney, Syndey Sparrow, had once defended Kitty Genovese on a minor gambling charge. This, Moseley maintained, created a conflict of interest; therefore, he didn't get the quality of defense to which he was entitled.

From the day Kitty Genovese was killed, up to this point, the Genovese family remained absent from courtrooms and kept themselves as far from the spotlight as possible. Perhaps given the legal basis of Moseley's argument, no matter how tenuous it seemed, Kitty Genovese's three brothers and one sister decided to attend this hearing and speak to the press. One of her brothers, William, fed up with society's indifference to the suffering of others, joined the marines not long after the murder and lost both his legs in Vietnam. Another brother, Frank, recalled the painful reminders of his sister's death when he read about it in college textbooks, in sections covering the Genovese Syndrome.

Yet, despite the anguish Winston Moseley inflicted upon the family, as well as the real or perceived apathy of an entire neighborhood, the poise and dignity the Genoveses retained throughout the ordeal was summed up in the words of William: "The question of apathy was with me throughout my time in Vietnam, and I came to be known for taking too many risks because I couldn't let anything go without trying to act," he told the *New York Times*. "The irony of being here today, thirty years later, is that maybe you begin to understand why no one wanted

THE BYSTANDER EFFECT

In 1968, a groundbreaking study inspired by news reports of the Kitty Genovese murder proved that when it comes to street crime, strength in numbers doesn't apply.

Dr. Bibb Latane and Dr. John Darley placed their subjects in separate rooms and had them communicate via intercom. Then they played out various scenarios involving possible life-or-death situations—smoke pouring through the vents of one of the rooms, recorded cries of distress from another. The phony emergencies were conducted involving various numbers of people. Results proved that the higher the number of participants, the less likely people were to help.

One reason for this, the doctors inferred, was that humans prefer to hand off responsibility to others when they can. Another, more depressing reason was that people are embarrassed to be seen as scared or anxious, which creates a catch-22 situation: If no one around you seems nervous in an emergency situation, you will likely pretend to be one of the crowd—but those people who seem calm and collected are probably faking their own confidence. And everyone fiddles as Rome burns.

to get involved. I appreciate the sensitivity of constitutional law, but, watching this proceeding here, I fear for the cynicism of the general populace."[15]

The judge in the new proceedings ruled against Moseley, concluding that despite Sparrow's previous representation of Genovese, her killer had been suitably defended.

Moseley has since struck out on every parole hearing, his last one taking place in February 2006. At the time of writing, he's in his early seventies and known as convict number 64A0102 at Great Meadow Correctional Facility in Comstock, New York. It's a safe bet that the killer of Kitty Genovese will die behind bars and razor wire in upstate New York.

seven

LAW & ORDER: A sweet-faced preteen and her slow-witted friend kill a little boy.

TRUE STORY: Two British ten-year-olds were charged with the abduction and murder of two-year-old James Bulger in Liverpool.

The video is slightly grainy, a bit too yellow. At first glance, it seems a touching family scene: an older boy gently leading his baby brother by the hand through the mall, their mother surely trailing behind, off-camera, pushing a shopping cart filled with groceries, happy that her sons get along so well. Another boy, perhaps a third brother or a schoolmate, walks ahead of the pair. The truth is far more sinister. The boys are strangers to the toddler. Off-camera, there is no mother following in their wake, just more strangers, shuttling by with packages in tow, oblivious to the youngsters. The older boys are friends, two ten-year-olds playing hooky from school, two ten-year-olds shoplifting candy and trinkets, two ten-year-olds kidnapping a toddler for fun.

February 12, 1993, begins as a gloomy Friday morning. In the working-class neighborhood of Merseyside, Liverpool, ten-year-old Robert Thompson thinks it's a perfect day for "sagging," the British term for playing hooky from school. He leaves home at the usual time and heads toward his elementary school, just in case his mother is watching. On the way, he encounters his schoolmate Jon Venables. It is Jon's turn to take home the class gerbil for the weekend but ultimately he decides to join his pal for a day of teacherless mischief. The boys toss their backpacks into the bushes and head to the nearby Boodle Strand Shopping Mall.

Dressed in their school uniforms, the boys arouse the suspicion of shopkeepers, a few of whom want to know why they aren't in school. It's a holiday, the boys answer, before making off with whatever trinkets and goods they can fit in their coat pockets—a toy soldier, fruit, a tin of blue modeling paint. They pass the school day shoplifting and running amuck in the mall, jumping on tables, harassing an elderly woman, and gobbling stolen candy and snacks.

Two-year-old James Bulger is also at the mall. His mother, Denise, treats him to a ride on a mechanical seesaw and half a sausage roll. James is a flaxen-haired child with a playful smile. He is his mother's pride and joy—her second chance. She miscarried her first child. Now, she watches James like a hawk. She doesn't leave his side. But today, James is particularly playful, knocking down merchandise from shelves and acting up. She lets him wait by the door, just for a moment, as she ducks into the butcher's shop.

Jon sees him first. A little boy, a baby, really, wearing a hooded sweatshirt and teeny, tiny sneakers. He looks like a doll. Earlier they'd talked about "getting a kid" for kicks. Robert, posturing, said it would be funny to get a kid lost in the traffic outside the mall. Jon said he wanted to let off some steam by bullying a child—he "hadn't hit one in a long time." At first it was just talk, two kids acting tough to impress each other. Then Jon tried to run off with a toddler in the clothing store. He was almost successful too, until the child's mother intervened.

But this little boy is all alone, standing there, eating candy. His mother is nowhere in sight.

"Come along, baby," they say. And he does.

James looks up, beaming at the two older boys. They are like him but bigger and stronger. One day maybe he will be as big and as strong. His fingers are still sticky from the sausage roll as he reaches out to take Jon's hand.

Security cameras capture the three boys walking together through the mall. Robert and Jon goof around, giggling and swatting at each other. The cameras follow them, recording their movements, the boys getting smaller and smaller until they are no longer visible onscreen.

Inside the butcher shop, Denise pays for her purchase. She is gone less than two minutes. Baby James is no longer standing by the door. Frantic, Denise runs through the mall, calling "James! James!"

With no real plan, Robert and Jon leave the mall and amble through town, little James at their side. They are an odd sight, two young schoolboys with a baby. Curious onlookers stare at the trio, wondering where their parents are. The boys walk for more than two miles. Along the way, they are stopped by several adults, including a woman who gives them directions to the nearest police station so they can drop off the wayward toddler they claim they found at the bottom of the hill. The woman considers accompanying them but chooses instead to stay behind with her young daughter—a decision that will come back to haunt her.

James, tired, starts crying for his mother and dragging his feet. He's beginning to get on the boys' nerves and they regret running off with him. They take turns carrying him; Robert holds him by his arms, Jon by his legs. Near a canal, they hit James and drop him on his head. They leave him there but the toddler, innocent and confused, runs after them. Robert takes James's hand. The boys pull his hood close around his face to conceal the bruises they've just given him.

An elderly woman watches from her window as the boys rough up the baby. She closes her curtains. Shortly after, a passing motorist witnesses one of the boys giving James a "persuasive kick." He's in a rush and drives off.

Later, the press will dub these witnesses the Liverpool 38, a reference to the Kitty Genovese case. In Forest Hills, New York, thirty-eight people listened or looked on, immobile, as Genovese was brutally attacked outside her apartment building. (See chapter 6.)

Around 5:45 p.m., the boys take James to the railway. There, they splash the stolen blue modeling paint in the baby's face. He is kicked and beaten with bricks and stones. Jon hits him with a twenty-two-pound iron bar he finds lying on the ground. They stick batteries in his mouth and pull down his pants. James appears to be dead when they move his tiny body onto the train tracks. In fact, he is still alive, though fading fast, as they cover his face with bricks. The boys want it to appear that a passing train killed the child.

The two boys head to the video store where Susan Venables, out looking for her truant son, finds them. Furious, she marches Jon down to the police station for a lecture. James Bulger's abduction had already made the news. Ironically, Susan had been worried that Jon was in danger of being kidnapped by the same scary stranger everyone assumed took the little boy.

On Sunday, Saint Valentine's Day, four young boys playing on the railway make a gruesome discovery: a body so small it appears at first to be a dead cat or a doll. Upon closer inspection they realize with horror that it is a dead little boy. The boy's body has been severed in half.

The autopsy reveals that James received forty blows to the head and body; the medical examiner is unable to determine which of these caused his death. The child was found naked from the waist down and had slight "abrasions" on his penis. His face bears the imprint of a shoe. Mercifully, James died before being run over by the train.

Heartsick residents turn the murder site into a shrine to James. They leave cards, candles, flowers, and toys. Robert, wracked by guilt, visits and leaves a single rose. The press quickly dubs the dead little boy "Jamie." Denise and Ralph Bulger have always called their son by his proper name; he was James, not Jim or Jimmy, and not Jamie. Strangers, neighbors, and newscasters now refer to their boy by this new name, a fact that upsets the grieving parents. It's a presumptuous but an innocent mistake. In calling him Jamie, it was as if the press—and the public— were claiming him as their own. His sweet smile beaming in photographs, the golden mop of hair, the tiny hands—he was too precious to be James. James was formal, adult. No, this sweet baby was Jamie. His smile won your heart; his death broke it.

James Bulger's murder is a horrific, brutal crime made all the more shocking when police release the video footage taken by the mall's security cameras. Viewers watch as James is led away not by some decrepit, middle-aged degenerate but by two nondescript, blurry boys. The image quality is poor, making it difficult to positively identify their faces. Even so, a Venables' family friend believes she recognizes them. She contacts the police.

Six days after the murder, acting on the woman's tip, police arrest Jon and Robert for the murder of James Bulger. Interviewed at separate police stations, both boys proclaim their innocence. The police are skeptical that two ten-year-olds are even capable of committing such a heinous crime. However, the boys' strange behavior gives them pause. Robert is truculent and combative with the detectives. He tells them, "If I wanted to kill a baby, I'd kill my own [brother Ben], wouldn't I?"[1]

Jon asks numerous questions about fingerprints and police procedure. He is preoccupied with Robert and whether or not the detectives have spoken to him. "It's that Robert Thompson," he tells them. "He always gets me into trouble."[2]

After several days of questioning, and being encouraged by their mothers to tell the truth, the boys break. Jon, crying hysterically confesses, "I did kill the baby." When he regains his composure, he tells detectives that "Robert done all of it mainly," and that Robert was "laughing his head off."[3]

Across town, Robert points the finger at Jon. It was Jon who lured the baby away from his mother, Jon who kicked and hit James with the bricks and the iron bar. Robert admits only to pinching the baby and touching him once to "get my ears against his belly to see if he was breathing." Then he moved him off the tracks "so he wouldn't get chopped in half."[4] Later, the imprint on James's face will be matched to Robert's shoe.

Jon Venables and Robert Thompson are indicted and tried for murder. Because of their ages, their names are kept secret. In the press they are referred to as Child A and Child B. Robert, Child A, is labeled the "ringleader." In truth, Jon has his own bad reputation, without Robert. He was a problem child and the bane of his teacher's existence.

What would compel two young boys—one of whom was fond of fuzzy troll dolls and lollipops—to brutalize and murder a two-year-old? What was the trigger? The "how," although gruesome, was easy enough to decipher. The "why" was not. A shocked community searched for answers—suspiciously eying everything from video games to television violence to mental defect, the former of which was ruled out after the boys "passed" a battery of tests proving they were not only "sane" but understood right from wrong. Psychologists theorized that the boys took out their frustrations on James, that James was a substitute for the siblings they resented, and for all that was wrong in their young lives.

Other, less liberal views held that the boys were just plain evil. Indeed, the press compared them to Saddam Hussein! The truth, though less sensational, was more likely that the murder was caused by a combination of factors. Both boys came from troubled homes, although the Venables' residence was considerably safer than the Thompson's.

By the time Jon was ten, his mother, Susan, had made two unsuccessful suicide attempts. She drank a lot and was frequently depressed. Susan and Jon's father, Neil, had separated and reconciled several times. Each time, the children, Mark, Jon, and Michelle, were forced to relocate. His parents' on-again-off-again relationship had a profound effect on Jon. The child craved attention and stability, sacred commodities in his family.

Although Mark was the oldest child, he required the most attention. Burdened with a learning disability and a cleft palate, the fifteen-year-old was a prime target for bullies. Mark often took out his frustrations on his younger brother Jon. Nine-year-old Michelle also struggled with a learning disability. Jon was kind to both siblings but may have resented them both, especially Mark.

Branded a troublemaker, Jon was really a troubled child crying out for help. He clearly needed counseling. One of his teachers remarked that she "had never come across a boy like Jon," in fourteen years.[5] At school, he butted his head against things, threw tantrums, rocked back and forth, made strange noises, and even purposely cut himself with a pair of scissors. He also attacked a classmate. Rather than address the problem, Jon was transferred to another school. He continued to act out. He also made a new friend, Robert Thompson.

At the time of the murder, Susan and Neil Venables were attempting reconciliation. Susan had her hands full at home. She cried easily and

A security camera captured the two British teens abducting two-year-old James Bulger in a Liverpool mall.
Photograph courtesy of CNN

was prone to fly off the handle, slapping the kids in the face. Her open-handed blows stung, but the only scars they left were emotional. These attacks were minor compared to the beatings that took place in the Thompson household.

Violence ruled the roost at the Thompsons' modest home. Ann and Robert Sr. had been raised in highly dysfunctional, abusive homes. When they married and started their own family, the chain of abuse continued. Theirs was a violent—and fertile—union. Together, the couple had five sons. The family would have been even bigger but Robert beat Ann so badly that she miscarried one of their children. He was a frightening character who was fond of scaring his kids. "See the evil in my eyes, twat," he'd say.[6] Robert, the youngest, was six when the father abandoned the family for another woman. Ann hit the bottle and, like Susan Venables, tried twice to kill herself. With the Thompson patriarch gone, the vicious cycle of violence continued. The second youngest in the family was removed from the home by social services after alleging that his oldest brother beat, tarred, and feathered him, and locked him in a tool shed.[7]

Eventually, Ann remarried and had another child, a son who displaced Robert as the baby of the family.

. . . .

Despite their ages, Robert and Jon were charged as adults and tried together at Preston Crown Court. The boys were so small that they could
not see over the court railings. To remedy this, they were seated on an
elevated platform constructed specifically for them. Seated here, they
were able to view the proceedings; they were also now very much on
display in the crowded courtroom. (This fact would be cited as grounds
for a retrial, a request the court denied.)

The defendants were so young, so small, and charged with such a
big, ugly crime. It defied belief. But then, they weren't the first prepu-
bescent kids to commit murder. Most notable before them was Mary
Bell. Like Thompson and Venables, Bell was British, and from an im-
poverished neighborhood. She was also ten when she killed her first
victim, a three-year-old boy. A year later, she and a friend murdered another toddler. Bell carved an M on the boy's stomach and mutilated
his genitals.

Child murder is always shocking, always heinous, and particularly
repellent to us as a society. When a child is murdered by another child,
the crime is all the more shocking and incomprehensible. And enraging.
Anger was the driving force behind the mob of protestors who waited
for hours outside the courthouse to get a glimpse at the little monsters who killed baby Jamie Bulger. The mob, several hundred strong,
screamed obscenities, and threw rocks and eggs at the police van trans-
porting the boys to court.

Jon and Robert pleaded not guilty; neither took the stand. Their
voices would be heard anyway. The courtroom listened in rapt silence
to audiotapes of the boys' police interviews (and in Jon's case, his confession). Jon cries often on tape, a high-pitched and at times hysterical
sound that members of the jury found almost unbearable. A few adults
were moved to tears. Robert, in contrast, sounds cocky and belligerent.
He doesn't cry on tape, nor does he cry in court, a fact that underscores
the public perception of him as a hardened killer. Raised as a Thompson, Robert learned early on to put on a tough façade. It was a survival
mechanism. He told his mother, Ann, that he was afraid to cry in court
because he was afraid to look "like a baby."[8] Adults who should have

known better viewed Robert's lack of tears and constant fidgeting as proof of his moral depravity. Jon fared better in the public's eye. He was portrayed as a weak, immature young boy who fell under the sway of a ten-year-old Svengali.

The psychiatrists and social workers who had evaluated the boys were not permitted to testify on their behalf. Although there were enough mitigating factors to win leniency for the boys—Robert's severely dysfunctional and abusive family, Jon's emotional problem and the lack of stability at home, to name just a few—the defense offered no defense. Instead, the boys' barristers (the British term for attorney) each blamed the other child for the crime.

Prosecutor Richard Henriques didn't buy it. He argued that both children were equally guilty. "Together they took James away from his mother and from the Strand, one holding his hand, the other leading the way," he said in his summation. "Together they abused James. Robert Thompson delivered a persuasive kick, while Jon Venables chose to shake James. They each heard each other lie to adults . . . If ever a crime was committed jointly and together then this was the crime."[9]

Further, Henriques contended that the crime was premeditated, a claim the defendants' barristers hotly contested. Robert's barrister, David Turner, argued that the boys would not have paraded James Bulger through their own neighborhood, past dozens of adults, if they had planned from the beginning to kill him. Turner suggested "an alternative intention. These boys were saddled by their own mischief with a little toddler who must have been tired out, as they were themselves." He suggested that the boys were silently hoping one of these adults would intervene and take the baby off their hands.[10] Tragically, none did.

The trial lasted seventeen days. No one was surprised by the jury's verdict. Robert, having lived with the stigma of being a Thompson, was certain he would be convicted. He was right. Both boys were found guilty as charged. Judge Michael Morland addressed the young defendants, "The killing of James Bulger was an act of unparalleled evil and barbarity . . . In my judgment your conduct was both cunning and very wicked." The boys were then sentenced to detention at "Her Majesty's Pleasure"—a clause under British law that allows the government to hold prisoners for an indeterminate time. Morland explained to the boys that they would be imprisoned for "many, many years until the Home Secretary is satisfied that you have matured and are fully reha- bilitated and until you are no longer a danger to others."

As the defendants were led from the courtroom, a spectator cried out, "How do you feel now, you little bastards?"

Jon Venables and Robert Thompson were the youngest convicted mur- derers in 250 years of British history. Their trial had been a highly charged, emotional event. The Venables and Thompson families re- ceived numerous death threats and were forced to go into hiding. Yet, time often cools tempers. At least one juror had a change of heart. "Looking back, I am ashamed that I allowed myself to be coerced by the judge and prosecution to agree to a verdict of guilty of murder," jury foreman Vincent Moss told *Guardian* reporter Libby Brooks. "A proper judgment would have been that they had behaved like confused, frightened, and stupid children caught up in a situation they had cre- ated but could not deal with. The judge's pronouncement that they were 'evil' was just wrong—they didn't have the moral and intellectual ca- pacity for this to be an accurate description."[11]

The boys served eight years in separate, secure youth detention fa- cilities. They were released in 2001. For their own safety, they were both given new identities.

eight

LAW & ORDER: The prime suspect in a brutal murder argues his innocence based on the fact that he was in an alcoholic blackout while committing the crime.

TRUE STORY: The murder of a married couple went unsolved for four years until Paul Cox confessed to the crime during an Alcoholics Anonymous meeting.

Shanta Chervu, a hardworking emergency room technician, was looking forward to completing her residency and beginning a career in geriatrics. Not that the life of a doctor is easy, but working as an EMT took a lot of energy and meant a lot of crazy hours. Shanta's husband, Lakshman Rao, worked hard as well, running the nuclear medicine program at Albert Einstein College of Medicine, earning enough money to live in Larchmont, New York, an upscale suburb in Westchester County. Life was good—hectic at times, but good.

Busy as the Chervus were, they always made time for their son, Arun, and daughter, Arati. Before she left for work in the morning, Shanta would gently coax Arati out of sleep by stroking her hair; a cup of tea would be awaiting the daughter in the kitchen. Lakshman, too, dedicated all his personal time to his family. He raised his children to place an almost religious value on education. They learned how to type before any of their friends did and understood algebra by the time they had reached sixth grade.[1] Eventually, they moved out of the house, established themselves, and started their own families.

Their patients and children weren't the only recipients of the couple's generosity and love. When the Chervus emigrated to the United States from India in the seventies, they didn't come alone. Between the two of them, Shanta and Lakshman had eight siblings, each of whom had their own families. The Chervus—financially better off than all of them—brought everyone to America with them and supported them all until they got on their own feet.[2]

Lakshman and Shanta's story was a textbook example of the American Dream gone right. They spent virtually every minute of the day helping others in one way or another, and they were beloved in return. They worked hard, built careers, bought a home, and raised their children to be productive members of society.

And it all came to an abrupt end on New Year's Eve in 1988.

In the early hours of December 31, twenty-one-year-old Paul Cox entered the Chervus' home while they slept and, in a blind, intoxicated fury, stabbed them to death in their bed. Cox had nothing against the Chervus, no motive for killing these people who had touched so many lives. He claimed later that he didn't even remember doing it. He wasn't on Angel Dust, Crystal Meth, or any other drug known for inducing randomly violent furies. Paul Cox was drunk. He killed these people, who had improved so many lives, in an alcoholic blackout. And, yet, strangely enough, it wasn't a "random" murder.

Paul Cox was born into a well-established Westchester family. His grandfather had been a supervisor of nearby Mamaroneck, and his father held a vice president position at Chase Manhattan Bank. Paul, however, didn't follow in their footsteps. In his earliest years of school, he had a penchant for stealing money from his parents and classmates, and in high school, he attempted suicide by overdosing on painkillers. After school, he joined the air force, but was discharged because of his suicidal tendencies. He then gave college a try and flunked out after his first semester.

But Paul Cox did one thing very well: he knew how to party. By sixth grade he had already begun working on his drinking problem; it saw him through all his failures in life. At the age of twenty-one he was a full-blown alcoholic working as a carpenter but expending most of his energy looking for the next buzz.

The night of December 30, 1988, began as any normal night. Cox got together with his friends and went to a keg party, where they knocked back one beer after another, chasing them with pitchers of kamikazees. When the keg was kicked, Cox, who had borrowed his mother's car for the night, drove his friends to Gary's Barleycorn, a bar in Larchmont, and they kept the party going. By two o'clock, even this hard-drinking crew had had enough and decided to pack it in for the night. They piled into the car and headed homeward. Speeding down a country road, Cox lost control and slammed into a guardrail. Everyone was okay, but the car was banged up. Worried that a cop passing by might have a Breathalyzer handy, Cox decided he'd better leave the car and walk home; his friends walked back to the bar.

Cox's route took him past his boyhood home on 36 Lincoln Avenue, the present home of the Chervus. The Coxes had sold it to the couple in 1974, when Paul was seven years old. Maybe he met the Chervus at some point during the sale, and maybe he didn't. But most likely, he hadn't thought of them since. Now, fourteen years later, Paul Cox walked up to the house, broke a window, and entered. As he passed through the kitchen, he picked up a knife.

Though the details of the murder are almost as hazy today as they were in 1988, investigators determined that the Chervus were not killed in their sleep. As they were stabbed repeatedly, they most likely put up a fight; there was simply too much blood around the room (even on the ceiling) to believe no struggle occurred. After killing the couple by cutting their throats, Paul Cox went to his parents' present home, where he was living at the time, and went to bed.

The next morning, Cox's mother woke up her son to inform him that the police had found her car abandoned miles away from her home. She demanded an explanation. Paul made up a story about a flat tire and went back to sleep. That night, he saw news coverage of the murder on TV and was surprised to see that it occurred in his old home.

The Chervus' bodies were found on January 2, 1989. Family and friends were thrown into a state of shock. In addition to grieving the loss of two beloved people, everyone was mystified. Lakshman and Shanta had no enemies whatsoever; people adored them. The police, confident they would find the killer, were eventually as baffled as the victims' family. With no leads to speak of, cops could discern no motive and although they lifted a palm print near the front door with the broken window, they couldn't find a match. The murder went unsolved for four years.

On November 11, 1990, Paul Cox decided to attend a meeting of Alcoholics Anonymous (AA). He had been blacking out far too often of late, and thought he might have a more serious problem than a simple lust for partying. Initially, the AA meetings were a little too freaky for him. There was a lot of talk about God, and he didn't see what God had to do with drying out.* But he figured he had two choices: either embrace the AA way or slide ever further down the slippery slope. There really was no choice. At the age of twenty-five, he had already been drinking heavily for more than half his life. Keeping it up would only put him in an early grave. He soon joined AA and embarked upon the twelve-step journey toward recovery.

Cox succeeded in ending the pattern of drinking that had thus far made his life story one failure after another. But as he sobered up, he said, he began to have intense dreams, some of which included disturbing images of killing his parents. (A psychiatrist had, in fact, diagnosed Cox as "matricidal" and "patricidal" in high school.[3]) Slowly, he claimed, he began to remember more details about that night in December, and soon realized that his connection to the Chervu murders was more involved than the fact that he had previously lived at the crime scene. As the weeks

---

*Out of AA's twelve steps, seven specifically mention God.

went by and the haze began to dissipate from his memory, he became more and more convinced that he had killed the Chervus.

Steps four and five of the twelve-step program require the alcoholic to make a "searching and fearless moral inventory" of himself and admit "to God, to [himself] and to another human being the exact nature of [his] wrongs."[4] It's the AA version of atoning for sins, like the Roman Catholic sacrament of confession. Cox decided that he must confess. First, he told his girlfriend,* who was also an AA member, about his strong suspicion that he was a murderer. Although refusing to believe that Paul was capable of such an act, she could plainly see that he was distraught over the issue, and she told him to talk to his AA sponsor about it.

Still upset, Cox called his sponsor on the phone and told him he had something of grave importance to confess. "What's the problem? How bad could it be, you didn't kill anyone did you?" the sponsor replied.[5] Cox was eerily silent on the other end. The sponsor felt a brick land in his stomach when he realized that his rhetorical question had an all-too-real answer. Everyone with whom Cox spoke passed him on to a higher authority. Eventually, he found himself a lawyer. In the end, Cox told no fewer than eight AA members and friends about the fact (and by now he knew it was a *fact*) that he had stabbed the Chervus to death.

AA being a quasi-religion/therapy organization, it takes anonymity very seriously. Cox's secret was well kept for years. Then his ex-girlfriend started seeing a personal therapist. When her analyst learned about her conversation with Cox, he urged her to tell the police. She did, and Cox was summarily arrested. The police only had to do one thing to be sure they had their man: take a palm print. It was a perfect match to the one found in the Chervus' doorway. Police then interviewed everyone with whom Cox had spoken about the murder. Every story matched. Paul Cox was sunk.

Or so it seemed. Before the trial, Cox's lawyer, Andrew Rubin, argued that his client's tale of the Chervu double murder had been related

---

*In the murder trial of Paul Cox, eight AA members testified anonymously; therefore, no names of AA members will be used here.

to fellow AA members in confidence. The success of AA requires complete anonymity, Rubin said, and conversations among members should be afforded the same privilege as those between clerics and congregants. Therefore, the police should never have interviewed Cox's fellow AA members; had they respected the confidentiality, they would have had no cause to pick up Cox in the first place and, therefore, would not have had access to his palm print. His motion to suppress the evidence was denied, but Rubin had set the grounds for appeal.

Members of the Chervu family were both bewildered and infuriated. While they had been mourning Shanta and Lakshman, struggling to find some sort of closure—a struggle made all the more difficult because the case had remained unsolved for so long—eight strangers had been walking around for years with the very knowledge that could have helped them deal with their loss. How could these people have kept quiet? Didn't the law—not to mention common decency—require them to reveal the name of the killer?

Having struck out on the privilege argument, Rubin changed course and went with an insanity defense, arguing that Cox had committed the crime in a psychotic state. His parents had pushed him so hard to succeed in life, and were so emotionally neglectful, that Cox had snapped. It was just a matter of time, given the stress Cox was under. On that night, Rubin argued, Cox reverted back to his seven-year-old self and murdered two people he believed, in his psychotic state, to be his parents. One psychiatrist who took the stand for the defense said, "Mr. Cox was in a severe blackout. Probably the most typical behavior during a blackout is finding the way home . . . It's almost as if he were going back in time and eliminating the people that he sought to blame for all his problems back when he was seven years old."[6]

New York State has two requirements for an insanity defense: (1) the defendant must prove he or she has a mental disease or disorder and (2) that the disease or disorder removed his or her ability to understand that his or her actions are illegal or immoral.

Eleven jurors had little problem identifying the holes the prosecution poked in the defense's argument, and each one decided that neither requirement for the insanity defense had been fulfilled. Eleven, not twelve. One juror insisted that Cox *might* be mentally ill and that the illness *might* have impaired his judgment. She dug her heels in. The holdout even argued Cox possibly didn't commit the crime at all—even though the defense admitted he did! Reports circulated that a war was raging in the deliberation room.[7]

At one point the jury asked the judge to provide the definitions of "moral judgment," "culpability," and "blamability." The holdout's request was written by the jury foreman, accompanied by an apology for "the ridiculousness of this request."[8] The judge looked the words up in a dictionary and read them to the jury. Still, the lone juror stuck to her guns. After seven days, the judge declared a mistrial. Many jury members broke down in tears when the verdict was read, and Cox walked . . . for now: the DA wasn't about to let it end there.

In November 1994, the second trial of Paul Cox began, and, again, the privilege was tossed. This time, Cox took the stand to explain his side of the story. He related his life story, with all its trials and tribulations—being sent to school with terrible sandwiches, his siblings' indifference to his birthdays, his parents' absence from his sports games. What did anyone expect him to do later in life but develop a drinking problem and commit murder?

This time, the jury had no renegades in its ranks . . . but it did have an iota of sympathy. The jury members found Cox guilty of murder, but considered him so completely screwed up that they lowered the charge to manslaughter in the first degree. Cox was sentenced to two 8⅓- to 25-year sentences, to be served consecutively.

Now it was Cox's turn to fight back. He had been keeping a version of the privilege issue in his back pocket, and it was time to use it—his wild card. He appealed his conviction on the grounds that the confessions he made to AA members fell under the cleric–congregant privilege recognized by New York State—and that the courts themselves had in the past treated AA as a religion. In one such case, *Warner vs. Orange County Department of Probation*, the court ruled that the probation department that forced a convict to attend AA sessions had violated the Establishment Clause, writing that "the Constitution guarantees that government may not coerce anyone to support or participate in religion or its exercise."[9] In effect, the Warner case had declared AA a religion.

Cox's prosecutors argued that AA is not a religion, and that its members aren't clerics. The federal judge who heard the case sided with Cox: AA can be considered a religion and, therefore, the confessions were privileged. Without the confessions, police would not have been led to Cox, would not have arrested him, and would not have taken his palm print. The manslaughter conviction was overturned.

Westchester County DA Jeanine Pirro was infuriated. Accepting AA as a religion for the moment—strictly for the sake of argument—she said that Cox's particular confessions "were not unlike going to church

SEPARATION OF RELIGION AND STATE

The type of argument Paul Cox used during his trial is practically as old as law itself. The religion versus state issue first reared its head in New York in the 1813 case of Daniel Phillips, a Catholic, who confessed to a priest that he had received stolen property. The priest refused to testify against Phillips, stating the church's position that a confession is a "secret" between the sinner and God. The court refused to make the priest betray his ecclesiastic oath, arguing that his constitutional right to practice his religion trumps all.

Fifteen years later, a Protestant tried to use the same argument in his murder case. Because confession isn't a sacrament in Protestantism, the court refused to grant the same privilege. Because this, in effect, meant that Catholics got preferential treatment, the New York State legislature quickly created a statute to extend the privilege: "No minister of the gospel, or priest of any denomination whatsoever, shall be allowed to disclose any confessions made to him in his professional character, in the course of discipline enjoined by the rules or practice of such denomination." And, thus, Paul Cox could argue that AA is a religion.

and having a cup of coffee . . . later with someone . . . and saying, 'By the way, I killed two people.'"[10] The DA bounced the privilege issue up to the U.S. Court of Appeals for the Second Circuit.

On July 17, 2002, the court handed down its decision. The three-judge panel scrutinized the state's definition of the cleric–congregant privilege, which was based on one main question: Were Cox's discussions with fellow AA members aimed at gaining spiritual guidance? The judges pointed out that, according to testimony, Cox had broken down in fits of tears during his first confession—the one to his ex-girlfriend. The court interpreted the confession as an emotional catharsis, not a desperate cry for spiritual advice. Later, Cox's so-called spiritual advisors—his AA sponsors—advised him to find a lawyer, which he did. This suggested to the judges that Cox and his sponsors considered the matter a legal one, not spiritual or religious. The rest of Cox's conversations were nothing more than a friend talking to friends.

The court of appeals ruled that privilege didn't apply in this case and overturned the previous appellate court's decision. Barring any future appeals, Paul Cox will serve his full sentence.

nine

LAW & ORDER: A soap opera star is attacked and left for dead by an obsessed fan.

TRUE STORY: Hollywood starlet Rebecca Schaeffer is murdered outside her home by a fan who had been stalking her for several years.

The script arrived by messenger. Rebecca Schaeffer signed for it and hurried back inside her apartment. She had just a couple of hours to prepare for her audition—and what an audition it was. The twenty-one-year-old was being considered for a coveted role in a sequel to Francis Ford Coppola's Oscar-winning film *The Godfather*. She would be reading for the director himself. Still a relative newcomer to Hollywood, Schaeffer could hardly believe how well her career was going. The doorbell rang. The intercom was broken so Schaeffer answered the door in person. A young guy wearing rumpled clothes and the oddest smile greeted her. In one hand, he clutched a publicity photo of the actress, in the other a letter. "I'm your biggest fan," he declared proudly, moving toward her. He was hyper and agitated—and too close for comfort. Startled by his visit and his demeanor, Schaeffer backed away. She thanked him for his support, and after explaining that she was very busy, politely asked him to leave.

There was little time to dwell on the brief but unnerving encounter. She needed to finish reading the script. An hour later, she was getting her clothes ready when the doorbell rang again. She put on a bathrobe and went to see who was calling. There was no one there . . . or so it seemed. Schaeffer opened the glass security door and stepped outside. Her biggest fan was back, rushing toward her from the side of the house. He was no longer holding her photograph. This time, he had a gun. Schaeffer's big eyes went wide. The stranger shot her point-blank with a .357 Magnum. She fell to the ground screaming as the hollow-point bullet exploded inside her chest.

Raised in Eugene, and later Portland, Oregon, Rebecca Schaeffer was the only child born to Benson and Danna Schaeffer. Smart, kind, and gorgeous, Rebecca was the kind of girl all the boys fell in love with and all the girls wanted to be like. Her lovely face was framed by a cascade of dark curls, and her big brown eyes projected both curiosity and intelligence. She epitomized the wholesome, archetypical girl next-door. But her innocent looks belied a strong determination and fierce independence. Schaeffer was still in her teens when she decided to pursue a modeling career. It was leaps and bounds from what she once wanted to be: a rabbi. During her junior year of high school, Schaeffer left Portland and her parents for New York City. She got an agent and enrolled in the exclusive Professional Children's School. Alone in a big city, Schaeffer was unfazed. When an overly enthusiastic admirer groped her on the street, Rebecca hauled off and hit him in the face.

She loved the fast pace of life in the Big Apple, even if her career wasn't working out as well as she had hoped. Too short to make it as a runway model, the five-foot-seven Schaeffer set her sights on acting. On camera, she was radiant. She landed a role on the daytime soap opera *One Life to Live* and had a small part in Woody Allen's *Radio Days*, although most of her scene wound up on the cutting room floor. Producers in Los Angeles saw her demo reel and cast her in a supporting role in the sitcom *My Sister Sam*. Schaeffer relocated to the West Coast, staying with costar Pam Dawber and Dawber's husband, actor Mark Harmon, until she found a place of her own. As Patti, the quirky, loveable younger sibling of lead Dawber, Schaeffer was a big hit with tele-

The apartment building where Schaeffer lived. On her way out to an audition that could make her career, Robert John Bardo shot her point-blank with a .357 Magnum. *Photo by Scott Michaels*

vision viewers. "Patti is more daring than I ever was, but like me, she's very positive," the actress told *Seventeen* magazine. "She expects things to go well, and so do I. I always think of good things happening to me—and they do." Still, Schaeffer admitted, "I never really thought I'd be doing television. But when this part came up, it was just too good to be true. I've still got a lot of time to fulfill my other dreams."[1]

Schaeffer was bombarded with fan mail. Some of the letters were sent to her agent, others to the studio. She piled the mail bags into her Volkswagen Beetle and took them home, where she would sift through them, reading as many as possible, her cat Katherine Hepburn at her side. Rebecca received over a thousand letters, more than a few sent by a young man named Robert John Bardo.

The youngest of seven children, Robert John Bardo was a loner with a long history of odd behavior. At thirteen, he became fixated on Samantha Smith, the young New Englander whose correspondence with Soviet politician Yuri Andropov during the Cold War earned her worldwide celebrity and the title "America's Youngest Ambassador." Hoping to meet the girl, Bardo traveled by bus to Maine. Police, alerted by Bardo's parents, intercepted him before he could make contact with Smith.

In high school, Bardo showed promise, earning high marks, but his mental problems got the best of him. He sent his teacher harassing letters signed "Dirty Harry" and "James Bond."[2] In the letters, he'd hint at killing her and then himself. Bardo was hospitalized briefly for mental illness. The teenager responded well to treatment and therapy. His parents, however, did not allow him to continue with treatment and Bardo's behavior worsened. His teacher described him as a "time bomb on the verge of exploding."[3] The teenager never graduated.

At seventeen, Bardo's life had stalled. He was in a rut; his dreary routine consisted of sleeping, writing letters to celebrities, and walking the two miles to and from Jack in the Box, the fast-food joint where he worked cleaning toilets and mopping floors. Then he discovered *My Sister Sam*. He became enthralled with the beautiful young actress who played Patti Russell. "She came into my life at the right moment. She was brilliant, pretty, outrageous. Her innocence impressed me. She turned into a goddess for me, an idol. Since then I turned an atheist, I only adored her," he would say later.

Each week he had eagerly awaited the new episode and the chance to gaze at Rebecca. Bardo was crazy about Schaeffer. He'd also been crazy about singers Madonna, Debbie Gibson, and Tiffany. But Rebecca was different. Although she was miles (and social classes) removed from him, Bardo felt Schaeffer was accessible, and maybe even interested in him. After all, she had replied to one of his letters, hadn't she? She enclosed an autographed photo along with a short note thanking him for "the most beautiful letter" she had ever received. Schaeffer signed off "With love from Rebecca."

Bardo cherished her reply. Holed up in his bedroom—a virtual shrine to the young actress—he read her words over and over. He watched the videotapes he had made of *My Sister Sam*, memorizing every curve and angle of Rebecca's lovely face. "When I think of her I would like to become famous to impress her," he wrote in his journal. Bardo bought a teddy bear and a bus ticket to Burbank, California. He arrived on the studio lot where *My Sister Sam* was filmed and made it past the front gate before security guards caught up with him. They escorted him off the lot. Bardo returned home.

Back in Tucson, Bardo really started to unravel. He shouted at strangers in the street, made obscene gestures at passing motorists, and menaced his neighbors, threatening to shoot one man for making too much noise. He also made plans for another trip to California. A month later, he was back at Burbank Studios. He'd brought a note for Rebecca and a knife, which he kept hidden from the security guards who, once again, refused him admission to the *My Sister Sam* set. The head of security felt sorry for Bardo and gave him a lift back to his hotel. On the way, he tried to convince the nineteen-year-old to abandon his quest to meet Schaeffer.

Bardo called him from the bus depot to thank him for his kindness and for "treating him like a father." Alone in his bedroom, Bardo was more sanguine, writing in his journal, "I don't lose. Period."

Meanwhile, *My Sister Sam* was failing in the ratings and after two years, the show was cancelled. Rebecca Schaeffer was disappointed, but now she was free to pursue a film career. She had a small part in *Scenes from the Beverly Hills Class Struggle*, a risqué farce that received mixed reviews. Her scene was a love scene. Schaeffer's star was on the rise.

In Tucson, Bardo rushed out to watch Schaeffer on the big screen. She was beautiful. She was also in bed with another actor, a fact that enraged the unstable young man who admired her innocence. His obsession with the actress quickly turned deadly. His fan letters, in which he addressed her now as "Miss Nudity Two-Shoes," took on a threatening tone. Schaeffer had become another "Hollywood bitch," whom "God was going to appoint me to punish," he told his sister. Bardo made plans to kill the actress; he sketched her body and marked off the places where he wanted to shoot her. He drew inspiration from Mark David Chapman, the loner who assassinated John Lennon, and from Arthur Jackson, the obsessed fan who nearly killed actress Teresa Saldana. Bardo wrote to Chapman in prison and the two men corresponded briefly. Chapman found Bardo's letters frightening and stopped replying. Bardo

The entryway to actress Rebecca Shaeffer's home where she was ambushed and murdered by an obsessed fan.
Photo by Scott Michaels

turned his attention to Jackson, a Scotsman who had become enamored with Saldana after seeing her in the movie *Defiance*. Jackson traveled across the ocean to kill the actress and get the death penalty so that they could be together in the afterlife. He hired a private detective agency to find out where Saldana lived and then attacked her outside her home, stabbing her dozens of times. A deliveryman intervened, thwarting Jackson's plans. Miraculously, Saldana survived the brutal attack. Jackson was sentenced to twelve years in prison. Upon his release, he was extradited to Great Britain where he was tried and found guilty of a murder he committed three decades earlier.

Determined to meet Rebecca, Bardo made another trip to Los Angeles. He'd packed light—the letter and photo the actress had sent him two years earlier, a cassette tape of U2's "Exit," a copy of *The Catcher in the Rye* (the book Chapman was carrying when he shot John Lennon), and the .357 Magnum revolver he convinced his older brother to buy for him. Before leaving, he wrote to his sister in Tennessee, "I have an obsession with the unattainable and I have to eliminate something that I cannot have."[4]

The sun was just coming up when Bardo arrived in LA. At first, he wandered the streets showing passersby Schaeffer's photograph and asking if they knew where she lived. Then he tried getting her address from her agent. When that didn't work, Bardo followed Arthur Jackson's lead and paid a detective agency $250 to track down Schaeffer— his "long-lost friend." Neither man knew it, but for a small fee, they could have obtained the information themselves from the California Department of Motor Vehicles.

Early the next morning, Bardo headed out to the actress's Fairfax neighborhood. He waited over an hour outside the Tudor-style building where she lived before summoning up the courage to ring the bell. Schaeffer answered the door. Bardo could hardly believe that he was face-to-face with her at last. He showed her the photograph she had sent him and handed her a note. She seemed startled so he tried to explain, "I'm your biggest fan." He had more to tell her but she said she was very busy. The actress was polite but asked him to leave. She shook Bardo's hand and returned inside.

Angry and disappointed, Bardo shuffled off in his well-worn sandals. He was bothered by the "cold look" on Rebecca's face and by his dismissal. From a pay phone, he called his sister in Tennessee and told her he planned to "stop Schaeffer from forsaking her innocent childlike image for that of an adult fornicating screen whore." His sister was alarmed but didn't think Bardo would actually harm the actress. She made him promise to leave Schaeffer alone. Bardo hung up and had breakfast—cheesecake and onion rings—at a diner nearby. He ducked into the restroom to load the .357 Magnum he'd been carrying inside a plastic bag.

By 10:15 that morning, Bardo was back on North Sweetzer Avenue. He rang Schaeffer's bell and hid out of sight. She answered, dressed in a black bathrobe, stepping outside to see who was calling. Bardo ambushed her, shooting her once in the chest with a hollow-point bullet.

"Why? Why?" Rebecca screamed, before collapsing at his feet. Bardo stood silent, watching the blood pool around her. A neighbor heard the commotion and ran outside to find Schaeffer lying on the ground. Bardo took off and bolted down the block.

The actress was rushed to Cedars-Sinai Medical Center where she died thirty minutes later. She was twenty-one years old.

The driver swerved to avoid the young man. In the process, he'd nearly plowed into another vehicle. He steered his car onto the shoulder of the road, rolled down the window, and honked the horn to get the young man's attention. It was incredible, the guy, still a kid really, was darting in and out of the traffic on the interstate! He must be mad, or stoned, the driver thought. Fortunately, the police arrived before the guy had time to cause an accident. Later, the driver would learn that the young man was a suspect in the murder of a television actress.

Robert John Bardo was dazed and disheveled but, amazingly, uninjured from his suicidal sprint onto Interstate 10. "I thought I owed it to Rebecca to kill myself after what happened," he told the officers who arrested him. Once in custody, he promptly confessed to killing Schaeffer. Preparations were made to hand him over to the Los Angeles police department. Bardo's public defender fought valiantly to block the extradition but filed her paperwork in the wrong court. LA County Deputy Assistant District Attorney Marcia Clark seized the opportunity to take custody of the defendant.

During an evaluation with his court-appointed psychiatrist, Bardo recounted his version of the murder. Rebecca Schaeffer, he said, "had this kid voice . . . sounded like a brat or something . . . said I was wasting her time! Wasting her time! No matter what, I thought that was a very callous thing to say to a fan, you know . . . I grabbed the door, gun's still in the bag, I grab it by the trigger, I come around and kapow! And she's like screaming . . . 'ahhhhh' . . . screaming, 'why . . . ahhhh' and it's like oh God."

Bardo was charged with first-degree murder. He pleaded not guilty and waived his right to a jury trial, a move that made him ineligible for the death penalty.

He opted instead to let Superior Court Judge Dino Fulgoni decide his fate. Bardo told the judge, "I could probably tell you what I did after I killed her, how I got sick and all, but I don't feel like it."

Prosecution witness Burbank Studios security chief John Eggers testified that he met with Bardo in 1987 and tried to discourage him from pursuing a relationship with Schaeffer. Rebutting defense claims that Bardo was insane, the security chief said, "He was one of the most lucid and intelligent types of people that I've ever dealt with." Eggers had felt sorry for the young man, whom he viewed as a lovesick, harmless fan. "I dropped him off [at his hotel] and told him the best thing would be for him to go back to Tucson. He said, 'I'm going to do that.' All in all it was a pleasant encounter. I felt I accomplished something."

Defense attorney Stephen Galindo did not deny his client killed Schaeffer. Instead, he disputed the prosecution's claims that the murder was premeditated. He also argued that the defendant's history of mental illness and his unhealthy family life were mitigating factors that should be considered. "It would not be inappropriate for this court to provide leniency" because of the abuse and mental illness Bardo "suffered through no fault of his own," he told the judge.

The cameraman who had observed Bardo running in traffic and acting "loony" testified that it was clear "Robert was a very sick young man." Forensic psychiatrist Park Dietz* told the court that the defendant was schizophrenic and afflicted with "Fan Obsession Syndrome," a psychological condition caused by repeated exposure to, and identification with, a particular celebrity. Dietz, whose role in several high-profile cases had made him something of a celebrity himself, said that Bardo's illness caused him to spontaneously shoot Rebecca Schaeffer.

Prosecutor Marcia Clark scoffed at the idea and criticized Dietz for believing Bardo's version of the crime. Clark, four years shy of O. J. Simpson stardom, said the defendant killed Schaeffer to become famous. She described the murder as the end result of "carefully controlled, methodical planning." Bardo spent "years of fantasizing about violence," she said. The defendant's strange behavior after the murder may have been due to other factors besides being "loony," argued Clark. For one, Bardo had been awake for two days straight.

---

*Park Dietz was called as an expert witness in the trials of Andrea Yates, Jeffrey Dahmer, the Menendez brothers, and Betty Broderick. He has also served as a technical consultant to *Law & Order* and *Law & Order: Criminal Intent*.

The judge ruled in the prosecution's favor. He declared Bardo guilty of first-degree murder, and of the special charge of "lying in wait" for his victim. "The idea that I killed her for fame is totally ridiculous," Bardo told the judge. "I do realize the magnitude of what I have done. I do realize what I did was irrevocably wrong. If you believe it is just and right to send me to prison for life, then I believe it is just and right." Robert John Bardo was given a life sentence without the possibility of parole, to be served at the state prison for the criminally insane at Vacaville.

ANTISTALKING LAWS

In 1990, as a result of the death of Rebecca Schaeffer and the near-fatal stabbing of fellow actress Teresa Saldana, California made stalking a criminal offense, punishable by jail time and a fine of $1,000. Previously, stalking wasn't considered a crime and a victim had to be physically attacked before he or she could press charges against the stalker. Under the current California Penal Code, a stalker is defined as "any person who willfully, maliciously, and repeatedly follows or willfully and maliciously harasses another person and who makes a credible threat with the intent to place that person in reasonable fear for his or her safety."

California's antistalking law was the first of its kind. Other states followed suit, enacting similar laws criminalizing stalking.

Additionally, new laws were passed making it more difficult for civilians to obtain personal information through the California Department of Motor Vehicles. A decade after Rebecca Schaeffer's death, her boyfriend, director Brad Silberling, made a film about how the tragedy affected him.*

---

*The 2002 film *Moonlight Mile* starring Susan Sarandon, Dustin Hoffman, and Jake Gyllenhaal was based on writer/director Brad Silberling's real-life struggle to come to grips with the murder of his girlfriend Rebecca Schaeffer.

ten

LAW & ORDER: A white, former ballerina is charged with shooting three black teenage boys on the subway.

TRUE STORY: On a winter day in 1984, Bernie Goetz shot four black teenagers when they approached him on the subway demanding money. Was it self-defense or vigilantism?

The bolt lock snapping shut echoed through the tiled hallway as the man locked his apartment door at West 14th Street in New York City. It was about 1:30 p.m. on December 22, 1984. He left the building and headed down the block toward the subway. Not too long ago, he had been mugged for expensive electronics equipment he was carrying and soundly beaten for good measure, leaving his knee permanently damaged; he hadn't felt completely safe on the street since. An unusually perceptive person might have noticed some latent tension in the man, but to most passersby he was just a regular guy walking down the street. A little gaunt, he had an average build, receding hairline, and wore pilot-style glasses and a blue windbreaker.

He headed to the downtown number 2 subway—the two train, as New Yorkers call it. He put his token into the turnstile and waited on the platform. The graffiti-covered train soon pulled up and he got on. The subway car wasn't crowded, and he sat down across from four black teenagers. As the doors closed and the subway began to move, the four youths looked at each other. The man tried not to make eye contact, but since there were so few people on the car, he inevitably caught

In December 1984, Bernie Goetz shot four teens who were about to mug him on a subway in New York. His actions divided a city fed up with rampant street crime: Either you were with the Subway Vigilante or against him.
Photo courtesy of EarthSave International

the eye of one of the kids, who gave him a smile. The man looked away; he didn't take it as a friendly gesture. This was New York City in the early eighties after all, one of the most violent cities in America.

The man had a love-hate relationship with the city he had called home for his entire adult life. Large cities afford a certain level of anonymity. No one cares what you wear, how you live, or what you do—as long as you don't do it to them. And that's how he liked it. Live and let live. But for years now, crime had been steadily rising in New York City and life, unfortunately, wasn't that simple anymore. For the average citizen, minding your own business wasn't always enough. You could be robbed or attacked any time, anywhere—and the police seemed unable or unwilling to prevent it. Violent crime in New York had spiraled so out of control that a former McDonald's night manager named Curtis Sliwa formed the Guardian Angels, a citizen's patrol group, five years earlier. New Yorkers concluded that because they couldn't depend on the cops to protect them, they would have to protect themselves—and they were getting angry about it. Something eventually was going to blow.

The man looked in the teens' direction again. One of them made eye contact again and said something about five dollars.

The man pretended he couldn't hear over the din of the train. "What?" he asked.

The teenagers stood up and walked across the subway car, surrounding him. "Give me five dollars," one of them said.

That's when a donnybrook ensued.

The man stood up, drew a snub-nosed .38 out of his quick-draw holster, and began firing at the teenagers. He shot one in the chest, one in the back, and one in the arm; his fourth shot missed. As quickly as it began, the explosive outburst ended—for a moment. Everyone in the subway car instantly fled to the next car, except for two women, who had hit the deck. The conductor, hearing the shots, pulled the emergency brake cord, and the subway screeched to a stop. It was eerily silent for a few seconds. Then the man approached the fourth teenager saying, "You don't look too bad. Here's another." He pulled the trigger and shot the teen in the spinal cord, instantly paralyzing him.[1]

The man told the terrified women lying on the floor that everything was okay. He sat down for a second, then, when the conductor entered the car, ran out through the rear door, jumped down to the tracks, and disappeared.

The tale of the subway gunman turning the tables on the would-be muggers might have come and gone if Bernie Goetz had been your garden-variety lunatic, or a hardened criminal himself. Shootings in New York were becoming less and less newsworthy these days. But Goetz and his gun struck a cord in the city. Though perhaps a little eccentric, Bernie was just another average middle-class New Yorker who wanted to make a living and mind his own business—but now he had single-handedly taken on four street thugs.

Born in 1947 in Kew Gardens, Queens, Goetz held a degree from New York University and ran his own electronics repair company. He was no doubt an educated and intelligent man. But was he "reasonable"? That question would sharply divide New York City during the subsequent trial of the so-called subway vigilante.

After scurrying down the subway tracks, Goetz emerged on the street and returned to his apartment where he packed some essentials. He quickly rented a car and aimlessly drove north. As cops scoured the city armed with sketches of the perpetrator's face, citizens long frustrated with rampant crime called the police to voice their support for the mystery man, saying their only regret was that the four teens were in a hospital and not six feet under.

The four teenagers—Troy Canty, Darrell Cabey, James Ramseur, and Barry Allen, each of whom was nineteen years old, except Allen, who was eighteen—hardly knew what hit them. Armed with screwdrivers, they had been on their way downtown to break into and steal money from coin-operated arcade games. Now they were languishing in hospital beds recovering from their wounds. Canty, the first to have approached Goetz, suffered from a chest wound; Allen, who had turned to run, caught a bullet in the back; Ramseur had been hit with two bullets—one in the arm, one in the chest; and Caby, the most seriously wounded of the four, was paralyzed from the waist down. He would eventually fall into a coma and suffer permanent brain damage.

On New Year's Eve, Goetz decided that ten days on the lam was just about enough. He entered a police department in Concord, New Hampshire, and announced that he was the subway vigilante. Against the advice even a high school criminal justice student would have offered, Goetz agreed to confess to his crimes on videotape. Sitting behind a table wearing a white-collared shirt, Goetz told his story, his anger building as he proceeded. "My problem was I ran out of bullets," he said leaning forward intently. "I was going to gouge out one of the guy's eyes with my keys." No, he didn't harbor the slightest regret for shooting the four teenagers. "I was vicious. My intent was to kill them." Bernie

Goetz showed the world that he was a bright, well-spoken guy who knew exactly what he was doing; he was clearly *not* insane.

When the confession was made public and people learned just how enraged and devoid of remorse Goetz was, many changed their minds about the Subway Vigilante. Maybe he should have controlled himself a little better, some people said. These were just kids, after all, and the only weapons they had been carrying were a couple of screwdrivers—which could hardly be called weapons.

Forget about it, argued the opposition. Those kids got what they deserved. And just look at the effect: Violent crime in New York plummeted after the shootings. Bernie Goetz had done the city a huge favor.

And so began the debate of self-defense versus vigilantism, spreading from the two train in New York to the four corners of the globe.

Bernhard Goetz was indicted for possession of an illegal weapon and numerous counts of attempted murder and assault—eighteen criminal charges in all. He was the talk of the town. Out on bail, the hitherto faceless electronics technician would turn the heads of passersby and was even approached by "fans" asking for an autograph. On every other street corner, he'd see an homage to himself: street vendors selling THUG BUSTER T-shirts, NEW YORK LOVES YA, BERNIE! graffito on a brick wall, bumper stickers praising the subway vigilante. Radio talk show callers invariably praised him. He was overwhelmed with offers to pay his bail. Goetz, for his part, turned down all offers of financial support; he wanted nothing of his overnight hero status and kept as low a profile as possible.

Anonymity, it turned out though, was simply impossible. And as more details about the shootings came out, the critics' voices grew louder. To be sure, the shooting was viewed by many as a racial thing, but the criticism didn't fall predictably along black-white lines. As Roy Innis, chairman of the Congress of Racial Equality, was proclaiming that black men should have shot the thugs that preyed in their neighborhoods long ago, newspaper columnist Jimmy Breslin was penning articles calling Goetz, and anyone who supported him, a racist.

High-profile defense attorney Barry Slotnick initially showed little interest in the case—that is, until he saw news reporters and cameras

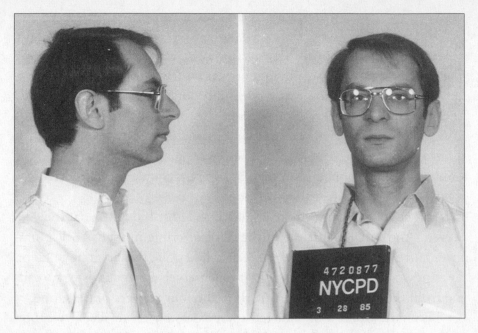

Hero or monster? New York City was sharply divided on Bernie Goetz, who shot four teenagers point-blank because he felt they were planning to mug him.
NYC Police Department

cluttering the sidewalk in front of Goetz's apartment. "I immediately understood that this had some significance greater than a subway shooting," he told the *New York Daily News*. "I decided I was going to represent the public's right to protect themselves."[2] Those words sum up his defense strategy. Slotnick would paint the four teens as predators of the worst kind—congenitally vicious and violent. Bernhard Hugo Goetz was simply protecting himself. Wouldn't each lady and gentleman of the jury do the same thing had they been in his situation?

Prosecutor Greg Waples's legal strategy was the reverse. Goetz was the predator here, a mean-spirited executioner who, by the way, had been walking around the city with an illegal weapon. While any reasonable person would share Goetz's fear during that fateful moment on the subway, no reasonable person would have responded to mere words with guns blazing. Sure, the teens all had been convicted of crimes, and they carried screwdrivers that could easily have been used to stab a person, but the gunman didn't know any of this at the time. The reasonable thing would have been to attempt to avoid confrontation or at least brandish the gun to ward off the so-called muggers. It could even be argued, the prosecution conceded, that Goetz had a right to shoot the first two young men—but to shoot one in the back as he attempted to flee and another who was probably playing possum after seeing his friends get shot? The answers were obvious.

During the seven-week trial, the jury viewed the videotaped confession; heard Canty's claim that they hadn't *demanded* five dollars, just *asked* for the money (Slotnick called him a liar); witnessed the testimony of Ramseur, whose words and body language made it crystal clear that he was indeed the thug that Slotnick was making him out to be (one juror later confessed that Ramseur gave her nightmares); and the words and theories of various experts.

After all was said and done, the jurors' decision rested on what they thought a "reasonable" man would have done in Goetz's situation. In essence, they had to decide if Goetz believed he was defending himself or cleaning the streets of unwanted criminals.

The jury of ten whites and two blacks, half of whom were victims of crime, turned in not-guilty verdicts for seventeen of the eighteen counts; they convicted Goetz of one count of illegal gun possession, for which he served less than a year at New York City's Riker's Island. The verdict hit the headlines everywhere, from the United States to France to Japan.

So Bernie Goetz had beaten the rap. He shot four people without warning, one of whom became paralyzed and brain damaged, fled the scene, was videotaped saying he wished he had shot them in the heads and gouged their eyes out—and got off scot-free.

Not quite.

Eleven years after the subway shooting, Bernie Goetz would find himself in court again—this time in the Bronx—as a defendant in a civil suit filed by Darrell Cabey. A heavy-hitting legal team of William Kuntsler, Ron Kuby, and C. Vernon Mason represented the plaintiff. Cabey filed suit in 1985 against Goetz for $50 million, based on the contention that Bernie Goetz was a racist who "deliberately, willfully and with malice aforethought" inflicted Cabey's life-altering wounds. The case went to trial in the spring of 1996.

Shortly before the trial, in 1995, Goetz told the *New York Times* that Canty, Cabey, Ramseur, and Allen "represented the failure of society . . . Forget about their ever making a positive contribution to society. It's only a question of how much a price they're going to cost. The solution is their mothers should have had an abortion."[3] Those words had come back to haunt him.

Portraying Goetz as the executioner New York prosecutors had failed to, Cabey's attorneys pointed out that three of the bullets in Goetz's chamber were "dum dum" slugs, "designed to cause a maximum of serious physical injury," which are prohibited by international treaty even on a battlefield. They also shared with the court some disturbing racist hate mail Cabey had received as a result of "defendant's said actions."

But the real clincher was Goetz himself. Kuby questioned him on the stand about various racially charged comments he had made over the years, including the abortion comment. At times Goetz appeared flustered and contradicted himself; at other points, he answered with a smirk on his face. Goetz's lawyer tried to save his client by referring to him as "a nerd, a peckerwood, a cracker," but who was decidedly not a "cool, calculating racist." It didn't work. Goetz's testimony struck a nerve in the jury, and he was ordered to pay $43 million. "After listening to him in person, the jury was ready to reach over and throttle him," Kuby commented after his victory.[4] (In later years, he would point out that this client had not received a penny from Goetz.)

In that 1995 *Times* article, Goetz portrays himself as a man who longs for the days when he was anonymous. Since that interview, however, he has thrown his name in the hat to run for mayor of New York City and as a public advocate, during which he advocated for power naps for city workers; spoken out publicly for animal rights; run a company that he named Vigilante Electronics; and appeared in a movie as a pot-smoking, vegetarian nutritionist for vampires.

The young men from the Bronx have led less-weird but more checkered lives. The brain-damaged Cabey remains in a wheelchair with the brain of an eight-year-old. Ramseur, soon after his release from the hospital, was charged and convicted for taking part in the rape of a pregnant eighteen-year-old girl in the Bronx. Canty has served time for crimes ranging from shoplifting to assault; and Allen was convicted of robbery in 1991.

After all the pain, suffering, investigations, legal wrangling, and racial turmoil, one person summed up the incident in two sentences. A woman from Harlem, commenting on the case, said, "It comes down to this: Five assholes met on a train. And one of them had a gun."[5] The rest is history.

POLICE LINEUPS AS EVIDENCE

On *Law & Order*, witness identifications in lineups are rarely challenged by the defense. In reality, attorneys often challenge lineup IDs—both through motions to dismiss and during trial.

Lineups are naturally flawed. Given the amount of detail witnesses need to retain in order to make a positive ID, it's crucial that lineup participants are gathered as quickly as possible. What are the odds of quickly finding a handful of people who look similar enough to keep a defense lawyer at bay? Pretty high.

Given the possible pitfalls concerning the length of witnesses' memories, the natural pressure people feel when viewing a lineup, and the general subjectiveness of this type of evidence-gathering, it's not surprising that lineups are frequently challenged. As a backup plan, police often have witnesses view a photo array prior to a lineup. The photo array can't be challenged.

eleven

LAW & ORDER: A police officer is stabbed to death in the park by a killer who finds religion after she's apprehended.

TRUE STORY: Death row inmate Karla Faye Tucker underwent a religious transformation and lobbied to have her death sentence commuted. Despite the support of Congressman Newt Gingrich and televangelist Pat Robertson, she was executed in 1998.

Karla Faye Tucker had been minding her business, biding her time. Then she found God. At least that's what she said. Quite a few people doubted her sincerity. A convicted murderess, Tucker had good reason to lie—she was on death row, after all. She wouldn't be the first inmate to feign religious conversion to gain sympathy and leniency. Joe Freeman Britt has witnessed this particular jailhouse con firsthand. As a prosecutor, he says, he "probably brought more people to the Lord than Billy Graham . . . they go to prison, they all find the Lord."[1]

Now that she had been reborn, Tucker believed she deserved clemency. Pope John Paul II agreed. He even asked then-governor of Texas George W. Bush to spare Karla's life. The pope wasn't alone in his crusade. Karla's cause had attracted an eclectic group of supporters that included speaker of the house Newt Gingrich, Moral Majority founder Jerry Falwell, former rock wife Bianca Jagger, and televangelist Pat Robertson, who made a plea for Karla's clemency on live TV. "Mercy trumps justice," Robertson told talk show host Larry King.[2]

Had Tucker truly repented? Or was she lying? And did it even mat-

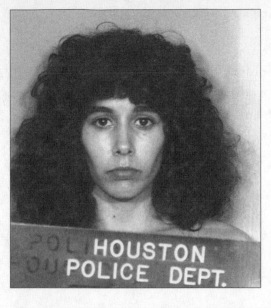

Karla Faye Tucker, the first female to be executed in Texas since the Civil War. Her claim of religious redemption fell on the deaf ears of then-governor George W. Bush. *Houston Police Department*

ter? Didn't the Bible, in which she believed, call for an eye for an eye? One thing was certain, with her pretty pixie face, big eyes, and impressive roster of supporters, Tucker made news. She didn't look like a killer. In fact, it was hard to imagine the smiling, soft-spoken woman even raising her voice. But in the spring of 1983, Karla raised far more than her voice. In a drug-induced frenzy, she had used a pickaxe to murder two people, raising and sinking the weapon into her victims dozens of times.

Karla Faye's parents Caroline and Larry Tucker had a stormy relationship. Their life together was an endless drama of breakups, makeups, and extramarital affairs. Karla Faye was conceived during one of those affairs; Larry wasn't her father. For years, Caroline kept her youngest daughter's paternity secret. Although she was a cute, petite child, Karla Faye often felt like the ugly duckling in the family. Her sisters Kari and Kathi were taller, fairer, blonder. Dark-haired Karla Faye would find out later in life that she resembled her father. Her biological father, that is.

The Tucker household was as tumultuous as the Texas sandstorms that blew through their Houston neighborhood. Left unsupervised, the Tucker girls ran with a tough, older crowd. Karla drank and did drugs, taking her first toke when she was eight years old. Soon after, she was shooting heroin and having sex with her sisters' friends, bikers who didn't let Karla's age dampen their enthusiasm. A full-fledged addict, she dropped out of school in the seventh grade and moved in with her newly divorced mother. Caroline taught Karla the right way to roll a joint.[3] She also taught her how to earn money as a prostitute.

At sixteen, Karla Faye met and married a fellow addict who worked as an auto mechanic. The marriage lasted six years. By her own admission, Karla was too restless to settle down for long. She didn't know it then, but her freedom would be short-lived.

In 1983, alarmed by a national epidemic of drug abuse, Nancy Reagan launched a media blitzkrieg on drugs. She urged Americans to "just say no" to drugs. Down in Houston, the first lady's message didn't reach the Tucker women. Caroline died of an overdose and her daughters loved to get high, especially Karla Faye, who sold her body for dope money. A few times a month, the native Texan would make the trip to Galveston to practice her trade.

She took a vacation the weekend of June 11, 1983. It was Kari's birthday and Tucker was intent on throwing her a party they would never forget. During the three-day celebration, Karla ingested, shot, smoked, and swallowed a staggering amount of drugs—heroin, marijuana, methadone, cocaine, speed, and handfuls of valium, percodan, and dialudid. Apparently, "no" was not a word in Tucker's vocabulary.

Fueled by drugs, sex, and alcohol, Tucker was wired. She hadn't slept for days. She looked like hell. But her friend Shawn Dean looked worse. Shawn's husband, biker Jerry Lynn Dean, had used her face as a punching bag before kicking her out. Bruised and wasted, Shawn cried on Karla's shoulder. The two women had been friends for sixteen years. Together, they had spent time on the road as rock groupies for the Allman Brothers Band. Karla was very protective of Shawn. She saw red every time she looked at Shawn's battered face.

Karla despised Jerry Lynn Dean. The feeling was mutual: Dean had banned Karla from his house. He seemed to enjoy pissing her off. Once, he had the nerve to park his motorcycle in her living room. Motor oil leaked into the carpet leaving a permanent stain. Another time, the biker ripped up the only photo Karla had of her and her mother. After exchanging heated words, Dean pushed Karla and she hauled off and punched him in the face. Friends broke up the fight before it got really ugly.

All weekend, Karla and Shawn talked about getting revenge on Jerry. Danny Garrett, Karla's new boyfriend, egged her on. Garrett suggested that the gang break into Dean's house and steal his prized Harley Davidson. Spewing curses through liquored breath, she vowed to make Dean pay for the job he'd done on Shawn.

Some time between two and four-thirty on the morning of June 13, Tucker, Garrett, and party guest James Liebrant set out for Dean's house. Shawn was passed out at the party; she had not noticed that Karla took her house key.

Noises coming from the other room woke Deborah Thornton from an uneasy sleep. For a moment she was confused, unsure of her surroundings. The thirty-two-year-old office worker had stormed out of her house after a heated row with her husband earlier that evening. She met Jerry Lynn Dean at a friend's party. He was friendly and attentive and Deborah was in no mood to go home. Instead, she accompanied Dean back to his apartment.

She heard Dean shuffling around the living room. She was about to call out to him when she realized he was still lying next to her. The noises grew closer. Deborah saw shadows moving toward them in the darkness. Awake now, Dean saw them too. Then, two narrow beams of light shone into the room. Flashlights. Scared, Deborah slid off the mattress, pulling the sheets with her.

Dean got out of bed. "Who's there?" he demanded.

A woman's voice, unfamiliar and hard: "Don't move, motherfucker, or you're dead."

Deborah cowered in the corner. Dean and the strange woman were talking. There was someone else there too. A man. Deborah's heart was beating so loudly she couldn't make out the words. Maybe she was dreaming. Maybe. Then, horrific sounds, sounds like nothing she had ever heard filled the room. She hid under the sheets, pulled herself into a ball. She prayed the people would leave, would not find her. They were just a few feet away. She understood now what Dean had been saying: Please. Please don't kill me.

Jimmy Liebrant hit the gas pedal and replayed the scene in his mind. He wished he had stayed in the car. Better still, he wished he had never left the party. He'd signed up to steal a motorcycle, maybe some cash. Not this.

Antsy and wondering what was taking Tucker and Garrett so long, Liebrant had left the car and entered Dean's place. It was dark but he could make out the Harley; it was in pieces on the living room floor. He found Garrett and Tucker in the bedroom. Dean was there too. He was lying on the bed, covered in blood, his head crushed. His body was riddled with holes, there were at least a dozen of them. It was a horrific sight but what really freaked Liebrant out was Karla. As Garrett cheered her on, Karla swung a pickaxe at something—or someone hiding under a sheet on the floor. Wild-eyed, Karla brought the weapon down again and again. As Liebrant backed out of the room, Karla turned and smiled at him.

Cable installer Scott Traver was scheduled to do a job with his neighbor, Jerry Dean. When Dean didn't show up, Traver made his way over to the biker's apartment. The door was ajar. Inside, a radio played. Dean was slumped over on the bed, badly beaten. At first, Traver thought Dean had gotten into a whopper of a fistfight. Then he saw the young woman. She was laying faceup in bed. A pickaxe embedded in her chest.

The medical examiner determined that Dean had been stabbed twenty-eight times. His skull had been fractured. Deborah Ruth Thornton had died from multiple stab wounds to the chest and back. The weapon wasn't a mystery. It would take two police officers to pry the pickaxe from Deborah's body.

Garrett was pissed at Jimmy Liebrant. Liebrant had split with the car, leaving him and Tucker at Dean's apartment. To get home, they'd taken Dean's truck—but not before loading the frame of his precious Harley into the back. To make amends, Liebrant helped them ditch the truck. Still, he was a liability. They toyed with the idea of getting rid of him to keep him quiet.

The double murder was all over the news. Karla and Danny were giddy with excitement, bragging about the crime to anyone who would listen: They were famous! They told Tucker's sister, Garrett's brother, and anyone who would listen. The couple's siblings turned them in to the police. Garrett's brother wore a wire and recorded Karla admitting to the killings. Six months later, Tucker and Garrett were arrested for the murders of Jerry Dean and Deborah Thornton. Jimmy Liebrant was granted immunity for his testimony.

Karla Faye Tucker and Danny Garrett were tried separately. The jury and the public were repulsed by the gruesome crime. And in Karla's case, they were nearly as repulsed by a comment she made right after the murder. She had bragged to friends that she had experienced multiple orgasms when she attacked the victims with the pickaxe.* At trial, Tucker tried to explain that it was just tough talk, a lie to impress the hardened criminals she hung around with.

It took the jury just over an hour to find Karla Faye Tucker guilty of murder in the commission of a felony. Tucker, now drug-free and apparently remorseful, testified against her lover at his trial. Danny

---

*Writer Florence King notes that "The murder occurred in 1983 when the multiple-orgasm craze was going full-tilt, when it was impossible to turn on the TV without hearing feminists talking about the female's 'superior capacity,' or read *Cosmopolitan* without finding an article on the mighty G-spot. I would bet anything that enough of this pop carnality filtered through to Karla Faye to inspire the trendy lie that sealed her doom." *National Review*, March 9, 1998.

Garrett received the same verdict as Tucker. Both were sentenced to
death. Garrett, however, would beat the hangman—dying of liver disease while awaiting execution.

Karla Faye Tucker sat on death row for fourteen years. During that
time, the murderess kept busy. She read the Bible, ministered to other
inmates, filed numerous appeals to have her sentence commuted, married minister Dana Brown, made television appearances on the *Larry
King Show* and ABC news. "Certainly you can't say that brutally murdering two people is good. It's not . . . but afterwards, what came from
that in me was good," Tucker told a reporter.[4]

She also made some surprising new friends. Ron Carlson, Deborah
Thornton's brother, was one of them. Carlson, a born-again Christian,
forgave Karla and became one of her staunchest supporters. Charley
Davidson (his real name) had prosecuted Tucker's accomplice, Danny
Garrett. Although he was a proponent of the death penalty, Davidson
was convinced that Tucker's life should be spared. "The Karla Tucker
who killed Jerry Dean and Deborah Thornton *cannot* be executed by
the State of Texas because that person no longer exists. The Karla
Tucker who remains on death row is a completely different person who,
in my opinion, is not capable of those atrocities. I am comfortable enough
with this belief that, if possible, I would welcome Karla into my house
to meet my family," Davidson said.

Davidson's co-prosecutor Rusty Hardin agreed. By 1985, Tucker
had already been rehabilitated and was definitely "not a late blooming
death row convert," Hardin insisted. "The fact that a person who has
already received a death sentence testified [against her accomplice] solely
because it was the right thing to do is extremely relevant," he wrote
in an affidavit requesting clemency for Tucker. "This unprecedented
step toward atonement should be strongly considered in assessing her
fate. It is very possible that if Karla Tucker's own jury could have fore-
cast that she was going to so honestly cooperate with law enforcement
even after she had been sentenced to death, they might have thought it

relevant to their determination as to whether she was a continuing threat to society."

Not everyone was impressed by Karla's conversion. Tucker wasn't the first person to be reborn on death row, nor would she be the last. Critics argued that had Tucker not been a pretty white female, her case would never have received the media attention that it did. They pointed out that no one seemed to notice the many men—a good number of them black—who had also found God in prison. It was a double standard, in reverse.

In Texas, the law allows the governor to grant a reprieve of a death conviction. The governor does not need the approval of the state Board of Pardons. Karla appealed for clemency to then-governor George W. Bush. In the letter she sent him, Karla wrote, "I don't really understand the guidelines for commutation of death sentences, but I can promise you this: if you commute my sentence to life, I will continue for the rest of my life in this earth to reach out to others and make a positive difference in their lives . . . I am seeking you to commute my sentence and allow me to pay society back by helping others. I can't really bring back the lives I took. But I can, if I am allowed, help save lives. That is the only real restitution I can give."

Karla's request was denied. Meanwhile, Tucker's supporters were hoping for an audience with the governor. Conservative pundit Tucker Carlson, who was interviewing Bush about his bid for the presidency, asked him if he had met with any of Tucker's camp. "No, I didn't meet with any of them . . . I didn't meet with Larry King either when he came down for it," he told Carlson. Bush had, however, watched King's television interview with Tucker. King, he said, had asked her what she would say to the governor, given the chance. What was Karla's answer? According to Carlson, Bush, "his lips pursed in mock desperation," whimpered, "Please, don't kill me."[5]*

On February 3, 1998, Governor George W. Bush rejected Tucker's

---

*Karla Faye Tucker, as the tape of the *Larry King* show proves, never begged George W. Bush to spare her life.

plea for a thirty-day stay of execution. Tucker would be the first woman executed in Texas since the Civil War. As a crowd of more than a thousand people gathered outside the prison, Karla finished her last meal: a peach, a banana, and a soft drink. At 6 p.m., she was strapped to a gurney and allowed to address her audience. Minutes before she expired, Karla apologized to the families of her victims. To her own family and friends, she said: "I love all of you very much. I'm going to be face-to-face with Jesus now." She sighed softly. And then she was gone.

twelve

LAW & ORDER: A woman dies at the hands of a privileged preppie with a penchant for rough sex.

TRUE STORY: Robert Chambers strangled Jennifer Levin in New York City's Central Park in what the press quickly dubbed "the preppie murder."

It's a balmy summer night in August 1986, and the vibe at Dorrian's Red Hand is electric. If you're a teenager, Dorrian's is the place to be. The bar is famous for opening its doors late at night to underage kids—*neighborhood* kids, that is. In order to get in, Jack Dorrian, the tavern's owner, needs to know you, or at least recognize you from the area. And it takes something special to live in this neighborhood: money—lots of money. Situated on the corner of 84th Street and Second Avenue, Dorrian's is on New York's Upper East Side, land of the rich.

The guys inside Dorrian's are dressed in polo shirts and khakis. They stand tall and relaxed, emitting that brand of cockiness peculiar to the New York City elite. That they'll all be making fortunes is a given; this is just a precursor of great things to come. They're all headed to Ivy League schools this fall. When they graduate, they're assured a six-figure job and, of course, a beautiful wife. Most of the gals in the bar will head to the East Coast's top liberal arts schools—Vassar, Brown, Wellesley—where they'll earn English or Art History degrees. They'll land a job through connections, work a couple years in the world of nonprofit, marry one of these handsome gentlemen, bear children, and keep the cycle of wealth rolling uninterrupted. There's no place on Earth quite like New York City's Upper East Side.

But looks can be deceiving. No matter what your bank account says, you are who you are. And on this night, August 26, 1986, these kids are all a little sad, as college-bound teenagers will be in the waning days of summer. Soon, when the freshman semester of college begins, the tight-knit Dorrian's gang will split up and go their separate ways.

It's well past midnight. A Dorrian's regular, Elizabeth Shankin comes in and sees her best friend, Jennifer Levin, sitting at a back table with the guy she's been dating for a couple of months. Elizabeth had been the matchmaker. Earlier in the summer this tall, strong-jawed guy had told Elizabeth that her friend was the most beautiful woman he'd ever seen. Elizabeth introduced them, and a summer fling quickly took off. Two months in the lives of teenagers, though, is plenty of time for feelings to change, and for people to get hurt. Now, as Jennifer animatedly talks to him from across the table, he seems distracted, aloof, as if Jennifer suddenly isn't the striking beauty she was when the summer began.

Elizabeth approaches the couple, which the guy uses as an opportunity to leave. She sits down in his place, and looks at her friend. Jennifer is truly beautiful. Dark shoulder-length hair, pretty smile, green eyes sparkling with life and constantly expressing her fun and compassionate nature. Tonight, though, Elizabeth sees also a sadness behind them. Jennifer tends to fall hard and fast for guys, and Elizabeth has helped see her through more than a couple broken hearts.

Jennifer is going off to Chamberlayne Junior College in Boston in a few days, but she still really likes this guy and wants to spend some more time with him before she leaves.

She tells Elizabeth that she just told the guy that sex with him was the best she's ever had. His reply was not what she had hoped to hear: "You shouldn't have said that." She asks Elizabeth to go tell him she'll be outside in twenty minutes, and that she wants to talk. Elizabeth agrees to deliver the message and approaches the guy, who is leaning on an ice machine near the bar slurping down a beer. Reluctantly, he agrees to meet the girl outside.

Jennifer Levin (right) and two friends. Murdered by Robert Chambers in Central Park, her memory was dragged through the mud by defense attorney Jack Litman, as well as the New York press. *Allan Tannenbaum/Polaris*

A few minutes later, Elizabeth's friend calls out to her, "Good night. I love you. I'll call you tomorrow," as she leaves with the guy.

"Where are you two going?" Elizabeth asks.

"Don't worry. It'll be all right." The two teenagers walk off.

At 6:10 a.m., about two hours after Jennifer Levin and Robert Chambers left Dorrian's Red Hand, a woman rode her bicycle into Central Park at Fifth Avenue. She pedaled up the path leading toward the rear of the Metropolitan Museum of Art. Under an elm tree, she spotted what she assumed was a homeless person—not an uncommon sight at this hour. On closer look, though, she saw that it was a young woman and that her clothes weren't those of a hobo. The bicyclist pedaled closer and saw that the woman's skirt was pushed up past her waist and her bra wrapped around her neck. A bloodstained, faded denim jacket lay next to her. She appeared to be dead.[1]

A small crowd began to form in the general area as police called to the scene examined the body of Jennifer Levin. One female jogger stopped and asked a young man sitting on a stone wall overlooking the scene what was going on. He had scratches on his face so prominent that the jogger thought he had been in an accident of some kind. "I think they found a body," Robert Chambers calmly said.

Robert Chambers talked the talk of a rich guy on the fast track to success, but in reality he had long ago begun to lag behind his fellow Upper East Siders. Raised by an Irish immigrant mother determined to get him the best education, and who seemed completely convinced that her blue-eyed son would be the next JFK, Chambers had struggled through prep school after prep school and was eventually accepted into Boston University—only to be kicked out after one semester due to poor grades and possibly stealing a credit card.

In 1985, he was stealing jewelry from apartments and had gotten off to a running start on his substance abuse problem. Coke was his drug of choice—and he chose it a lot. By that fateful August night, Chambers was so far off the path to success, he was lost in the forest.

Needless to say, a law firm partnership just wasn't in the cards for Robert Chambers, which became fully apparent to his doting mother when police knocked on the door of her West 90th Street brownstone looking for her son. They got his name from Dorrian's patrons and wanted to know what he and Jennifer Levin did last night and at what time they left the bar together.

When Chambers appeared in the doorway of his apartment, police didn't have to do too much questioning before hauling him down to the precinct. Not only did they see right through Chambers's initial lies, they also couldn't help but notice the multiple scratches running down his face. In no time, Chambers was in the NYPD's Central Park station house trying to get his story straight. "Where did you get those wounds on your face?" detectives asked him. His cat had scratched him, Chambers told them. When one cop made it clear that he could easily discern wounds inflicted by an animal from those by a human, Chambers did a

Robert Chambers, the so-called "Preppie Killer." After serving most of his fifteen-year sentence for murdering Jennifer Levin, he was released on Valentine's Day 2003. Less than two years later he was back in jail for cocaine and heroin possession.
NYC Police Department

one-eighty: "I got them from Jennifer." Although he denied he had left the bar with her shortly before her death, he told his interrogators they had had a fight at Lexington Avenue and 86th Street. When cops told him that no one in the donut shop on that corner had seen him, he changed the location to Park Avenue and 86th. Then he tried in vain to pass the buck, by claiming they had bumped into some friend of Levin's (the guy's name, of course, slipped Chambers's mind), and that Levin had left with him.[2]

The cops thought Chambers's story was pretty lame so far, but this was only a warm-up for what they were about to hear. On a videotaped confession to his crime, Chambers pled self-defense. Jennifer Levin, he claimed, had sexually assaulted *him*! Levin had tied him up, climbed on top of him, and fondled him. "She hurt me," he said. "I told her to stop. She wouldn't." Chambers dramatically pulled up his shirt to show police the scratches on his chest, and told the tale of how he valiantly struggled to fight her off, momentarily forgetting that he was seven inches taller than Levin and outweighed her by a hundred pounds. He said that he finally got hold of her neck and flipped her back over his shoulder. That must have been how she died. He never meant to hurt her. "I kept waiting for her to get up," he innocently said. Police laughed out loud. One cop later quipped that Chambers claimed to be the first man ever to be raped in the park.

Chambers probably came up with the cockamamie story in a panic; little did he know that he was setting the groundwork for his entire defense strategy.

The next morning, Chambers's attorney Jack Litman, who cut his teeth as a celebrity defense lawyer in the Bonnie Garland case nine years earlier, called the precinct and ordered police to stop questioning his client. "It's too late," the detectives said. "We've already made your client a movie star."[3]

But Chambers was in good hands. Jack Litman had a history of successfully defending sexual predators. He had a knack for putting images of short-skirted women with voracious sexual appetites into jurors' minds, dazzling them into forgetting about the defendant and focusing on the victim. However, the prosecutor, Linda Fairstein, head of the DA's sex crimes unit, was a worthy opponent. She had begun her career as an assistant to Jack Litman, who was then a prosecutor. Fairstein knew him, and she knew his tactics. Just as press-savvy as her opponent, she exposed Litman's blame-the-victim tactics for what they were every time he opened his mouth.

On bail day, Litman presented the judge, Howard Bell, with numerous letters attesting to Robert Chambers's high moral character, including one from Catholic Archbishop Theodore McCarrick. Jennifer Levin's parents wrote one to the judge, as well, pleading for remand. Bell read them all and set bail at $150,000, with the stipulation that Chambers couldn't live at home while on bail. He would have to stay at the Church of the Incarnation in Manhattan, under the supervision of the monsignor of the parish, Thomas Leonard, who volunteered to keep an eye on the lad.*

Litman's first big move in defending Chambers was to request Jennifer Levin's diary as evidence. He claimed that Fairstein had told him it contained tales of "kinky and aggressive sexual activity by Jennifer Levin with many others." No doubt, Litman planned to run with it, dragging the memory of Jennifer Levin through the mud. Fairstein denied giving Litman this information.

The judge read the diary and found nothing more than the thoughts and dreams of an average teenager. He found it irrelevant to the case and ruled it couldn't be used as evidence. This didn't stop an eager press from labeling it the "sex diary." In fact, newspapers ranging from the notoriously sensationalist *New York Daily News* to the long-respected *New York Times* had gone wild from the day Jennifer Levin was murdered. As the story broke, reporters seemed to enjoy themselves a little too much over the bawdy details. Then they unknowingly began to do Litman's work for him, presenting Chambers as a likeable, soft-spoken preppie loved by everyone—especially women. Levin was a temptress, a sexually aggressive woman who, God forbid, liked to stay out late partying. One *Daily News* article, shamefully titled "How Jennifer Courted Death," drew the most criticism for implying that Levin was to blame for her own death. But it was only one of many such stories.

Litman didn't need the press to help him develop a strategy, anyway. No doubt, he planned to vilify Levin from the get-go. In his opening statements, he suggested that Levin was a sexual predator and said she had, in fact, assaulted his former altar-boy client.

---

*None of this looked good to the man in charge of the Catholic church in New York City—John Cardinal O'Connor. In an attempt to quell any ideas people might get that church officials were conspiring to protect one of their own (Chambers was Catholic and a former altar boy) involved in a crime against a Jewish woman, he wrote an article for a weekly Catholic newspaper explaining that the monsignor and priest were doing what priests were supposed to do; however, he stated, "[i]f I were Jewish, and the media were saturated with what Catholics are purportedly doing for a Catholic, I might well feel troubled." He also wrote to the Levins explaining his position; the Levins were unimpressed. (Information from the *New York Times*, "O'Connor Fears Split With Jews," Robert O. Boorstin, 10/13/86, p. B1.)

The trial began on January 4, 1988, and New York City was ready for it. Tabloid reporters titillated their readers with tales of the "sex diary"; the Guardian Angels and the National Organization of Women (NOW) joined Bonnie Garland's father and Marla Hanson, a model who had had her face slashed, outside the courtroom to protest the smear campaign everyone knew Litman had planned for the murder victim; the Levin family fended off the press; and Robert Chambers strolled in with his lawyer through the crowd, hearing both jeers and shouts of support ("Go get 'em Robbie!").

Litman knew his audience well, and he was all too familiar with society's double standards when it comes to the behavior of men and women.

Chambers was constantly referred to in the press as a ladies' man. Reporters fell over each other to get more information on just how much all the women of the world loved him. He hung out and drank with his friends, as guys do. It was all meant as a compliment. Levin was good-looking, as well, and she, too, liked to stay out late; but this would be held against her. Brooklyn law professor Elizabeth M. Schneider put it best: "[T]he fact that Jennifer was young and appears to have been sexually active added a whole new dimension to the case," she said in a *New York Times* interview. "Somehow we'd be more at ease if Chambers had dragged her unwillingly into the park."[4]

Litman did a spectacular job exploiting the double standard, steering as many cross examinations as possible away from his client and toward Jennifer Levin. The jury heard innuendo after innuendo suggesting Levin was a sex-crazed vamp. Her "bad-girl" behavior clearly led to her death. In his closing statement, Litman actually said, "It was Jennifer who was pursuing Robert for sex . . . that's why we wound up with this terrible tragedy"[5]—conveniently forgetting the fact that it was Levin, her family, and her friends, not the collective "we," who suffered from the "tragedy."

When the jury retired to deliberate, problems arose. Jurors fought among themselves, constantly requested more information, and sent notes to the judge begging to be released from the jury. Added up, it spelled out "mistrial." Litman had only summoned five witnesses for the defense (against the prosecution's twenty-six) during the three-month-long trial, and yet he had cast enough doubt into the jury's mind that after nine days of deliberation it still couldn't come up with a verdict.

But neither side wanted to take a chance with another trial, and the Levins said they simply couldn't go through this again, disappointing as a plea bargain was to them. After two days of negotiations, Chambers agreed to plead guilty to first-degree manslaughter, as well as to the robbery he was involved in previously.[6]

One requirement for his plea bargain was allocution. Chambers stood in front of the packed courtroom to admit that he had killed Jennifer Levin—and that he had intended to do so. The judge had to prod him three times before he would actually utter the words. He was stiff and formal and the words, when they finally came out, sounded rehearsed. Had he broken down, cried, or at least presented himself as sincere and a bit sorry, the Levins might have had some consolation, however little. But Robert Chambers took even this away from them. For his part, Jack Litman gave the world a big I-told-you-so afterward, saying, "This affirms what we've said all along, that this is not a murder case and never was."

Chambers exited the courtroom into a city that was a little less ambivalent about exactly who he was. There were more jeers coming from the crowd than when he first entered the courtroom thirteen weeks previous. The Guardian Angels were there, as they had been during the entire trial. They now serenaded Robert Chambers—"They're coming to take you *away*, ha, ha . . . They're coming to take you *away*!"[7]—as he walked out the door to begin his fifteen-year sentence.

If there were any pro–Robert Chambers holdouts at this point, clearly nothing would faze them—not even the airing of a home video taken while he was supposed to be in the custody of the Catholic church. During the first days of his trial, Chambers, fully clothed, was videotaped partying with some young women who, for some reason, were wearing nearly no clothes. They were reportedly friends of Chambers *and* Levin.

The videotape was aired on television by the tabloid news show *A Current Affair* a few months after his guilty plea. At one point, Chambers picks up a small doll and twists its head, saying in a high-pitched, mock female voice, "My name is . . ." As the doll's head comes off in his hand, he says, "Oops, I think I killed it." His audience bursts into laughter.

PLEA DEALS

In one episode of *Law & Order*, ADA Jack McCoy makes a unique deal with a defendant. In return for the locations of his murder victims, he offers the defendant his freedom. Sweet deal, but it's too sweet for the judge, who refuses to recognize it even after the locations of the bodies are revealed. The defendant, of course, goes crazy, screaming, "We had a deal! We had a deal!" He did have a deal with McCoy, but he didn't have one with the judge. It makes all the difference.

When both sides appear before the judge after a plea has been agreed upon, the judge has the discretion to either accept it or not. If he doesn't, the defendant has the opportunity to withdraw his plea. An accepted plea is always subject to change until sentencing day.

This public display of a judge wielding his or her power over a DA can be personally humiliating to the DA and it can seriously affect his or her credibility at the next plea. When it comes to plea bargaining, a DA's credibility is everything.

And as with many aspects of the law, plea deals are subject to politics. What can occur is that while the defendant is awaiting sentencing, his or her crime becomes a political hot-button issue, in which case it's very possible that the mayor will put pressure on the DAs and judges to prosecute heavily. This is often how would-be deals are reneged upon. It's a dirty game.

thirteen

LAW & ORDER: A white supremacist is prosecuted after a teenager is badly beaten by members of a neo-Nazi gang.

TRUE STORY: A civil jury found White Aryan Resistance founder Tom Metzger and his son guilty of inciting the murder of Ethiopian immigrant Mulugeta Seraw.

Mulugeta Seraw was a long way from home. At the age of twenty, he had made the long journey from his native Ethiopia to the United States. Sponsored by an American family, Seraw began a new life in Portland, Oregon, living for a time with his uncle, Engedaw Berhanu, who, like Seraw, had come to the States to get a proper education. After Berhanu earned his degree in social work, he moved to California. Seraw stayed behind, attending Portland Community College where he studied engineering and business. In Portland, Seraw made new friends, many of them fellow Ethiopian immigrants. But he missed his family, especially his six-year-old son, Henok, whom he had left behind in Ethiopia. Seraw worked as a shuttle bus driver at the airport, sending his meager earnings to his family. His country, located in the Horn of Africa, had fallen on hard times and Seraw hoped the money would help make life easier for his relatives.

Seraw's wide smile belied the pain and heartbreak he'd already experienced in his young life. His mother, whom he adored, died when he was ten years old. When Seraw was a teenager, the Ethiopian emperor was overthrown by the Derg, a Marxist military faction. The country was thrust into a violent, bloody civil war that claimed the lives of thousands of Ethiopians, including many of young Seraw's friends and neighbors. During a two-year period known as the Red Terror, the Derg slaughtered men, women, and children—anyone deemed an enemy of the state. The dead, broken bodies were left, like litter, in the streets. Seraw saw all this. But he had survived—the loss of his mother, the famines and droughts, the Marxists who patrolled the towns with guns drawn. Yes, he had survived all that—only to have his life cut short at twenty-eight by a group of racist skinheads on a Portland street.

It was after midnight on November 13, 1988, and Mulugeta Seraw was sitting in a car outside his apartment with two friends. Earlier, the three Ethiopian immigrants had attended a party, an informal get-together really, thrown by a mutual acquaintance. Seraw had to work in the morning and so Tilahun Antneh had given him a lift home in his car. Wondwosen Tesfaye, who knew Seraw's family back in Ethiopia, came along for the ride. The three men were saying their good nights when a car full of neo-Nazi skinheads came barreling down the narrow street. Antneh's double-parked car was blocking their way. The skinheads began shouting at the Ethiopians to move the car. An argument ensued.

Kyle Brewster, Steve Strasser, and Ken Mieske, members of a ragtag racist club called East Side White Pride, were drunk and wound up from a night spent knocking back beers and handing out racist literature. The skinheads, egged on by their like-minded girlfriends, welcomed the opportunity to attack three black immigrants. Seraw attempted to diffuse the situation, urging everyone to stay calm. It was too late. The skinheads attacked the Ethiopians with their fists and kicked them with their steel-toed boots. Mieske grabbed a baseball bat from the car, which he used to smash the taillights and windshield of Antneh's car. Fearing for his life, Antneh drove off in a panic, leaving his friends behind. Mieske charged at Seraw, hitting him again and again with the bat until the Ethiopian lay crumpled on the ground. The skinheads continued to kick Seraw as their girlfriends cheered them on with shrill cries of "Kill him! Kill him!" When it was over, Wondwosen needed stitches; Mulugeta Seraw was dead.

"Ah, that we were all Oregonians, loving, hospitable with an open-heartedness that envelops the stranger like a great coat. I am positive, from all that I have heard, that Saint Peter, who greets us with a smile and a handshake as we knock at the golden gate, is surely an Oregonian," read a letter to the editor of the *Oregonian*, circa 1905.[1] But Oregon was not so welcoming to everyone. At various times, the state banned blacks, Asians, and the Native Americans who had lived on the land for thousands of years. In 1850, Oregon became the first state to enter the Union with an exclusion law, banning blacks from owning land, written into its constitution. And then there were the infamous Lash Laws, which called for blacks—free or enslaved—to be beaten twice a year "until he or she shall quit the territory."

Oregon today is a peace-loving, earth-loving, hippie state—most residents would like to distance themselves from their home state's past. The state, however, remains predominantly white; in the eighties, it was more than 80 percent white. Apparently, that wasn't white enough for the members of the East Side White Pride. Bored, aimless, disgruntled, and drunk much of the time, these young people were angry at the world. Racism provided a way for them to channel their anger. Minorities, of which there were few, served as a perfect target.

Ken Mieske, nicknamed "Ken Death" for his love of death metal music, was the de facto leader of East Side White Pride. Mieske, a musician, lived with his girlfriend in her parents' basement. The couple decorated their subterranean digs with swastikas, photos of Adolph Hitler, and other assorted Nazi paraphernalia. They talked about getting married and naming their first child Joseph, in honor of Mieske's favorite Nazi, Josef Mengele.[2]

Kyle Brewster had been prom king in high school, but with his glory days behind him, he eagerly embraced a new identity: skinhead. Steve Strasser was a follower, a punk rocker turned racist who had been arrested for menacing a group of black men at a nightclub.

East Side White Pride was one of many loosely knit groups of skin-heads popping up in America in the late eighties. The skinhead subcul-ture had originated in Britain in the sixties. Back then being a skinhead had nothing to do with race. Named for their shaven heads, the skin-heads formed as a response to flashier, wealthier, and more fashionable mods that swept England. For the most part, the mods had money, while the skinheads, most of whom hailed from the working class sec-tions of the country, did not. These skinheads weren't interested in racial politics. For them, the skinhead movement was a way of life—it was about music, dance, parties, and solidarity. Years later, a splinter group of skinheads would be recruited by the radical right—and the term "skinhead" became a synonym for racist. By the eighties, the skin-head movement had run out of steam in the United Kingdom. But across the pond, skinheads began to dot the landscape of the American West.

This new breed of racist hadn't escaped Tom Metzger's watchful eye. For decades, Metzger, a television repairman by trade, had been cultivating his own brand of white supremacy. Born in Indiana, Metz-ger moved to California in 1961 and joined the John Birch Society, an ultraconservative organization that opposes socialist, communism, and leftist ideology. Metzger left the organization because he couldn't "crit-icize the Jews." He signed on with the Ku Klux Klan and was appointed Klan Dragon for the state of California. After a falling out with Klan leader David Duke, Metzger struck out on his own.

In 1983, Metzger founded WAR—White Aryan Resistance. From his new bully pulpit, he preached his own brand of violent and pro-active racism: "WAR is strictly racist. A house or race divided cannot prosper."[3] The Anti-Defamation League describes Metzger's philoso-phy as a mixed bag of totalitarianism, and left- and right-wing revolu-tionary thinking. A family endeavor, WAR's youth division, Aryan Youth Movement, was run by Metzger's son, John.

Most Americans hadn't heard of Metzger until he was involved in the on-air melee that left TV host Geraldo Rivera with a broken nose. But to Ken Death and his pals, Tom Metzger was a superstar. The WAR president used their adulation to his advantage. East Side White Pride was unruly, unfocused, and violent. While others dismissed them as hooligans, Metzger saw them as potentially valuable and powerful tools. He made plans to recruit them into his fold.

Ken Death was honored to receive a phone call from Tom Metzger inviting East Side White Pride to join WAR. A letter followed informing the skinheads, "Soon you will meet Dave Mazzella, our national vice-president, who will be in Portland to teach you about how we operate and to help you understand more about WAR."[4]

Armed with racist literature, Dave Mazella traveled to Portland to indoctrinate the skinheads. It wasn't an easy task. When it came down to it, East Side White Pride was more interested in parties than politics. According to WAR's vice-president, "Tom Metzger said the only way to get respect from skinheads is to teach them how to commit violence against blacks, against Jews, Hispanics, any minority. The word will spread, and they'll know our group is one you can respect."[5] Mazella had the East Side White Pride boys hand out WAR's newsletter on the streets of Portland. Several hours later, while Mazella was settling into bed, three members of East Side White Pride beat Mulugeta Seraw to death. Mazella promptly christened Ken Mieske "Batman."[6]

A week after Seraw's death, the killers were turned in by an anonymous tipster, a fellow skinhead motivated by the $10,000 reward offered by the Jewish Defense League. The evidence against the skinheads was overwhelming. Their attorneys tried and failed to have evidence of East Side White Pride's racist views excluded. There were the incriminating photos and the racist tattoos Brewster sported, and then there was the matter of song lyrics penned by Mieske, which included the lines "Victims all around me/I feel nothing but hate/Bashing their brains in is my only trade."[7]

Ken Mieske, the leader and the skinhead who had wielded the bat against Seraw, was charged with first-degree murder. In a brief filed by the prosecution, Mieske is described as "a radical, white supremacist. He is a Nazi. He advocated violent enforcement of his views. He views blacks as 'subhuman.' He knows no moral obstacle to racial violence . . . He was prepared for it, armed for it, and primed for it; defendant acted on his white supremacist beliefs on November 13, 1988. As a direct result, Mulugeta Seraw died."[8]

Shortly before the case was to go to trial, the district attorney's office brokered a plea bargain with all three defendants. Ken Mieske, charged with first-degree murder, admitted in court that he "unlawfully and intentionally killed Mulugeta Seraw because of his race." He was sentenced to life in prison. Kyle Brewster and Steve Strasser both pleaded guilty to first-degree manslaughter and were given twenty-year sentences.

Many Oregonians felt gypped by the plea bargain. They wanted closure, wanted to show the world that they were far removed from the settlers of the early days. For many, it was a crushing disappointment. Portland has "tolerance for different lifestyles as long as they're liberal lifestyles," Portland Gang Enforcement officer Loren Christensen told *Time* magazine. "There's no tolerance for skinheads."[9]

Enter Morris Dees. The Southern-born Dees was a lawyer and the founder of Southern Poverty Law Center (SPLC), a nonprofit firm specializing in civil rights issues. Dees wanted to make those responsible for Seraw's death pay—literally. On behalf of the Ethiopian immigrant's family, the SPLC filed a civil suit against Mieske and Brewster—and Tom and John Metzger. Steve Strasser, whom Dees hoped would testify for the plaintiffs, was not named in the suit.

The Metzgers were confused. They hadn't lifted a hand against Seraw, how could they be responsible for his death? While that was true, Dees explained, the Metzgers had set in motion the actions that caused Seraw to die that fateful night. The civil suit alleged that they were engaged in a conspiracy with East Side White Pride that led to Seraw's death. According to the plaintiff's complaint, the Metzgers "encouraged members of East Side White Pride to commit violent acts against blacks in order to promote white supremacy."

Sure, Mieske and Brewster were skinhead punks before the Metzgers got involved, but their crimes were fairly innocuous—kicking garbage cans, bar brawls with other gangs, and scaring, not harming, minorities. Dees contended that the Metzgers were equally responsible for the Ethiopian immigrant's death. "The bat that hit Mulugeta Seraw in the head started in Fallbrook, California," Dees argued. But would a jury agree?

Tom Metzger, perhaps not realizing the gravity of the situation, chose to represent himself in the civil trial. He saw the trial as an opportunity to showcase his beliefs. As a layman with a poor understanding of the law, Metzger was grossly outlawyered. He hadn't done his homework and did not research the case. From the start, he seemed to treat the trial as an aside in his life. It seemed that Metzger didn't consider the very real possibility that he might lose. At pretrial proceedings, he objected to the presiding judge, whose name sounded Jewish. The judge was replaced by Ancer Haggerty, who to Metzger's shock and chagrin, turned out to be black.

The crux of the Metzgers' defense was that their racial rantings were protected by the First Amendment. They claimed that "negligent and reckless speech . . . while recruiting for their organization is protected under the Oregon and U.S. constitutions." Dees countered, "Nothing in the First Amendment prevented imposing liability if such a conspiracy could be established . . . Our argument to the jury . . . would be simple: under our Constitution, you have the right to hate but not to hurt."[10] Dees admitted that he was hoping for a big payday, but greed wasn't the motivating factor. Dees and the Seraw family hoped the judgment would be significant enough to bankrupt Metzger's entire organization. They hoped to put WAR out of business for good. "Ladies and gentlemen, you know the America that Tom Metzger believes in is an America that never existed. Our nation is great because of our differences, because of our diversity, not in spite of it," Dees told the jury. "This case is important for this community. It's important for the state. And it's important for this nation. Because the verdict that you're going to render is going to have very far-reaching effects. We hope that the verdict will tell Tom Metzger and his organization and all other people who peddle and preach hate and violence in this country that this jury says 'No!' We are going to nip you in the bud."[11]

Throughout the trial Tom and John Metzger made racist remarks. During his closing argument, Tom Metzger was unable to hide his contempt for both the trial and the plaintiffs. He flailed his arms, raised his voice, and appeared menacing. He told jurors, "I don't think there's four people in this jury that have the guts to find with Tom and John

Metzger and go home and tell your family, 'I decided they were not liable.' Let's face it. 'They were not guilty.' Because it's a civil trial but you might as well call it a criminal trial. I know what's cooking here."[12]

The jury found the Metzgers had lit the fuse that caused East Side White Pride to explode and ultimately kill Mulugeta Seraw. The Metzgers, Brewster, and Mieske were each found equally liable. The jury awarded Seraw's family $12.5 million. Tom Metzger appealed and lost. His business, home, and private assets were seized to help satisfy the court's judgment. Although the plaintiff's family is unlikely to receive the bulk of the money, the judgment has helped put Seraw's son Henok through school.

DEADLY FORCE

Compared to those on most other cop shows, the detectives of *Law & Order* aren't real gunslingers. They spend much of their time doing what detectives really do—canvassing neighborhoods, interrogating suspects, and shuffling paperwork. On occasion, they'll have to draw their weapons.

Police departments have strict regulations concerning the discharge of firearms, and would view the behavior of most TV cops as irresponsible, reckless, and oftentimes criminal. According to the NYPD patrol guide, "[p]olice officers shall not discharge their firearms to subdue a fleeing felon who presents no threat of imminent death or serious physical injury to themselves or another person present." Other guidelines forbid firing warning shots and shooting at a car, unless the perpetrator is basically shooting a gun out the window while he's driving. In essence, it's always better to let a perp run away than to shoot him.

fourteen

LAW & ORDER: A young girl is killed during an unconventional psychological treatment session.

TRUE STORY: Candace Newmaker, a ten-year-old Colorado girl, was smothered to death during a rebirthing session with her therapists.

Candace Tiara Elmore's middle name was chosen by her stepgrandfather, David Davis, who said the word meant "precious jewel." He was wrong, but it didn't matter. And it didn't matter that David wasn't a blood relative. During the short time he knew Candace, he treated her as a precious little jewel. David loved his granddaughter more than he ever loved anyone. He read to her, kidded her, and laughed with her. Little did he know during these moments that Candace would eventually be taken from her home by social services, and that she would be adopted, issued a fake birth certificate, and given a new name—and that her new mother would stand back and watch as four strangers took Candace's life.

Candace was born on November 19, 1989, in Lincolnton, North Carolina. She never stood a chance for leading a normal life. Her grandmother on her mother's side had been abandoned on a street corner in a West Virginia town when she was a young child, and grew up in multiple foster homes. She was in her teens when she gave birth to Candace's mother, Angie. Convinced she couldn't adequately care for the child, she, too, abandoned her child. Rather than leave her on the street to fend for herself, though, she gave her away to social services.

Like her mother, Angie was raised by various foster parents, and she didn't have fond memories of any of them. "These people didn't love me," Angie once said. "I was a paycheck." As soon as she was old enough—seventeen—she got herself out of foster family hell the only way she knew how, by getting married. Angie's escape route, though, was in some ways worse than what she was escaping. Her husband was an angry, controlling man who couldn't hold a job to save his life. To make himself feel better, he liked to beat Angie up; the feisty toddler Candace would sometimes try to pull him away from Angie. It wasn't a shock to anyone when he eventually ditched the family.

Given Candace's father's fierce temper and frequent run-ins with the law (mainly misdemeanors, but enough to earn him a reputation as a local troublemaker), plus child services' knowledge of Angie's anger issues, which she developed from being bounced from one foster home to another, it was almost inevitable that the vicious cycle would continue. At five years old, Candace, along with her little sister and brother, was taken away from her parents and placed, like her mother and grandmother, in foster care. There had been no record of abuse or neglect.

The difference this time was that Candace was forcibly taken away, not abandoned. Angie attempted to get her children back, but her own record from foster care alarmed the judge. Her case file documented just too many instances of violent behavior when she was a youth. Angie, the judge ruled, simply couldn't be trusted to raise children. For the good of the children, the judge ruled, they would remain in the care of Lincoln County, North Carolina. Candace would never see her mother or siblings again.[1]

Like her mother, Candace had frequent bouts of anger and often threw tantrums. Her foster parents complained that they couldn't take care of her. One foster parent after another quickly had their fill of the temperamental child and handed her back to the state.

Then, at the age of six, Candace hit pay dirt, or so it seemed. She was adopted by a Durham, North Carolina, woman named Jeane Newmaker, a responsible single woman who worked as a pediatric nurse practitioner at Duke University Medical Center and desperately wanted a child of her own. Candace's birth certificate was sent from the county of her birth to the state capital, where it was kept from anyone who didn't have a judge's order. She was issued a new, fake birth certificate that said she was born in Durham and that her name was Candace Elizabeth Newmaker.

Newmaker had plenty of money and was willing to spend it on her new treasure. She sent Candace to private school, bought her boatloads of toys, and, because Candace loved horses, enrolled her in horseback riding school. The little girl appeared to be happier than ever and had a sweet side to her. She was affectionate with animals, quickly made friends at school, and liked to help handicapped students get around.[2]

Some adults who dealt with Candace at this point in her life noted a cold side to the girl, an emotional vacancy. But people can't work miracles, especially six-year-olds. For someone with Candace's background, emotional healing would take lots of time, and there would likely be scars that just wouldn't heal at all. The important thing was that, by all outward signs, Candace was getting better. Of course, she missed her mother. Of course, she missed her siblings. Of course, she had occasional tantrums. But it seemed that she was finally beginning to learn what happiness was about. Candace was coping.

The scene behind closed doors, according to Jeane Newmaker, was a completely different story. Candace, she said, was impossible to deal with. She wouldn't behave and just couldn't be handled. She was often mean, cruel, and violent. Newmaker said that Candace destroyed things and even set fires inside the house. Clearly, something had to be done, and fast. But unlike Candace's foster parents, Newmaker couldn't return her adopted daughter for a better one. Candace was broken, and she needed to be fixed.

Newmaker took Candace to a host of therapists. The girl was diagnosed by one as bipolar; another, as suffering from post-traumatic stress disorder; and still another, Reactive Attachment Disorder (RAD), a condition that prevents a child from forming a bond with her parent, and particularly common with adopted children. RAD children can turn out to be so cruel and devoid of conscience that they're sometimes referred to in the field as "future Ted Bundys." Indeed, many therapists theorize that numerous serial killers in fact suffered from RAD. Over the next few years, Candace was given an assortment of psychotropic meds. But everything failed; Candace was still Candace.

At long last, Jeane Newmaker found her salvation. She discovered an organization called ATTACh (Association for Treatment and Training in the Attachment of Children), and attended one of its seminars in Virginia. There she met Bill Goble, a therapist from North Carolina specializing in Attachment Therapy (AT), and discussed the possibility that Candace was afflicted with RAD.* Newmaker was handed a Randolph Attachment Disorder Questionnaire, a short, standardized checklist pertaining to a child's behavior. Designed to aid therapists in coming up with an accurate diagnosis of a child, the RADQ** is one tool in a more involved process. Ideally, anyway. After reviewing Newmaker's answers, Goble believed that Candace was, in fact, a RAD child, and a pretty severe case at that.[3] Goble's diagnosis was an incredible feat, considering that Candace wasn't even there! She was back in North Carolina. Goble, apparently, didn't need to meet the child. According to the "test," all the pieces fit. And so, while Candace rode her bicycle, played with her friends, and walked her beloved dogs back in North Carolina, her fate was being determined for her, by total strangers.

Goble's schedule was booked, and he couldn't take on Candace's case. Instead, he referred Newmaker to a therapist named Connell Watkins,[4] who practiced at Colorado's Evergreen Attachment Center, the mecca of attachment therapy. Watkins was a student of Foster Cline, a physician, psychiatrist, and guru of AT, who also practiced out of the Evergreen facility. Cline, an unflappable advocate for AT, is worshipped by his supporters and energetically denounced by his critics. Watkins was an entrenched member of the former camp.[5] Her schedule was wide open and for $7,000 she would conduct an intensive two-week AT program with Candace and Jeane—two weeks to fix problems stemming back, literally, generations.

---

*RAD is a widely recognized disorder and defined by the *DSM-IV* (Diagnostic and Statistical Manual of Mental Disorders), which is published by the American Psychiatric Association and is the profession's and insurance industry's accepted manual of disorders.

**The RADQ has since been modified.

Watkins, technically unlicensed because she had let it lapse, and Julie Ponder, a licensed California therapist, would start by treating Candace (or inflicting on her, depending on one's point of view) to textbook "holding therapy," a procedure linked with Rage Reduction Therapy, in which the patient is forcibly restrained by a therapist, or a team of therapists, and then goaded into a physical or psychological rage. The goal is to have the patient listen to the therapist as she's experiencing rage and learn that lashing out will do her no good. Even some of its adherents liken it to training an animal.

Of course, this practice has come under severe criticism. Today, even Evergreen is careful to point out on its website that its therapists don't practice this brand of holding therapy. "We do not use physical stimulation, nor do we use the heavy confrontation from the early years," Evergreen points out; instead, "the child is safely contained in a nurturing holding position" and will only be restrained if she's "out of control."[6] But this surely wasn't the case in April 2000.

On April 10, the therapy began. First, the resident psychiatrist changed Candace's medication, taking her off the antidepressant she was on and doubling her dosage of an antipsychotic medication she was taking.[7] Then the sessions with Watkins and Ponder commenced. As the week progressed, the therapy became more intense. Watkins and Ponder screamed at the ten-year-old, cut her hair off, and said they'd give her a tattoo if she didn't get her act together. They vilified her birth mother, Angie, and ordered Candace to erase her from her memory. Angie cared nothing for you, they said. The girl also endured sessions of "strong sitting," during which she was forced to sit motionless and silent for up to a half-hour.[8] To the surprise of Watkins, Ponders, and Jeane Newmaker, Candace showed little interest in bonding with her adoptive mother after this treatment.

So they changed tack from tough love to rage reduction. The therapists had Jeane lie on top of Candace for over an hour and frequently lick the girl's face, all the while threatening to abandon her. This was meant to incite rage. Afterward, the girl was instructed to crawl over to her mother and sit on her lap. Ponder and Watkins interpreted the fact that Candace did as she was told a breakthrough. Candace was ready to be "rebirthed," the next and most critical phase in the treatment.

Rebirthing is a method used by particularly zealous attachment therapists, in which the patient quite literally reenacts her birth. If a child
playacts the process of emerging from her mother's womb, these therapists say, she will relive and, therefore, *erase*, traumas experienced in her
infancy. The patient will come out the other end a brand-new person
who isn't afraid to love or be loved by her caretaker. To this day, people
ranging from therapists to psychics advertise their ability to remake a
client through rebirthing, claiming that the hour-long process will un-
equivocally obliterate any attachment issues you may be harboring.

When Candace arrived at Watkins's office to be reborn on the morning of April 18, she told Ponder that she hadn't slept well. She had had a
nightmare that someone was murdering her. This might have been a result of the fact that she had curiously been put back on the antidepres-
sants the day before, or maybe was simply freaked out from the therapy.
But Ponder assured her that no one was out to hurt her, *especially* Jeane
Newmaker, who wanted nothing more in life than to forge an emotional
connection with her new daughter. Ponder told Candace all about rebirthing and how it would achieve this. Rebirthing was the last step on
the path to happiness. The ten-year-old agreed, and the video camera set
up to record the little girl's second entry into the world was turned on.

Candace was told to lie down on the floor in the fetal position. Then
others entered the room—Jeane Newmaker; Watkins; Brita St. Clair,
Watkins's office manager; and Jack McDaniel, an out-of-work construction worker engaged to St. Clair. (Neither St. Clair nor McDaniel had
any medical training, yet they had acted as Candace's therapeutic foster
family since the beginning of the Evergreen therapy, meaning that Candace lived with them, away from Jeane. They fed her, put her to bed,
and even dispensed her medication.)

Ponder wrapped Candace tightly in a flannel sheet, bunching up the
corners and twisting them together, forming the "rebirthing womb." Then
the others piled pillows on top of Candace and began to push down on her
to simulate the muscle contractions of childbirth. Their combined weight
was 673 pounds; Candace weighed about 70 pounds. Candace's job was to
fight her way out of the womb and into the hands of Jeane, who would be
waiting for her with open arms at the end of the "rebirthing canal."

Candace complained that they were pressing down on her head too hard and soon said she didn't want to go through with it. The therapists decided that more "tough love" was in order. Being born isn't easy for anyone they told the girl. Candace would have to fight for her life if she wanted to be fixed. Jeane Newmaker played her part, announcing that she was thrilled that she would soon have a new baby girl. She would love Candace and "keep her very safe." One of the therapists asked Candace how she felt about her mother's commentary. "Happy," said Candace. Well, then, get down to it, she was told. "If a baby doesn't decide to be born, she will die," Watkins said. Ponder added that Jeane would die, too, if Candace didn't get out.

Ponder, Watkins, St. Clair, and McDaniel all put their weight onto Candace, sometimes pushing with their backs and using the couch or hearth as leverage. A few minutes later, Candace asked who was sitting on top of her. "I can't do it," a muffled shout came from under the pillows. She began to cry. "My hands come out first?" she asked. Watkins told her that it can take up to eighteen hours to be born.

Candace began to panic, screaming the way only ten-year-old girls can. The "therapy" session continued. "I can't breathe!" she shrieked. "I can't do it! I can't do it!"

Ponder asked her if she would rather stay in there and die, then. "I can't do it!"

"Do you want to die?" Ponder asked.

"No, but I'm about to," Candace replied.

Twelve minutes into the rebirthing session, Candace pleaded: "Please, I can't breathe."

A minute later, Watkins asked Newmaker, "Are you feeling the contractions, Mom?" Newmaker said she did.

"Where am I to go? Right here? Right here? I'm supposed to go right here? Please. Please. OK, I'm dying. I'm sorry . . . I want to die . . . Can you let me have some oxygen? You mean you want me to die for real?"

"Uh-huh," Ponder said.

"Die right now and go to heaven?"

"Go ahead and die right now," the therapist replied.

"OK, I'm dead." Still, the "contractions" didn't let up. Pleading for her life wasn't enough for them; Candace had to fight four adults for it. "Get off. I'm sick. Where am I supposed to come out? Where? . . . You said you would give me oxygen."

"You have to fight for it," Watkins told her. Then Candace vomited.

"I gotta poop. I gotta poop," she told them.

"Go ahead," said Ponder.

"Stay in there with the poop and vomit," Watkins added.

In the background Newmaker was saying, "Baby, I love you already. I'll hold you and love you and keep you safe forever . . . Don't give up on your life before you have it."

A half-hour into the rebirthing, Ponder tried to get Candace's attention, but got no response. She repositioned a pillow over Candace's head. "She needs more pressure over here so she can't—so she *really* needs to fight," she told her colleagues.

"Getting pretty tight in here," Watkins said.

"Yep, less and less air all the time," replied Ponder.

Five minutes later, the therapists began to make fun of Candace for lying there in her "puke and poop," calling her a quitter.

"Do you want to be reborn, Candace?"

The little girl spoke her last word—a muffled "no"—from under the blankets.

The therapists, convinced that Candace was being her typical manipulative, controlling self, continued pushing on the girl and taunting her. They called her a quitter repeatedly and said things like "This baby doesn't want to live." St. Clair and McDaniel took a break as Ponder and Watkins sat atop Candace's body, talking shop, gossiping about a colleague, discussing a piece of land that was being sold and how they'd love to build a dream house.

At one point, Watkins signaled to Ponder that they should make sure Candace was still breathing. Ponder put her hand under the blankets and touched Candace's now sweaty face. "She's pretty sweaty, which is good," she said. At this point, Newmaker was asked to leave the room. Watkins theorized that Candace might be channeling Newmaker's negativity; Newmaker watched the rest of the rebirthing on a monitor in the next room.

A few minutes later, Watkins said, "Let's talk to this twerp in here." They unwrapped Candace from her "womb."

Initially, the therapists believed Candace was just playing another one of her control games. "Oh, there she is sleeping in her vomit," Watkins said. The girl didn't stir. Her face was blue. She wasn't breathing. Jeane Newmaker ran into the room. Newmaker and Ponder gave her CPR, as Watkins called the paramedics. The therapists hadn't checked the girl's breathing until twelve minutes before they unwrapped her. Candace was airlifted to a local hospital and placed on life support, but it was too late. She was pronounced dead of asphyxia the next morning, the victim of lethal egos and unrestrained arrogance. As she had lived much of her life, Candace Newmaker died alone; the nightmare she had dreamt only hours previous had come true. "The videotape's going to hang us," Watkins said soon after. For once, she was right.[9]

The two therapists and their assistants were arrested, each held on $250,000 bail. Ponder and Watkins were charged with reckless child abuse resulting in death, similar to second-degree murder. They faced sixteen to forty-eight years in prison. St. Clair and McDaniel were charged with the same crime. Jeane Newmaker was also arrested for negligent child abuse resulting in death, a four- to sixteen-year prison term.

As Candace's memorial service was going on in Durham, North Carolina, Angie Elmore was going about her business 150 miles away in the town of Hickory, totally unaware that her daughter had been smothered in Colorado. Her home was filled with pictures of Candace and her other children, and she constantly thought of being reunited with Candace. Her abusive husband was out of her life and, although she had made some big mistakes with her children, she felt there were much worse mothers out there, mothers who didn't even love their children, and they were allowed to raise them.

It wasn't until five months after Candace's death that Angie learned of it. She broke down. "No, no, no. Not Candace. Not Candy. Not Candy. Not Candy Doll," she cried.[10]

St. Clair and McDaniel plea-bargained their way down to ten years and one thousand hours of community service. Newmaker opted to testify for the prosecution in the Ponder-Watkins trial. In exchange, her testimony couldn't be used as evidence against her in her own trial. She then pled guilty to the charge and received the minimum of four years. The judge deferred the sentence, saying that Newmaker was only trying to help her daughter; she and Candace were victims of quack psychology. As for the prosecution's request that her right to practice nursing be revoked, the judge said it would be pointless. Newmaker had to serve four hundred hours community service and attend grief-counseling sessions.

Someone had to answer for Candace's death. It would have to be Watkins and Ponder.

The prosecution's star witness—the seventy-minute videotape capturing the entire ordeal—made life extraordinarily difficult for the defense. But they gave it the college try. Rather than plead out, Ponder and Watkins stood trial together in March 2001. The jury was to either come up with an innocent verdict or decide guilt on one of three crimes: reckless child abuse resulting in death (sixteen to forty-eight years); criminally negligent child abuse resulting in death (the same as Jeane Newmaker's charge—four to sixteen years); or child abuse resulting in bodily injury (a misdemeanor).

The prosecution painted the therapists as monsters and torturers who acted with complete disregard for Candace's well-being. If these people were so bent on helping the poor child, why didn't they heed her cries for help? Why didn't they check on her breathing until twenty minutes after she stopped crying for help? Why didn't they take obvious precautions? It was up to the defense to prove that this particular rebirthing session was routine.

Attorneys can be crafty, but they aren't miracle workers. Instead, the defense bypassed those questions and focused on some key details. First, Watkins and Ponder clearly didn't intend to harm Candace Newmaker. They introduced as witnesses former patients who testified that the therapists had changed their lives for the better with attachment therapy. These women weren't murderers, they were professionals who dedicated their lives to helping children in need. They made a mistake, plain and simple.

Candace Newmaker with her beloved dogs soon after being adopted by Jeane Newmaker. The ten-year-old was smothered by two therapists and their assistants during a "rebirthing" session on April 18, 2001. *Rocky Mountain News/Polaris*

Then the defense lawyers proceeded to blame everyone except their clients for Candace's death. Because her little brother was known to have a heart condition, Candace likely had one, too, defense lawyers claimed, which was really the cause of death, not asphyxia. They dismissed the autopsy report as inaccurate. It hadn't been performed by a forensic pathologist. So now, the real answer could never be known. And while they were on the subject of hearts, why not talk about Candace's birth parents, who had given their daughter away? Watkins's lawyer, Greg Lawler, switched from a medical argument to a metaphorical one: "They stole her heart," he dramatically proclaimed. And, anyway, what was the psychiatrist thinking when he increased Candace's antipsychotic meds . . . right before the rebirthing? That couldn't have helped her heart. And let's not forget, Candace was being rebirthed at the Evergreen facility in Colorado—over 7,000 feet above sea level. Not good. Someone should have thought of that. (Apparently, though, not Watkins and Ponder.)

Blame-the-victim-and-everyone-else-she-knew was the only viable strat-egy, and it didn't work. One serious problem was Watkins and Ponder themselves. When they took the stand, the therapists dug their heels in. They came across as cold and unfeeling, refusing to take responsibility for their actions. Watkins described her brand of therapy as necessary in Candace's case—which meant that she personally had to admit to meting out brutal treatment. She seemed confused and nervous, but always defi-ant about any claims that she did anything wrong.

Ponder, too, showed no remorse. For five hours on the stand, she was forced to relive the details of Candace's death, and to defend the procedure of rebirthing. She said that she had been rebirthed a few times in the past and that it was a wonderful experience. "It felt like be-ing held, if you can imagine being held by a group of people who love and care about you," she said.[11]

Ponder insisted that Candace could breathe through the flannel sheet. "The whole thing is an air-hole," she said. "It's not like wrapping someone in plastic." When pressed by the prosecution to explain why she believed Candace was grunting as if really trying to push her way out of the simulated womb, Ponder responded, "At times, I think they were manipulative."[12] (This was a vastly different Julie Ponder than the distraught one who said, "It's my fault. It's all my fault," when she real-ized Candace had died.)

The situation was a catch-22 for the defense. The therapists couldn't be apologetic when their entire defense was based on the claim that they simply weren't responsible; yet, by insisting they had done nothing wrong, they came across as cold-hearted.

The defense tried valiantly to plant the seed of doubt, but once the jury saw the video, all bets were off. As the video of Candace's torture and death played, there wasn't a dry eye in the courtroom—except, of course, those of the defendants. After all, why should they feel bad when they weren't involved?

Within five hours, the jury found Watkins and Ponder guilty of the most serious charge. One juror commented, "I was waiting for at least any glimpse of remorse or sorrow or regret that they had ignored Can-dace, and I was quite shocked that that just never happened." Nevertheless, the judge sentenced them to the minimum of sixteen years, based on the fact that there was no evidence that Ponder and Watkins intended to harm Candace.

At the sentencing, Ponder said, "I have to live the rest of my life knowing that Candace was dying next to me and I wasn't aware of it."[13] Watkins professed her "sorrow, regret, and remorse" and even accepted "full responsibility." Too little, too late. When she was led out in handcuffs to begin her new life as a convict, Watkins finally found a reason to cry.

CANDACE'S LAW

When the story of Candace Newmaker made the rounds, public outcry for a ban on rebirthing was almost instantaneous. During the Watkins-Ponder trial, the Colorado state legislature drafted a bill designed to stop the controversial therapy, and one day short of the year anniversary of the deadly rebirthing session, Colorado Governor Bill Owens signed it into law. Candace's grandparents, David and Mary Davis, stood at his side.

The carefully worded law prohibits the practice of rebirthing if it's a "psychodrama" that employs "physical restraint." Those caught practicing rebirthing will face a misdemeanor charge for the first offense and felony charges for the second and subsequent offenses.

Interestingly, the law pertains to registered or licensed therapists. Connell Watkins wasn't licensed. To sidestep this grim irony, the law states that lay people will be charged with a misdemeanor for practicing or even recommending rebirthing to patients.

Of course, Colorado police don't stake out therapists' offices, waiting to kick in the door when they detect a rebirthing in progress. In essence, Candace's Law was little more than political posturing. "If you try to micromanage every cuckoo, cockamamie intervention that Americans can dream up, you are going to have a law book that will extend from one end of the continent to the other," said Dr. Arthur Caplan, Director of the Center for Bioethics at the University of Pennsylvania, in a *New York Times* interview. "And everybody who believes in the therapy will find ten ways to circumvent it so that it doesn't meet what's on the law book." In other words, rebirthing doesn't kill people; people kill people.

fifteen

LAW & ORDER: Two men are executed in a trendy Italian restaurant after someone insults a patron as she's singing.

TRUE STORY: Mafia wise guy Louis "Louie Lump" Barone, a regular at the exclusive Harlem eatery Rao's, shot and killed a fellow patron for insulting him.

New York City is notorious for pricey real estate but twenty grand to lease a table? Now that takes the cake—or in this case, the cannoli. That's how much a table at the famed East Harlem eatery Rao's went for on the auction block. To call Rao's exclusive would be an understatement—Madonna couldn't get a table nor could Bill Clinton. The tiny restaurant is home to just eleven tables, tables that co-owner Frankie Pellegrino permanently assigned to his regular customers.

Pellegrino was tired of juggling reservations and turning people away—an unfortunate necessity that had earned him the nickname "Frankie No." Assigning tables made his life easier (and made the place an even hotter commodity). Pellegrino distributed tables based on loyalty. Tommy Mottola, former head of Sony Music, and Ron Perelman, chairman of Revlon, got tables, as did ex-cops Bo Dietl and Sonny Grosso, and a dozen people from the neighborhood.

If you don't own a table, the only way in is an invite from someone who does. This system makes for strange bedfellows; at Rao's it's not uncommon to find an opera singer sitting at the same table as a plumber from Brooklyn, an ex-cop, a Hollywood director, and a fat guy with a wad of cash, a pinkie ring, and no discernible career. When Bill Clinton finally dined at Rao's, he was there as a guest.

Those who are lucky enough to get in the door are treated to Sunday dinner, no matter what day it is. The food, old-world Southern Italian fare, is only part of the allure. Rao's reputation for being a mob hangout is equally enticing. The thrill of being in the same room as a guy who just might know where to find Jimmy Hoffa has celebs and average Joes alike clamoring to get in.

Rao's rep is not without merit. In 2001, two Lucchese wise guys were caught on wiretap in a major beef over table rights. They were just the latest in a long line of diners with connections to the mob. Lucky Luciano, Gambino boss Paul Castellano, and his successor John Gotti ate at Rao's. Fat Tony Salerno ate there too, but even he couldn't always get a reservation. According to mob folklore, Salerno kidnapped Rao's chef and set him up in another restaurant, one where he was guaranteed a good seat.

Located on the corner of 114th Street and Pleasant Avenue, Rao's is one of the last vestiges of Harlem's Little Italy. Today, East Harlem is a predominantly Hispanic and black neighborhood. However, in the early twentieth century, East Harlem was home to nearly 90,000 Italian Americans. There, everyone spoke Italian and everything a local needed was available within this tiny insular world that stretched from 96th to 125th Street, bordering the East River. The son of Italian immigrants, Charles Rao was raised in East Harlem. His fluency in English served him well and granted him access to many avenues closed to his non-English-speaking, Italian-born elders.

Rao was proud of his heritage—and his surname, which he promptly bestowed on the small corner saloon he purchased in 1896. Predating consumer refrigerators, Rao's did a brisk business selling beer by the pail to locals who would stop by each evening for fresh, cold brew. When Rao died, a decade later, his brother Joseph assumed control of the bar. Despite the odds, and the difficulties posed by Prohibition, Rao's not only remained open, it remained in the family.

Over time, Charles Rao's little saloon blossomed into a first-rate restaurant, one with a loyal following of regular customers, almost all from the neighborhood. Today, the restaurant is run by Frankie Pellegrino and Ron Straci, both descendants of Charles Rao.

Louie "Lump Lump" Barone was a familiar fixture at Rao's. The sixty-seven-year-old was in his twenties when he first started dropping by. He'd nurse a drink, or two or three, and shoot the breeze with the staff. Barone considered the place his second home. Four decades later, he still didn't own a table, although Frankie No had said yes a few times. For his birthday one year, Frankie gave him a table. Madonna had been turned away. But Louie got a table. Frankie understood about loyalty and respect.

Loyalty and respect meant a lot in the hardscrabble world Louie Barone grew up in. Nowadays, though, such things were as hard to come by as a Rao's reservation. Born and raised in East Harlem, Barone was a tough kid. He often got into fights, fights that left him with bruises and lumps that earned him the nickname "Lump Lump." He could still be a bit of a pitbull at times. Rumor had it that Barone had ties to the Genovese Family. He also had a rap sheet for gambling, assault, and weapons possession.

While Barone no longer lived in East Harlem, he made it a habit to visit often. He'd drive from his Pelham Parkway condo in the Bronx, see some familiar faces, and drop by Rao's for a few drinks.

Three days before Christmas 2003, Louie Barone made what would be his last visit to Rao's. The city was dressed to the nines in colored lights, bows, and wreaths. On Fifth Avenue, hordes of revelers gathered outside Macy's famed holiday windows. Uptown at Rao's the mood was equally festive. Frankie Pellegrino held court, chatting and greeting diners. Later, honoring a Rao's tradition, he would sing a song. A part-time actor with a recurring role in the HBO smash *The Sopranos*, Pellegrino loves the limelight.

As always, the crowd was eclectic. Former French Connection cop Sonny Grosso was there along with tenor Michael Amante, chief clerk of Nassau County Surrogate Court Al Petraglia, Broadway chanteuse Rena Strober, deli owner Johnny "Roastbeef" Williams, who had a supporting role in Martin Scorsese's *Goodfellas*, and actor Len Cariou.

Barone bellied up to the bar and chatted with bartender Nicky the Vest, an affable fellow known for his extensive collection of vests. Louie also noted the newcomer in the black leather jacket. Nicky said the guy's name was Al. Barone didn't know him but it was clear that this Al was connected. The young guy's body language spelled m-o-b. Barone nodded amiably in Al's direction and went back to his drink and the impromptu floor show.

Al was Al Circelli Jr., a handsome thirty-seven-year-old who lived with his mother and grandmother in Yonkers. Friends and family knew him as a businessman and a fitness buff who swore off salt and sugar and worked out regularly. According to his ex-fiancée, Circelli ran a private ambulance service and an extermination company. The FBI, however, had a much different take on Circelli. They had pegged him as a midlevel soldier who had just received his "button" from the Lucchese Family. To the FBI, Circelli was an exterminator all right, just not of insects.

Circelli owned a fleet of cars that included a Ferrari and the Lincoln that he drove to Rao's that night. At six foot four, he had a good view of the crowd from his perch at the bar. By the time Michael Amante sang "O Sole Mio," a cappella, Circelli had tossed back a few drinks. Amante, whom Tony Bennett dubbed the "fourth tenor," received a great round of applause for his performance. Around ten o'clock Rena Strober rose to sing one of Frankie No's favorites, "Don't Rain on My Parade." Strober, a soprano and Monday night regular, had played Cosette in *Les Misérables*.

Apparently, Strober's voice was good enough for Broadway but not good enough for Circelli. Later, his neighbors would describe him as quiet and unassuming. That night, though, he was anything but as he heckled Strober from across the room. He'd had a bit too much to drink and was behaving like a bad drunk. Rolling his eyes, Circelli complained loudly, "Someone shut this fucking broad up." A few feet away, Barone felt his blood pressure rise.

Barone put his finger to his lips to shush the younger man. Circelli,

In the famous East Harlem restaurant Rao's, Louis "Lump Lump" Barone murdered a purported Mafia hitman for heckling a patron as she sang "Don't Rain on My Parade."
NYC Police Department

---

in response, heckled Strober some more. Barone didn't care how connected this guy was—somebody had to teach him some manners. "Watch your mouth, there's a lady singing," he said. Circelli bristled and spat out a string of expletives. "Don't you ever raise your fucking finger at me," witnesses heard Circelli say. He threatened to break off Barone's finger and put it where the sun don't shine. Nicky the Vest ran interference, trying to diffuse a volatile situation.

After a few more nasty exchanges, Barone clammed up; Circelli had thirty years and half a foot on him. "He could have twisted me into a pretzel," the five foot eight gray-haired Barone told a reporter from the *New York Daily News*. "He was intimidating. I was scared . . . The things that were coming out of his mouth . . . I've never spoken to a man like that."[1]

To Nicky the Vest, it appeared that the dispute between the two men was over. Barone, however, was quietly steaming. He fingered the Smith & Wesson he'd stashed in his pocket earlier that day. The gun, Barone claimed, was to protect him against terrorists—the security level having been elevated recently to Code Orange in New York City. Those who knew him knew Barone simply liked to carry a gun.

Circelli paid his tab, peeling off twenties from a big roll of cash. He turned to leave. "I was really mad at this point," Barone admitted later. "I had blood in my eyes." Barone pulled out his gun and shot Circelli in the back. Wounded, Circelli stumbled some twenty feet and collapsed on diner Al Petraglia. Barone shot again, missed his intended target, and hit Petraglia in the foot instead.

Rena Strober, her song long over, took cover under the table. There was pandemonium in the small restaurant. Circelli lay bleeding on the floor, Petraglia clutched his foot in pain. All around them, people were screaming. Len Cariou's grandson had an asthma attack. Barone, in a scene reminiscent of *The Godfather*, calmly walked out of the restaurant.

Two cops from the twenty-third precinct happened to be in the area. They heard the shots and arrived just as Barone was making his exit. "There's been a shooting inside," he said in his best deadpan. The ruse fell flat. By now, Sonny Grosso and other diners had rushed outside to identify Barone as the gunman. He was taken into custody as paramedics arrived to treat his victims. Al Petraglia would limp for a while but he'd survive. Albert Circelli was not so lucky; he died in the ambulance on the way to the hospital.

HOSTILE WITNESSES

During trial, Jack McCoy will often ask permission to "treat the witness as hostile." What exactly does this mean? When a witness is called to the stand, his testimony is expected to support the argument of the side that subpoenaed him. If the witness becomes evasive or changes his testimony on the stand, the lawyer is given permission by the judge to treat the witness as if he were called to the stand by the opposing side—which legally changes the nature of the questions and language the lawyer uses to ask them. That is to say, the direct examination becomes a cross examination, allowing the DA to use leading questions, giving the lawyer more latitude to suggest how the witness should answer.

. . .

On Christmas Eve, Barone was arraigned in Manhattan Criminal Court. He pleaded not guilty to second-degree murder, assault, and possession of a deadly weapon. Prosecutors weren't worried. Barone had made a statement to police confessing everything. Barone spent the rest of the winter, and then spring and summer stewing away in jail at the Bernard B. Kerik Complex. Faced with the possibility of life behind bars, he decided to accept a plea bargain offered by Assistant District Attorney Gary Fishman. In August 2004, looking sickly and infirm, Barone pleaded to manslaughter in exchange for a reduced sentence of fifteen years. State Supreme Court Justice Budd Goodman called the crime "a senseless killing." Barone declined to make a statement before the court. Noting his client's age and failing health, defense attorney Thomas Lee decried the ruling was "a death sentence."

Uptown, the murder hasn't been a death sentence at all for Rao's. Business is better than ever.

sixteen

LAW & ORDER: An exorcism performed on a troubled teen causes the young girl's death.

TRUE STORY: In Milwaukee, eight-year-old Terrance Cottrell was smothered during a church exorcism intended to cure his autism.

Eight-year-old Terrance Cottrell liked to go to the home of his neighbor Denise Allison, knock on the door, and, when she opened up, yell, "Tickle!" He would run inside, and Allison would give him a newspaper, which Terrance would fold into intricate designs. When he was finished, he would playfully throw punches at his twenty-five-year-old friend.[1] Most people didn't take to Terrance the way his neighbor did. When he wanted to play, they tended to back off. They seemed afraid of him, uneasy, unsure of what to say to him. But Allison had a way with Terrance. She knew he was only playing. "Tickle" was one of the few words Terrance could articulate to express his feelings and desires, and throwing his fists at people was the only way he knew how to express affection. Terrance was autistic. The ministers of his church, however, weren't convinced that autism was Terrance's only problem—if it was even a problem at all. The youngster's real crisis was a spiritual one: They were convinced he was possessed by demons.

Pat Cooper, a single mother living in Milwaukee, struggled to provide for her two children—the autistic Terrance and his two-year-old sister. She fed them, clothed them, sent them to school (Terrance was to enter a third-grade special education class in the fall) and was somehow able to hold it all together. But it wasn't easy. When Cooper wasn't worrying about Terrance hurting himself, she was worried that he would hurt his sister. And she was convinced his autism was getting worse. What kind of future would her boy have? How does an autistic child make it in the world? Years of worry and sleepless nights were beginning to wear on her.

Then, one day, everything changed. As Cooper was dealing with a particularly out-of-control Terrance on the street in front of her home, a member of the Faith Temple Church of the Apostolic Faith happened to be walking by. She offered to help Cooper restrain Terrance and told her that her church could provide "spiritual" healing for the boy, who was clearly tormented.[2] For Cooper, the church was an instant support group. It was like a fairy tale.

Cooper promptly became a member of Faith Temple Church of the Apostolic Faith. Located in a Milwaukee strip mall, along with a pizza place and dry cleaners on Fond du Lac Avenue, and a stone's throw from the Chicago and Northwestern train line, Faith Temple was a storefront church. It may not have been a glamorous house of worship, but the members had big hearts.

Church members would show up at Cooper's house in a van and take Cooper and Terrance to the church for prayer sessions. They would help with household tasks, clean, wash dishes, and take care of the children.[3] It seemed to Cooper that she had found her salvation; out of nowhere, God had sent these caring people to help her climb out of the pool of despair she would surely have drowned in. Now, she was getting a glimpse of the light, and the future, finally, seemed bright. God works in mysterious ways.

But, curiously, the more involved Cooper became with the church, neighbors noticed, the more haggard her appearance became. She ceased to be the friendly neighbor they had come to know, spending most of the summer holed up inside. As for Terrance and his sister, they looked more and more unkempt and were frequently seen wandering around the neighborhood without shoes. Faith Temple Church was, without a doubt, helping Cooper in some ways, but what else was going on, some neighbors wondered. One feared that Cooper was being brainwashed by her fellow congregants.[4]

The prayer sessions were intense affairs, held three times a week during the summer of 2003, and for up to two hours at a time. Church members put all their spiritual effort into helping Terrance become a normal boy. They prayed over him constantly, asking God to intervene and save the boy from a life of torment. The sessions went on for weeks, but Terrance showed no signs of improvement. He would constantly act up, kicking his feet and punching and scratching the congregants, who would try to calm him down. Often, they would physically restrain him, holding his arms and legs down to the floor; sometimes, they removed his sneakers to avoid being kicked by them.

Finally, one of the ministers, Ray Anthony Hemphill—the church founder's brother—concluded that Terrance was without a doubt possessed by demons, and he offered to exorcise them from the boy. The forty-five-year-old was on summer vacation from his job as a school janitor, but was willing to dedicate the rest of it to curing Terrance. At her wit's end, Cooper agreed.

The boy was brought, kicking and screaming, to a number of exorcisms in summer of 2003, which usually consisted of Ray Hemphill pinning Terrance down and commanding Satan's minions to evacuate the innocent boy's body. Cooper claimed to have heard the evil spirits speaking through her son's mouth: "Kill me! Take me!" But time after time, nothing changed. The demons held fast, and Terrance kicked harder. Finally, Hemphill decided to give one final, grand effort to discharge the demons from Terrance's body.

On Friday night, August 22, 2003, a small group of Faith Temple Church members arrived at Terrance's home, hoping and praying that tonight was the night their efforts would pay off. Terrance got in the car to be taken to the church.

One of the congregants noticed the boy was unusually quiet this time. With almost every moment a struggle to keep the autistic Terrance calm in the past, tonight was completely different. Rather than fight to get up off the car seat, determined to go nowhere in particular, Terrance calmly looked out the window. Was this a sign that the demons tormenting Terrance were losing their strength? Were they finally ready to give in to Hemphill's commands on this blessed night?

Or was Terrance just exhausted after weeks of fighting to free himself from the grips of people twice his size while a strange man stood above him shouting words from a book?

They pulled up to the storefront church. Cooper led the oddly quiet child to the front doors by the hand. A peaceful calm descended upon the congregants.

Inside the church it was warm, muggy, and humid. The air was still and tense, as if the church itself were holding its breath in anticipation of what would soon unfold. Ray Hemphill was waiting for them, preparing himself for his final combat with the Beast. Cooper and two other congregants laid Terrance down on the floor in front of the altar. The exorcist knelt down, removed the boy's sneakers, and began to pray. And Terrance started to act up. He began kicking and flailing his arms, struggling to communicate his torment. He spoke in a language unknown to anyone but himself. The congregants held him down as Hemphill commanded the Dark One to free Terrance from his grip. Each volunteer pinned a leg to the ground, while Terrance's mother restrained her son's left arm. The 160-pound Hemphill lay on top of the boy, holding his right arm and head to the floor, increasing the level of his incantations and songs. One woman would periodically press on Terrance's abdomen, while Hemphill lifted some of his weight off the boy's chest, as if to literally squeeze the diabolical spirits out of him.

An hour passed. Then one of the congregants noticed that Terrance was no longer struggling and that his breathing had slowed. Minister Hemphill pulled himself up off the child. Hemphill's shirt was drenched in sweat. Terrance, too, was soaked with sweat; his face was blue.[5] In an instant, everyone knew that the exorcism had gone terribly wrong. God had not intervened, and the demons hadn't exited the boy's body in the maelstrom of fury as they had expected.

At this moment, the church members' extreme religious beliefs evaporated into thin air, and they attempted to revive Terrance with a time-proven, scientific method called cardiopulmonary resuscitation. Perhaps Terrance hadn't been possessed after all; perhaps his problem all along was what the doctors said it was: autism—nothing more, nothing less. Someone called 911.

Terrance Cottrell didn't survive his final and most intense exorcism. He lay on the floor of Faith Temple Church of the Apostolic Faith in his shorts and T-shirt, shoeless, motionless, dead from asphyxiation. The storefront church was hot as hell.

Minister Ray Hemphill remained silent after his arrest and indictment for "child abuse recklessly causing great bodily harm," a crime that carried five years imprisonment and five years court supervision. His brother, David Hemphill, and sister-in-law, Pamela Hemphill, did the talking for him—to the press before the trial and to the court during the trial. Seventeen years older than his brother, David had founded Faith Temple Church in 1977, and he and his wife had run it ever since. No others present at the prayer service were charged.

David had personally ordained his younger brother, who had no formal training in religion. His reasoning went like this: "If a person believes that the King James Version of the Bible is the word of God, you just read it and you believe it," David explained on the stand at his brother's trial, which began in July 2004. "It's nothing you have to go to school for. You believe it, that's it."

This belief system of the church founder begs the question, then, of what "ordainment" means; why would someone need to be "ordained" in the first place if personal faith is the only prerequisite? How does one prove one's faith? By these standards, shouldn't anyone in the church who professes powerful faith be "ordained"? As the deadly exorcism proved, there's more to being a minister than possessing strong faith.

But religion holds a peculiar place in the law. Defendants who commit a crime in the name of religion are granted more leeway than other defendants, and prosecutors hesitate to go for the throats of "ordained ministers"—even those who smother third graders. Not only was the original charge of child abuse against Hemphill relatively minor, given the outcome of the exorcism, but as the trial began, prosecutors instructed jury members that they could opt to convict Hemphill of "child abuse-recklessly causing bodily harm" a lesser crime than the initial one of causing great bodily harm.

"If a child had died in a home, there would be a whole array of charges, maybe including child abuse but also homicide or manslaughter. When a religious entity enters the picture, prosecutors get very nervous," said Marci Hamilton, a law professor at New York City's Benjamin N. Cardozo School of Law, commenting on the case.[6]

And Hemphill's status as a minister of the church wasn't the prosecution's only problem; Hemphill's intent was key to his defense. After all, he had obviously meant no harm to Terrance; not even his most vociferous critics could claim that his actions stemmed from anything but good intentions. Hemphill's behavior could be described as ill-advised, foolish, and even arrogant. But malicious? No one could prove that and, to be sure, no one wanted to try. The prosecution stuck with the basic facts of the exorcism.

The medical examiner who performed the autopsy on Terrance testified for the prosecution that he had found higher levels of drugs in the boy's blood, but they certainly weren't at a level that could be considered "toxic." He also described the severe hemorrhaging he found on the rear of Terrance's neck and in his right eye—bolstering the prosecution's claim that prolonged pressure to his body was what had killed him.

The defense argued that Hemphill had nothing to do with the boy's death: that Terrance had died from the drugs he was taking for his autism. Creatively combining religion and science, the defense called to the stand a toxicology expert, who testified that the levels of antihistamine brompheneramine and dextromethorphan (two chemicals found in cough medicine), mixed with the ziprasidone (an antipsychotic drug), could very well have been responsible for Terrance's death; then they called David Hemphill to the stand, who explained away his brother's action with his perverted brand of theology. God took Terrance's life, not minister Hemphill. "If I lay down on somebody and they pass away, God took him, I didn't," pastor David Hemphill said under cross examination. "[Terrance] just passed away," he added. "God is a mysterious person, and if he wants to call a life back, he does."

That wasn't the only theological somersault performed by Hemphill's defenders. Prior to the trial, Pamela Hemphill had stated that her brother-in-law's technique of lying across Terrance's body came right from the Bible itself.[7] Specifically, Kings 17:21: "And [Elijah] stretched himself upon the child three times, and cried unto the Lord, and said, 'O Lord my God, I pray thee, let this child's soul come into him again.'" Ironically, Elijah was attempting to help the child in the passage because the child was so sick that "that there was no breath left in him," (17:18) not because he was kicking and screaming, like Terrance was. Maybe Elijah was performing an ancient version of resuscitation. Maybe the Holy Spirit *was* working miracles through Elijah. Or maybe the story has gone through so many translations that the King James Version doesn't even resemble the original. One thing's for certain, though: literal readings of ancient books have been the cause of more than a few deaths in history.

Even Pat Cooper and the so-called innocent congregants at the prayer sessions looked to the Bible for clear-cut instructions on how to cure the autistic third grader, using the good book's words to defend their flagrantly un-Christian behavior. For instance, church members might have had in mind Proverbs 23:13–14—"Withhold not correction from the child: for if thou beatest him with the rod, he shall not die/ Thou shalt beat him with the rod, and shalt deliver his soul from hell"—when, according to neighbor Denise Allison, they took turns beating Terrance with a belt during a prayer session in his home. "I told Pat it was wrong," Allison said, explaining how she looked in Cooper's window during a prayer session and saw them abusing Terrance, "but she said the Bible told her you're supposed to chastise your children."[8]

In the end, the jury decided that Terrance Cottrell hadn't been the victim of the "mysterious person" called God, and that a minister's good intentions aren't enough to excuse his smothering of a little boy. Ray Hemphill was found guilty of recklessly causing *great* harm to the boy. Prosecutors were satisfied with the verdict. Others, however, including Terrance's father and grandmother, felt that the holy man got away with murder.

seventeen

LAW & ORDER: The repressed memory of an emotionally fragile woman holds the key to a thirty-one-year-old murder.

TRUE STORY: Californian George Franklin was tried and convicted of the murder of an eight-year-old girl based on his daughter's recovered memory of the crime.

Susan Nason was looking forward to the weekend. On Saturday, the little girl would turn nine years old and her mother had planned a birthday party to celebrate the occasion. Susan invited a few girls from school and, of course, her best friend Eileen Franklin. Like Susan, Eileen was often teased about her red hair. In Foster City, California, nearly everyone had blonde or brunette hair. Susan and Eileen sometimes felt like odd ducks and banded together, two freckle-faced girls with flame-colored hair most women would envy.

Margaret Nason was sewing a dress for Susan to wear to the party when her daughter returned home from school, carrying a pair of sneakers that Margaret did not recognize. The sneakers belonged to Cecilia, a classmate who lived nearby. She had left them behind at school and Susan volunteered to bring them by the girl's house. Margaret told her to come straight home after her errand. Susan, still wearing her school clothes—a blue print dress, white bobby socks, and brown shoes—set off for Cecilia's house.

When dinnertime arrived with no sign of Susan, Margaret began to worry. She learned that Susan had not stayed at Cecilia's house to play, as Margaret had assumed, but had dropped off the sneakers and left. Frantic, Margaret pedaled through the neighborhood on her bicycle looking for her daughter. Eventually, she returned home alone, and called the police. Search parties were organized, residents were questioned, missing posters of Susan dotted the town. Soon, hundreds of leads flooded the police department but turned up no new clues. Donald Nason's employer offered a $10,000 reward.

Saturday came and went. Susan's birthday presents, clad in colorful paper and tied up in ribbon, remained wrapped, gathering dust in a back room. Not knowing where the little girl was agonized her family. Margaret was a bundle of nerves, and wracked with guilt. What if she hadn't let Susan go out that day? She watched her eldest daughter Shirley like a hawk. Susan's father, Donald, took to the bottle. Even Snoopy, the Nason's dog, sensed there was something deeply wrong. The dog would wait at the door for Susan, but she never came home.

A San Francisco water department employee was making his rounds when he found her, or what was left of her. The tiny body lay at the bottom of the embankment of Half Moon Bay Road. It was badly decomposed, but from the size of the skull, and the bits of clothing that remained, it was clear that this was once a young girl. It was also clear that she had died a violent death. The coroner confirmed everyone's fears: the dead girl was Susan Nason. The cause of death appeared to be a severe blow to the head. The redheaded child had been missing for seventy days, and according to the coroner, she'd been dead just as long.

"We had not prepared ourselves for this," Donald Nason told reporters. "We always thought she was being cared for by someone— somebody who wanted a child and kidnapped her."[1]

The murder stunned the close-knit community of Foster City. In 1969, the city was felony-free: there had been no rapes, no assaults, and no murders reported. "This is going to be a tough case to crack," Foster City Police Chief Gordon Penfold said.[2] He had no idea how prophetic his words would prove to be.

Susan Nason was buried on December 9 under a headstone that read: SO SMALL, SO SWEET, SO SOON. Her murder would go unsolved for twenty years.

· · ·

In 1989, Charles Etter had just a year to go before retirement. An inspector with San Mateo's District Attorney's office, Etter had seen and heard it all—or so he thought. Then he got the call. The guy said his name was Barry and that his wife had witnessed a murder. Etter listened attentively, jotting down notes. Murders, unfortunately, were not uncommon in Etter's line of work. This one would turn out to be a different story—and a different decade. The murder, explained Barry, took place in the fall of 1969, two decades earlier.

Over the next few days, the mysterious caller and his wife "Mrs. Barry" phoned six more times. While her story was fantastic, "Mrs. Barry" did sound credible as she recounted the murder of eight-year-old Foster City resident Susan Nason. Unlike other crimes, there is no statute of limitations on murder. Detectives were assigned to look into the case. A rudimentary investigation confirmed what the woman had told Inspector Etter.

Mrs. Barry was actually a California homemaker named Eileen Franklin-Lipsker. She and her husband Barry Lipsker had two young children. Eileen said she was frightened that the killer, a close family member, would seek revenge if she testified against him in court. After being promised protection in the event of a trial, she consented to a police interview at her home.

On November 25, 1989, detectives drove out to Eileen's home to interview her in person. They were taken aback by the attractive, strawberry-blonde woman who answered the door. It was her twenty-ninth birthday and Eileen was miles and years away from the awkward-looking girl with the bright red hair she had once been. But, she had never forgotten her childhood or her childhood best friend.

Eileen explained that on the morning of September 22, 1969, her father, George Franklin, decided to drive her and her sister Janice to school in his Volkswagen van. (Eileen's memory about the time would prove to be inaccurate.) They spotted Susan Nason walking and offered her a ride. Franklin told his daughter Janice to leave the van. He dropped her off on the sidewalk. Driving off, he declared they were going to play hooky that day. He headed toward Half Moon Bay while the girls jumped up and down on a mattress in the back of the van. Franklin pulled off the road near a reservoir and joined the girls in the back, sending Eileen to sit up front. A few minutes later, Susan cried out, "Stop! No, don't!" Eileen turned and saw her father straddling Susan and pushing the little girl's dress up. The next thing she remembered was being outside the van. Susan was sitting at the bottom of a hill, crying.

Eileen said she watched in horror as her father raised a large rock into the air and brought it down on Susan's head. "I think I screamed," Eileen said. "I did something that made Susie look up at me. She met my eyes." It was a look that would come back to haunt Eileen. Susan raised her hand to protect herself as Franklin hit her again with the rock. The second blow crushed her hand and the ring she wore on her finger.

Franklin grabbed Eileen and pushed her toward the van. This was all her fault, he hissed. If she hadn't wanted to give Susan a ride none of this would have happened. He warned her to keep her mouth shut, or else he'd kill her. And so, for twenty years, Eileen kept the terrible secret to herself.

It was a compelling, horrifying story. Except that it wasn't exactly true. What Eileen didn't tell the investigators was that she had only recently "recovered" the long-repressed memory of the crime. This fact would emerge in time.

Twenty years can be brutal on a murder investigation. Evidence is lost or damaged by the ravages of time, witnesses and suspects move away, or worse, die. Those that can be located no longer have fresh memories of the event. Still, investigators are always hopeful of cracking cold cases. Surprisingly, much of the evidence from the Nason murder remained remarkably intact. The case file and coroner's report provided detectives with the information they needed to verify Eileen's story. The report noted that Susan's remains had been found under an "old box spring mattress." Two rings had been found on the skeleton. One was missing a stone.

Deputy District Attorney Martin Murray told Eileen she described what "only a person who saw the crime would know." He found her credible and mistakenly believed that she knew facts about the murder that were not made public. In reality, the case had received extensive media coverage in 1969 and the facts Eileen offered up were public knowledge. Given that Susan had been Eileen's best friend, it stands to reason that Eileen would have followed the case or at least been aware of the facts as the case unfolded. She told Murray that she never read or listened to accounts of the crime. However, she told her therapist that she had.

From the start, there were problems with Eileen's account of the crime, which changed to fit each new set of facts uncovered by the investigation. Initially, she said her sister was in the van. Then when Janice disputed this, she changed her story. She was wrong about the clothes Susan was wearing, and wrong about the time and place the crime occurred. The district attorney didn't know it yet, but his star witness was about to drop a bombshell on him.

Retired and divorced from Eileen's mother, George Franklin was enrolled in college and living alone in a rented apartment in Sacramento. He was in between classes when detectives arrived to question him about Susan Nason's murder. Franklin, undaunted, asked, "Have you talked to my daughters?" His statement aroused their suspicion and would later be used to incriminate him in court. Franklin refused to speak to the detectives. He was arrested and taken into custody. A search of his apartment turned up a large stash of hardcore pornography, including magazines and books with themes of incest and bestiality. Former girlfriends told police that Franklin liked to be called "Daddy" during sex.

Franklin certainly fit the profile of a predator pedophile. But if Murray thought he had an airtight case, he was about to be surprised. After the arrest, his star witness confessed that she had only recently "recovered" the memory of Susan's murder. As Eileen explained it, in the days after the murder, she kept the terrible secret to herself. Scared and traumatized by what she had seen, she managed to repress the memory completely.

Two decades later, she was playing with her young daughter and something clicked. It was the way her daughter looked up at her. She had seen that expression before. The red hair, the freckles, the puzzled look on her face—it was so familiar to her. Eileen says it was as if she was looking at Susan Nason. "I was sitting on the sofa in my family room, and I was holding my son. And my daughter said something to me, which caused me to look down at her, and I matched her gaze. And at that moment she very closely resembled Susan. And I remembered seeing Susan there and seeing my father with a rock above his head," she said.[3] This latest account contradicted what Eileen had previously told her family. She told her brother she had recovered the memory while under hypnosis. Eileen's sisters and mother were led to believe the memory came to her in a dream. In truth, Eileen had recalled the repressed memory not in a thunderous epiphany but while under hypnosis in her therapist's office. This was an important distinction. According to California law, "the testimony of a witness who has undergone hypnosis for the purpose of restoring his memory of the events in issue is inadmissible in all matters relating to those events."

But was it really possible to repress the memory of such a terrifying event? And was it possible to recall the memory in detail twenty years later? By the late 1980s, a growing number of therapists and patients believed it was. Further, they believed that the phenomenon was much more common than anyone realized. The Franklin case brought the subject of repressed memory to the forefront of public consciousness.

The psychiatric community was bitterly divided over the issue. *Science Today* and *Psychology Today* magazines dubbed the rift the "Memory Wars." Even members of the task force assembled by the American Psychological Association to investigate the burgeoning recovered memory movement couldn't agree on the issue. Instead, they agreed to disagree and released two reports, one supporting the syndrome, the other debunking it. "At this point, it is impossible, without corroborative evidence, to distinguish a true memory from a false one," read the statement released by the association.[4]

Behind closed doors, in therapists offices and group sessions across the country, patients were suddenly uncovering memories of childhood sexual abuse on an epic scale. Soon came the tales of horrific abuse at the hands of satanic cults. Patients routinely offered up bizarre "memories" of satanic ceremonies that involved rape, and murder. They "remembered" being buried alive, impregnated by Satan, forced to partake in human sacrifice and cannibalism. It was not uncommon for one recovered memory to begat another and another, each new recovered memory more horrific than the last.*

District Attorney Murray was about to find this out himself. Eileen Lipsker-Franklin excitedly reported that she had recovered more memories of more murders and rapes—all involving her father. Either his star witness was not the levelheaded person he thought she was, or George and Eileen had quite a sordid résumé. These newer claims, none of which could be verified, shed doubt on Eileen's original repressed memory of seeing her father kill Susan Nason. If the district attorney had any misgivings about going to trial, he kept them to himself.

Was Eileen lying? By all accounts, the Franklin family *had* been severely dysfunctional. George Franklin was known as an abusive, hostile husband and father. His wife, Leah, was a wreck emotionally. Eileen was seven years old when Leah had a nervous breakdown. While Leah was in the hospital, the Franklin children were left to fend for themselves, and according to Eileen, fend off their father. As adults, three of Franklin's daughters alleged that he had sexually abused them as children. Eileen claims he told her that "Little girls are really sexy."[4] At the firehouse where he worked, coworkers described Franklin as a sexual deviant who wasn't shy about his predilection for young girls. Friends recall Franklin being obsessed with pornography.

Based exclusively on Eileen's testimony, George Franklin was indicted for the 1969 murder of Susan Nason. He pleaded not guilty. Bail was

---

*As some experts point out, it is frighteningly easy for a therapist to induce a false memory. Richard Ofshe, one of the recovered memory movement's most vocal detractors, has described it as "the psychiatric psychological quackery of the 20th century." (Maria Shriver interview.) Napa Valley winery exec Gary Ramona sued his adult daughter's recovered memory therapists after she accused him of sexually abusing her as a child. The jury found the therapists guilty of negligence and awarded Ramona $500,000 in civil damages—a small consolation to a man who had lost his job, his reputation, and his family.

set at two million dollars; unable to raise the money, Franklin remained in custody throughout the trial. Eileen visited her father in jail, in an attempt, she said, to persuade him to confess and spare the family the pain of a trial. She claimed that her visit was sanctioned, and even encouraged, by DA Murray. The jailers, as a favor to Murray, awarded her special treatment, Eileen said. Murray disputes this. "I told her I didn't have the power to tell her that she couldn't [visit Franklin], but please don't do it." During the short, strained visit, Eileen asked Franklin why he had killed Susan. In response, he pointed to a sign in the visiting room that said, "Conversations may be monitored." Eileen left without the confession. The next time they met would be in court.

Meanwhile, Eileen was enjoying her status as a celebrity. Her picture was published in the papers and her phone rang off the hook with offers to tell—and sell—her story. With her lovely red hair and slim build, the attractive woman was definitely media-friendly. Reporters weren't the only ones eager to interview Eileen. The talk shows came calling and Eileen appeared on *Oprah* and *Today*. She got an agent, signed a book deal, and sold the rights to her life story.

In January 1990, George Franklin was tried in Sacramento Court for first-degree murder. Assistant prosecutor Elaine Tipton, who took over the case from Deputy DA Murray, told the jury that Eileen knew facts about the case that had not been reported in the media. Defense attorney Doug Horngrad had evidence to the contrary—newspaper clippings, news recordings. However, the judge, in what would prove to be a costly decision, denied Horngrad's motion to introduce the evidence. As a result, the jury was not informed that Eileen's "privileged" information had been widely reported at the time of the murder.

On the witness stand, Eileen described in chilling detail how she had witnessed her father rape and bludgeon Susan Nason to death when she was eight years old. She demonstrated how Franklin had raised the murder weapon, the rock, in the air and brought it down on little Susan's head. Eileen also told the jury about her jailhouse visit, about how Franklin had refused to speak about the case because he thought they were being recorded. The prosecutor made it clear that an innocent man would have nothing to hide.

During cross-examination Horngrad tried his best to trip up Eileen but she held her ground. Although she was combative with the defense attorney, Eileen came across as sympathetic, and truthful. Clad in an ultra-conservative dress, her hair pulled back in a tight bun, Eileen looked like a prim schoolmarm. The jury had no idea that she had a criminal record with arrests for prostitution and drug possession. This information was kept from the jury, and, as it turned out, from the defense.

The jury received a crash course on the nature of memory. In a battle of experts, both sides called on the big guns. The prosecutor's expert, Lenore Terr, was a well-known child psychiatrist who treated the Chowchilla schoolchildren who had been kidnapped and buried alive in California in 1976. Terr, who, years earlier had contended that it was not possible to repress traumatic memories, had recently reversed her position on the subject. Although some people are haunted by their painful memories, others cannot remember them at all, Terr now believed. She testified that Eileen's memory of seeing her father kill her best friend had been buried so deeply that it took twenty years for it to surface. Terr then kept the jury spellbound with a story about writer Stephen King, who as a child had witnessed a friend get hit by a train. According to the psychiatrist, King's movie *Stand By Me*, which features a recurring train motif, was inspired by the writer's repressed memories of the traumatic event. King, consciously or not, was reliving the event over and over.

Elizabeth Loftus, a pioneer in the field of cognitive research who had been named one of the twentieth century's top one hundred psychologists by the *Review of General Psychology*, testified for the defense. As a cognitive psychologist, Loftus had conducted numerous studies on human memory. What she found, she told to the jury, was that memories can be distorted over time and, more significantly, that false memories can be easily implanted through suggestion, dreams, or even a vivid overactive imagination. In one experiment, the psychologist set out to convince participants that they had gotten lost in the mall as children. By the end of the experiment, nearly all of the participants had created false memories of this fictional event. Many even described the mall and the anxiety of being separated from their parents in great detail. The moral of the story, Loftus explained, was that memory was extremely malleable. In the end, Terr, who would go on to collaborate on a book about the case with Eileen, won the battle.

George Franklin did not take the stand. Throughout the trial, assistant prosecutor Tipton made repeated references to Franklin's refusal to speak—to the detectives when they arrested him, and to his daughter when she visited him in jail. An innocent man would not be concerned that his conversations were being monitored in prison, Tipton insinuated to the jury.

Defense attorney Horngrad shocked the court by alluding to his client's guilt—not in the murder but in the sexual abuse of the Franklin children. "When you live in a home where there is a bad guy in the home—Dad—and you associate him with acts of sex and violence and something happens to your best friend, where she disappears and turns up dead as the victim of a violent sexual act . . . how many bad guys are there in your universe? In your home? Well, Dad is a bad guy. Did Dad do this too? Did Dad take away my best friend? Is it Dad's fault?" Horngrad said in his closing statement.

Apparently, the jury believed that Dad *did* do it. George Franklin was found guilty of the first-degree murder of Susan Nason. His conviction made legal history. It was the first time a defendant had been convicted of murder based solely on the recovered memory testimony of a single witness. "You are a depraved and wicked man," San Mateo county judge Thomas McGinn Smith told Franklin before sentencing him to life in prison.

In 1995, an appeals court ruled that George Franklin had been deprived of his constitutional right to a fair trial. U.S. District Judge D. Lowell found that the trial judge had committed two serious errors. The first error was not allowing the defense to introduce evidence of media coverage of the crime to challenge the prosecution's claim that Eileen had information about Susan Nason's death that was never made public. "It is likely that this error had a critical effect on the jury inasmuch as it served to make the testimony of the key prosecution witness seem irrefutable," Jensen said in his decision. The second error occurred when the jury was told that they could consider Franklin's silence during Eileen's jailhouse visit an admission of guilt. Lowell chided the trial judge, saying, "It is difficult to imagine a more egregious error or one that so infected the conduct of a trial." Lowell overturned Franklin's conviction.

After serving six years of his life sentence, George Franklin was released from prison. By then, there were serious doubts about Eileen Franklin-Lipsker's credibility. Janice Franklin told the district attorney that both she and Eileen had been hypnotized before her father's trial. Eileen had lied to the prosecutor about not being hypnotized and DNA tests had cleared her father in another rape and murder she claimed to have witnessed. Flummoxed by these transgressions, the district attorney declined to retry Franklin.

POLICE LINEUPS: PROCEDURE

Surprisingly, there are no set rules for how criminal lineup participants (fillers) are chosen. Usually, though, other cops stand in; occasionally, police will find people outside the police house and pay them to appear in a lineup.

In New York City, at least five fillers are required for a lineup. Police officers are instructed to inform suspects that they *don't* have a right to a lawyer if one is requested for the lineup and to prevent the defense attorney from communicating with witnesses during the viewing. Unless otherwise informed, defense attorneys aren't even allowed in the same room when the lineup is conducted.

Detectives on the case are responsible for selecting lineup participants. New York City requires fillers to be of the same sex and race as the suspect, and they must be close to the same age and dressed similarly. Cops who participate in a lineup have to ensure that clothing, badges, or anything else identifying them as police offers are covered. If the suspect is wearing something distinctive, that must be covered up, too. Suspects are allowed to choose their own spot in the lineup.

In the case of suspects who are so injured or sick that they might die before a standard lineup can be conducted, police can conduct an "identification showing" during which a witness identifies the suspect in a "one-on-one display."

eighteen

LAW & ORDER: A gangster is the number one suspect in the murder of a businessman, but the FBI stymies the cops' investigation.

TRUE STORY: Whitey Bulger, head of Boston's Winter Hill Gang, spent decades murdering, robbing, and extorting his neighbors at will, thanks to an old neighbor in the FBI.

At first glance, he looks like an average old man, a grandfather perhaps, eyes peering out from behind tortoiseshell pilot-style glasses. What's left of his hair is pure white. Any minute, he might climb into a Buick and drive off to the local diner's early bird special. You don't think twice about him. On closer look, though, you see that he's not "peering" at all; he's staring right at you. You realize there's an icy intensity in these eyes—a meanness—that makes you want to look away. And he's not even in the room. You're just looking at a picture—a mug shot, a surveillance photo, an FBI wanted poster. At every known point in his life, from his teenage years to old age, James "Whitey" Bulger has possessed a coldness, a total disconnect with those around him. But don't be fooled. He's anything but aloof. Behind those cold blue eyes staring through the camera, a mind is hard at work.

Whitey Bulger was born and raised hell in New England's first public housing projects, Old Harbor Tenements, in the tough, working-class neighborhood of South Boston, or "Southie." Quiet but not shy, Whitey (so-named because of his blonde hair) possessed an evil temper and was the most ferocious fighter in the projects, a place where such skills earned the utmost respect. But he was smart, too. While other Southie street toughs wielded their power indiscriminately, Whitey Bulger beat the hell out of people only when they deserved it. By his late teens, he had earned a reputation for being the "good bad-guy," someone you could trust with your life, as long as you were smart enough not to cross him, and as long as you came from Southie.

Southie was (and, in large part, still is) as tight-knit and insular as a city neighborhood gets. Outsiders are never trusted, but locals always are. During the time Whitey Bulger was growing up, Southie was almost entirely Irish-Catholic, and the family unit was the strongest bond; the neighborhood bond was the second strongest; and strangers be damned. The people might not have much money, but Southie would take care of itself, thank you very much.

Only in such a neighborhood could the number one criminal's younger brother be a powerful politician—with no one batting an eye. While Whitey was engaging in high-speed car chases with police, facing judges in juvenile court, and, later, killing for money, Billy Bulger kept his nose buried in books of Roman philosophy, earned high grades in school, and went on to attend college. And while Whitey went AWOL from the air force and served ten years in the toughest federal prisons, such as Alcatraz and Leavenworth, for robbing banks, his brother attended law school, started a family, and got himself elected to the Massachusetts House of Representatives and, later, the State Senate, where he became president and one of the most powerful men in Massachusetts.

Yet, the two weren't complete opposites. Both sought and gained extraordinary power. Whitey with fists, knives, and guns; Billy, with education, connections, and persuasion. They also shared fierce family loyalty. Though Billy never made a peep about his brother's criminal activities, there's no evidence that he ever used his connections to help Whitey (besides getting him a job as a courthouse janitor once).

Whitey seemed to be the ultimate Southie boy. He wanted and needed no one's help, relying solely on street smarts and quick fists. Although his business was dishonest—he especially excelled as a loanshark enforcer—he worked his way to the top of it honestly, in the classic honor-among-thieves tradition. Meanwhile, he kept an eye on his beloved neighborhood, making sure to shield the innocent, hard-working people of Southie from his activities.

But it was all a lie. When Whitey saw an opportunity, he seized it, and he didn't give a rat's ass about who suffered. One day around Christmas in 1983, Bulger and his partner Steve "The Rifleman" Flemmi decided they needed a new base of operations. Driving around South Boston, they spotted an old gas station that a couple, Stephen and Julie Rakes, had recently purchased and converted into a liquor store. Each had grown up in Southie, and Julie had gone to the same church as Whitey when she was younger. The store, Stippo's Liquor Store, was situated in a heavily trafficked area and offered plenty of convenient parking. This was it, the couple thought. They'd have to work longer hours than ever, and they had invested over $100,000, but Stippo's would bring in the money to keep them financially secure.

The Rakeses' two daughters were too young to leave home alone, but the store had to be open all the time in order to make money. So while Stephen worked at the store, Julie stayed home; when Stephen came home, he took the kids and Julie went to the store. Relatives helped out when they could, but basically it was all Stephen and Julie.

One night when Stephen was feeding his daughters dinner, Bulger, Flemmi, and one of their lackeys, Kevin Weeks, showed up at his door. Without an invitation, they walked into the house. Bulger sat down at the kitchen table. Rakes recognized all three of them. One of his brothers happened to be married to a sister of Weeks. And he knew Flemmi and Bulger from Triple O's bar—ironically, the very base of operations the gangsters were looking to drop for the more favorably located Stippo's Liquor Store.

Bulger, opening and closing a pocketknife he held in his hand, calmly announced that he was going to buy the store. When Rakes protested that it wasn't for sale, Bulger lost it. He jumped up and screamed that he would kill Rakes and just take the store. One of Rakes's daughters came in to see what the commotion was all about; Bulger immediately calmed himself down. Flemmi took out a gun, put it on the table, and took the little girl onto his lap. "Isn't she cute," he said, as she played with the gun. "It would be a sin for her not to see you."[1]

Rakes's problem, Bulger explained, was very simple. Either sell the store or die. Rakes didn't need it explained again. He accepted the paper bag filled with $67,000 that Bulger held out. On his way out, Bulger told Rakes that he was lucky to get even *that* much for the store. "Now, go away," Bulger said as he walked out the door.[2]

No, Whitey Bulger didn't look out for the neighborhood or his fellow Southie residents. He lived and breathed one thing: Whitey Bulger. Sure, he held the doors open for old women he had known since he was a kid and handed out Thanksgiving turkeys to his neighbors, but at the same time, he was collecting a percentage of the proceeds on every last gram of coke and every dime-bag of pot sold on the streets of Southie. Each and every drug dealer in South Boston knew the price of his trade: Pay Whitey Bulger or end up in a garbage bag, in pieces. Whitey made the cost of business as simple for them as he did for Stephen and Julie Rakes.

Whitey Bulger was no *Cosa Nostra* don sipping an espresso in the back room, while his henchmen did his bidding. He liked to get his hands dirty, throwing himself full force into the violent life he chose. Once a thug, always a thug.

Boston's problem, though, was that he was more than *just* a thug. He had a little more in common with his brother than it might have seemed. For Whitey, too, was a voracious reader. While serving time in federal prison, he developed an appreciation for World War II history. He made a point of comparing battle strategies and tactics of each side to learn what works in the world of combat and what doesn't. He read up on the generals, and became an especial fan of George Patton and the Third Reich's great tank commander Erwin Rommel. Nicknamed the Desert Fox, Rommel was a master tactician and had a knack for slipping out from under the enemy's grasp when cornered. He once said, "A risk is a chance you take; if it fails you can recover. A gamble is a chance taken; if it fails, recovery is impossible." Whitey Bulger's greatest criminal strength was that he took risks—murdering his rivals, shaking down business owners, strong-arming people who owed money—but he didn't take gambles. Bulger never made the mistake of many higher-level criminals by expanding his business too far. He didn't start wars with the Italian Mafia, which far exceeded Winter Hill in terms of money, manpower, and connections. He kept a loose affiliation with them—using them when he needed to and ignoring them when he needed to. He seemed to be happy as king of the neighborhood, Southie's one and only despot. Bulger conducted business at night and then went home to his mother's house, where he lived until he went on the lam.

Smarts, however, wasn't the only thing Bulger had in his favor. His connections were his *real* ace in the hole. One day, at the age of nineteen, he was hanging around in a neighborhood drugstore. A group of young kids came in and he heard one whisper in awe, "There's Whitey Bulger." The big-shot Bulger turned around and told the kids he'd buy them some ice cream. One of them, an eight-year-old named John Connolly politely said that he wasn't supposed to accept anything from strangers. Bulger laughed and explained to him that since they're both Irish and live in the same neighborhood, they're not strangers at all. He lifted the young boy up to the counter where he enjoyed his bowl of ice cream.[3]

John Connolly must have been starstruck after this encounter. He knew and looked up to Whitey's younger brother Billy, who was six years older than Connolly. He would trail Billy through the neighborhood, fascinated by the books he carried and wondering what was in them. But by this time, Whitey was a legend in Southie, and a sighting of him was rare. Connolly only had one more encounter with Whitey during his youth, but remained in touch with Billy, who talked Connolly into attending Boston College. After completing his education, Connolly joined the FBI, and met the Southie's bad boy once again— but not in the expected capacity of law enforcer and criminal.

In 1975, Connolly received his greatly desired transfer from the New York City FBI office to the agency's Boston location. Although his parents had moved him out of Southie when he was twelve years old, he would always consider himself a Southie boy at heart. It didn't take him long to contact Whitey Bulger and make him an offer that, Whitey Bulger being Whitey Bulger, wouldn't dare refuse. Connolly wanted to make him a confidential informant, or CI, for the agency. The agency wanted to target the Italian Mafia in Boston, and Bulger, with his loose affiliation, would be the perfect man to help take them down. Bulger didn't have to think too long about the deal. It was perfect. "The Mafia can play checkers; we'll play chess," he said to Connolly at one point in the discussions.[4] The deal was sealed. While Connolly became the star FBI agent in Boston, busting one flashy Italian mobster after another, Bulger could sit back and watch his rivals go down one by one, then scoop up the extra business.

Developing CIs is considered one of the "arts" of law enforcement; organized crime can't be fought without it, and great handlers are valued by law enforcement agencies. But time after time, Connolly crossed ethical and legal lines when dealing with Bulger. When Julie Rakes's uncle, Joseph Lundbohm, a Boston detective, approached Connolly about Whitey Bulger's extortion of his niece, nothing came of it—other than Whitey contacting Stephen Rakes to tell him it would be in his best interest to shut his mouth from here on in. Although Lundbohm couldn't prove it, he assumed Connolly had tipped off Bulger. (To add insult to injury, Connolly's FBI office purchased liquor at a discount from Bulger's new store for their Christmas parties.)[5]

Innocent liquor store owners weren't the only ones who suffered. Law enforcement agencies were constantly foiled by Whitey Bulger, and it's suspected that Connolly played the part of tipster all along. In 1980, the Boston Police Department, Massachusetts State Police, and federal drug enforcement agents created a joint operation to take down Bulger and Flemmi, who were operating their criminal business from a front called Lancaster Foreign Car Service.

Acting on intelligence about which office Bulger used to conduct business, the law enforcement team obtained a warrant to bug the garage. They rented a room directly across the street from the front and

staked it out. After one failed attempt to install the bugs, they were finally successful. In the middle of the night, they waited for everyone to
leave the garage, broke in, and planted three bugs. Now they would get
the great Whitey Bulger on tape incriminating himself. Except for one
thing. Whitey clammed up. He completely stopped talking about anything that could incriminate him while he was in the garage. He and
Flemmi would sometimes walk outside and gaze up at the apartment
where the cops were staked out.[6]

It was clear to the team why Bulger had suddenly changed his routine, and why he was so interested in one, single nondescript apartment
across the street from his "business." Connolly had tipped him off, they
insisted. But, as usual, no one could prove it. Bulger skated once again.

In another case—one that would eventually come back to haunt
them all—an Oklahoma millionaire named Roger Wheeler purchased a
company called World Jai Alai, based in Connecticut. Jai Alai is an ob-
scure sport—something between lacrosse and handball—on which bet-
ting was legal in Connecticut. Winter Hill, it turned out, was skimming
off the profits à la the company's former president John Callahan. Bulger
and Callahan knew Wheeler would find out when he began as the new
president, and wanted to solve the problem sooner rather than later.

Brian Halloran, a Winter Hill goon, was summoned to a meeting at
Callahan's apartment. Bulger and Flemmi were there with Callahan.
They explained their problem and communicated to Halloran that
they'd like him to kill Wheeler. Halloran was nervous. He dealt coke,
knocked around gamblers who owed money, and was even indirectly
involved in at least one murder. But he had never pulled the trigger on
someone; he was a desperate Irish galoot, a Southie hood, a two-bit
thug—and he didn't really have the nerve for the high stakes of contract
murder. He said he'd have to think about it. Bulger, he knew, didn't like
him and glared at Halloran as he exited Callahan's apartment.[7]

A couple weeks later, Callahan met with Halloran again. He apologized for involving him in his scheme and told him that Bulger and
Flemmi were going to take care of the job themselves. As a consolation
prize, he handed Halloran twenty-thousand dollars. Halloran readily
accepted the cash and blew through it in less than a week. Nothing's as

sweet as free money, Halloran thought. When he heard that Wheeler had been shot dead outside his country club in Tulsa, a .38 bullet between the eyes, Halloran finally put two and two together, realizing that Whitey Bulger doesn't give things away for free. Halloran knew that if he didn't take action soon, the price was his life.[8]

Halloran had one choice. Go to the cops, rat everyone out, and try to get an immunity deal and protection. He approached the Boston FBI and told agents the whole story, along with information about other murders he knew Bulger and Flemmi (who was also acting as one of Connolly's CIs) had committed. He provided mountains of details implicating the Winter Hill duo, which inevitably got back to Connolly via John Morris, Connolly's supervisor, who was, by then, also in deep with Winter Hill. Law enforcement had suspected Bulger and Flemmi all along, so Halloran's tale wasn't far-fetched at all. Nevertheless, after spilling his guts about everything, Halloran was summarily dropped by the FBI and sent back out into the lion's den. Everyone knew Halloran's days were numbered. One agent involved with the case put it bluntly to a colleague: "I would not want to be standing next to this guy." As he exited a pub a couple weeks later, Halloran was shot dead. Callahan was murdered a few months later.[9] Agent Connolly's CIs had cleaned up the entire mess.

It would take over a decade, but the sordid tale of Connolly, Morris, Flemmi, Bulger, and others would finally come to light. The FBI finally began to officially investigate the situation that so many cops and agents had been complaining about for so long. It didn't take long for investigators to reach Morris, who instantly copped an immunity plea. He told story after story about late-night dinner parties, payoffs, gift-giving, doctored agency reports, illegal tip-offs, and everything else that goes into a corrupt relationship between powers on opposite sides of the law. Morris spilled all the beans about how he, Connolly, and other agents scrambled to put out fires for their prized informants, even if it required them to shanghai the efforts of their own colleagues or other law enforcement agencies.

For his part, Connolly to this day refuses to admit any wrongdoing. "We got forty-two stone criminals by giving up two stone criminals," he said, referring to the Italian Mafia. "What's your return on investment

The elusive, psychopathic James "Whitey" Bulger, former kingpin of the Irish mob in Boston and second only to Osama bin Laden on the FBI's Top 10 Most Wanted list. *FBI*

Perhaps the only photo of Whitey Bulger with a smile on his face. In his seventies, he remains on the lam, avoiding numerous murder and racketeering charges. *FBI*

there? Show me a businessman who wouldn't do that?" As it turned out, though, Connolly gave Bulger way more credit for helping take down the Mafia than he deserved. A close look at his reports (not to mention Morris's testimony) shows that Whitey provided little more than street gossip that even the lowest-ranked Mafia soldier had access to.

Indictments were handed down for Whitey Bulger and Steve Flemmi for a host of crimes. Typically, Connolly, by then retired from the FBI and working as a highly paid security consultant for a Boston firm, tipped them off. Flemmi was caught before he could flee and will likely spend the rest of his life behind bars. Connolly, too, eventually landed in prison, convicted for receiving bribes and leaking the indictment information to his pals. Bulger, though, slithered away and remains slippery as ever in his old age. He is on the FBI's top ten most wanted list and has been spotted in Louisiana, California, and Long Island, New York. There is a one-million-dollar reward for his capture.

As Whitey Bulger had gleefully told John Connolly over thirty years ago, he and the FBI had started a high-stakes game of chess after that fateful meeting. What Connolly didn't realize at the time, though, was that there can only be one king. That's Whitey Bulger. Connolly and the FBI were just lowly pawns sent out on a suicide mission, as pawns always are. Is the king dead? Or is he out there collecting more pawns and planning their next moves? Somebody surely knows, but they're not talking . . . yet.

CONFIDENTIAL INFORMANTS

Confidential informants, or CIs, are almost always up to no good, so federal and local law enforcement agencies have strict guidelines for developing and maintaining a CI. It's all about paper trails; cops are never allowed to simply go out on their own and befriend or bribe a criminal who's willing to rat out friends or rivals. Though the exact requirements vary according to jurisdiction, they all hold certain similarities.

First, the informant must be officially registered with the department as such. He or she will often be interviewed by the contact's supervisor and undergo a background check. Once the CI is registered, the police contact is to maintain detailed files on the informant's relevant movements; the CI isn't allowed to take part in criminal activity unless it's under the supervision of the law enforcement agency. As time goes on, a committee of higher-ranking officers will periodically review the CI's information to make sure it's both credible and valuable enough to maintain CI status. If the CI is violating any of his or her conditions, CI status is supposed to be terminated. The Whitey Bulger case, though, shows that things aren't always done according to the book.

nineteen

LAW & ORDER: Two punks commit a random murder, leaving Assistant DA Jack McCoy searching for a motive.

TRUE STORY: New Jersey teens Thomas Koskovich and Jason Vreeland ambushed and killed two pizza deliverymen for the "thrill" of it.

The deserted road was eerily silent as the two young men stood admiring their handiwork. Three weeks shy of his twentieth birthday, the older one had dreamt of this moment for so long. Having realized his dream, he could barely contain his excitement.

"I can't believe we just did that!" he shouted.

The younger one was happy too, but for a different reason. He didn't have many friends and he longed for his companion's approval. Although he was three inches taller, he looked up to the nineteen-year-old. This night had brought them closer together. They'd bonded! The younger one was flush with emotion.

"Yeah, I love you man," he replied.

They embraced, two friends rejoicing at their achievement, like football players after winning the Super Bowl.

The younger one added, "I think I finished off the passenger."

They headed back to their car. It was close to 11:00 p.m. as they drove away—away from the blood, the bullet casings, the pizza slices, and the two dead men sprawled on the ground.

. . .

There's not much to do in Franklin. A sleepy hamlet in northwestern New Jersey, Franklin has a population of five thousand and the lowest crime rate in the state. Most residents appreciate the peace and quiet. Others, primarily teenagers, find the town's rural charms less than charming. Franklin's pride and joy is its mineral museum. Known as the fluorescent mineral capital of the world, the town sits atop a rich ore body that is home to nearly two hundred minerals. The museum, however, isn't much of a draw with the under-twenty set. Bored kids with too much time on their hands cruise the roads looking for excitement before ending up at the usual haunts—the strip mall, bowling alley, Dunkin' Donuts, Burger King, a vacant lot.

Nineteen-year-old Thomas Koskovich was born and raised in Franklin. Abandoned by his parents as a child, young Thomas shared a house with his grandmother, Bertha Lippincott, and various relatives. The boy's uncle, Leonard, lived there too when he wasn't incarcerated. A career criminal, Leonard was well-known by Franklin police. He had a long rap sheet and a drug problem. Thomas idolized him. Leonard, in turn, shared his booze and drugs with his nephew.

As a teen, Koskovich developed an addiction to painkillers such as Fiorcet and Percocet, prescription drugs he stole from his grandmother. He dropped out of high school and spent his days holed up in his bedroom or getting high with his friends, fellow dropouts who were as bored and aimless as he. In early 1997, Koskovich got engaged and enlisted in the army. He didn't make it to the altar, or the army base. By August, that year, he would be in jail awaiting his trial for murder.

Of course, Koskovich didn't know that in April when he came up with an antidote for his endless boredom. The key ingredients? Guns and ammunition. Getting them was easier than he had imagined. With his pal Michael Conklin, Koskovich broke into Adventure Sports. The alarm system was broken and the two made off with a .45 and a .22 caliber.

All they needed now was a victim, Koskovich declared. Conklin figured Tom was just playing tough, as he often did. Koskovich liked to brag about being crazy and he was always obsessed with murder and with the Mafia. His goal was to become a hit man, he'd tell any-one who would listen. No one really took him seriously. Half of the time, Koskovich was stoned anyway, and when you're stoned you talk shit.

Like Koskovich, Jayson Vreeland was a high school dropout who did drugs and courted trouble. The lanky seventeen-year-old vandalized mailboxes, destroyed mail, and stole a motorcycle. His poor grades and frequent altercations with other students got him expelled from voca-tional school. He got a job at Burger King but was fired for not show-ing up. In March 1997, Vreeland was arrested for shooting a fellow teen with a pellet gun.

Vreeland, who had dyed his hair blonde and wore a half-dozen ear-rings, was desperate for approval. Koskovich was only an acquaintance but Jayson hoped to win his friendship. He told his girlfriend that he and Koskovich "would be best friends." When the older teen asked him if he wanted to help commit "the perfect crime," a flattered Vreeland said yes.

In nearby Hardyston, boredom was a luxury Georgio Gallara couldn't afford. The enterprising twenty-four-year-old owned and man-aged Tony's Pizza and Pasta. Eager to build up the business he had bought four years earlier, Gallara routinely worked twelve- and fourteen-hour days. Although he employed a sizeable staff, he did much of the work himself. He took orders, balanced the books, made deliveries, and pre-pared the tasty pizza and Italian favorites that kept the locals coming back. When he wasn't at work, Gallara spent time with his fiancée and their four-year-old daughter.

Jeremy Giordano worked for Gallara delivering pizzas and helping out in the restaurant. Twenty-two-year-old Giordano was a kind soul who was always ready and willing to help out a friend or family mem-ber. He came from a close-knit Italian family and lived with his parents in a house across the street from Tony's Pizza and Pasta. Naturally gre-garious and upbeat, Giordano was well suited to the service industry. He loved people and hoped to own a restaurant one day. Like Gallara, Giordano was also engaged to be married. He was excited about what the future held.

Saturday, April 19, 1997, had been a busy day. Giordano's parents had even ordered a pie, which Jeremy delivered himself. After the dinner rush, someone called to ask if Jeremy was working that night. Gallara confirmed that he was and the caller hung up. Gallara thought nothing of it. He and Giordano were closing up when the phone rang. They were about ready to go home but Gallara, good-hearted as always, agreed to fill one last order. The caller wanted two plain cheese pies delivered to Scott Road, over in Franklin. Since it was the last delivery of the night, Gallara decided to ride along with Giordano to the unfamiliar address.

Much of Scott Road was under construction. Giordano steered his Chevy Impala over the rough road, as Gallara held the two freshly baked pizzas on his lap. The pizzas were still piping hot, the heat radiated from the square cardboard boxes. Giordano squinted to make out the numbers on the houses. He found the address but something wasn't right. The house looked abandoned.

Thomas Koskovich stepped out of the shadows. Jayson Vreeland, following in his wake, recognized Giordano. "That's Jeremy!" he exclaimed. Koskovich approached the passenger window. They ordered the pies, he said. Gallara told him the bill was $16.50.

Koskovich turned to Vreeland, and asked, "Have you got any money?" He didn't wait for an answer. Koskovich reached into his front pocket and pulled out a .45-caliber handgun.

"I've got your money," he said before opening fire on his stunned victims. Vreeland ran forward and began shooting with a .22 caliber.

The Chevy Impala rolled forward into a marsh a few feet away. Giordano and Gallara were silent and still. The teenagers pulled both men from the car and shot them each once more in the head, execution style. Then they riffled through the dead men's pockets, looking for cash.

Vreeland tried to back Giordano's car out of the marsh but the vehicle was stuck. He grabbed one of the pizza boxes and tossed it through the air like a Frisbee. Pizza slices scattered everywhere.

Koskovich surveyed the grotesque scene. He was on cloud nine, high on adrenaline and painkillers. "I can't believe we did that!"

New Jersey youth Thomas Koskovich, ringleader of the so-called "thrill kill" duo who murdered pizza deliverymen Georgio Gallara and Jeremy Giordano.
New Jersey Department of Corrections

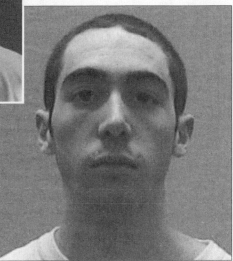

Koskovich's accomplice, Jayson Vreeland. Thanks to their ceaseless bragging about their actions, the two killers were picked up and charged with murder.
New Jersey Department of Corrections

The teenagers hugged in celebration and then headed to the bowling alley to meet with some friends. Afterward, they made a pit stop at a Presbyterian Church where they touched the front door and made the sign of the cross "for forgiveness."

They couldn't stop talking about the crime. "How'd you like to shake the hands of a murderer?" a proud Koskovich asked Michael Conklin, his accomplice in the gun store burglary. Christine Slater read about the killings in the newspaper and suspected her ex-boyfriend, Thomas Koskovich, was responsible. She went to the police. Based on her statement, police obtained a search warrant for Koskovich's house.

The police found Georgio Gallara's ID and wallet in Koskovich's bedroom along with a bag filled with bloody clothing. The blood was matched to Jeremy Giordano. Witnesses recalled seeing Koskovich and Vreeland using the pay phone in Dunkin' Donuts. An employee there told police the teenagers had asked for a phone book, which he'd given them. The calls from the donut shop were traced to five different pizzerias. The teenagers had called Tony's Pizza and Pasta twice, once to find out if deliveryman Jeremy Giordano was working, and a second time to order two pies. They had been unsuccessful in convincing the other pizzerias to take such a late-night order for delivery to a remote address. The call sounded hinky; it wasn't uncommon for kids to send pizzas to unsuspecting friends and neighbors as a prank. Koskovich told one wary pizzeria employee "We'll make it worth your while" to deliver. The employee hung up. The kindhearted Gallara was the only one willing to take the order.

Forensic experts determined that Koskovich had fired seven times, Vreeland twice. Koskovich's bullets had wounded Gallara but Vreeland's had killed him; fragments from his gun were found in Gallara's brain. Giordano had been killed by bullets fired by Koskovich.

Koskovich and Vreeland were arrested and charged with the double homicides of Jeremy Giordano and Giorgio Gallara. In police custody, the teenagers immediately confessed. Koskovich, the wannabe gangster, couldn't keep his mouth shut. He said he had taken several doses of the painkillers Percocet and Fioricet that day.

Koskovich told the police that he'd been planning the crime for a long time. He recruited Vreeland after he and Michael Conklin robbed the gun store. Koskovich claimed that robbery had been the motive for the murder. But Vreeland and other friends knew the truth—Koskovich just wanted to kill for the thrill of it, to see what it felt like to take a life. Apparently, he also believed the killings would help him gain entry into the Mafia.

"I stuck the gun right here on the right side of [Gallara's] head," he said, motioning to his temple. "There was a hole in his cheek. The guy starts screaming 'Oh! Oh!' and the glass on the driver's side shattered. I freaked out when the guy started screaming. I kinda blacked out."

Jeremy Giordano was just delivering a pizza. Little did he know that two teenagers who wanted to kill "for the thrill of it" were lying in wait for him. *Theresa Navarro*

According to Koskovich, Vreeland hadn't wanted to kill Giordano, whom he knew casually from the neighborhood. When the car carrying Giordano and Gallara pulled up Jayson had screamed, "That's Jeremy! That's Jeremy!" He'd fired his weapon anyway. Afterward Vreeland felt bad because he knew Giordano. Koskovich though, had "no remorse because I didn't know the guys."

In his confession, Jayson Vreeland told police that he never intended to kill. "I just wanted to prove I was a friend. I was pretty much shooting toward the dashboard." Prosecutors would prove that Vreeland's gun killed Gallara. He died from a bullet to the back of his head.

Vreeland tried to pawn the blame on Koskovich. "He was talking about offing a couple of pizza guys because he had this thing about always wanting to kill someone," he told police. "I guess they were an easy target."

The defendants were tried separately. Koskovich was tried first for capital murder. If convicted, he could face a death sentence. Because of his age, Vreeland was ineligible for the death penalty. While awaiting trial, Koskovich attempted suicide with pills obtained from a fellow inmate. After a short hospital stay, he was declared competent to stand trial. He pleaded not guilty and turned down an offer of a plea bargain.

Assistant Prosecutor Michael Briegel made a strong case that the crime was premeditated. He refuted the defense claim that Koskovich was too high on drugs to know what he was doing. In fact, Breigel told the jury, the defendant spent weeks planning the crime before luring the victims to their deaths "like lambs to a slaughter." And in the days prior to the killings, Koskovich and Vreeland practiced shooting the stolen guns to familiarize themselves with the weapons. They also scouted locations for the crime, eventually deciding on desolate Scott Road in Franklin.

"This was not a robbery gone bad," said Briegel. "It was a simple, well thought out plan." After ambushing the deliverymen, Koskovich and Vreeland "stopped and hugged and exulted over carrying out their plan to murder two innocent men."

"Thomas Koskovich committed these murders so he would know what it felt like to be a killer, so he could be a big man," Briegel said. "The plan was to escape to Florida where Mr. Koskovich wanted to live as a fugitive."

Defense attorney Pamela Brause granted that her client "bears significant responsibility" for the crime, but, while his confession was "a very bad and upsetting statement, Mr. Koskovich never said this was a plan to kill anyone."

Brause argued that Koskovich's judgment was impaired on the day of the crime because he had taken numerous doses of Fioricet, the painkiller he stole from his grandmother. A defense psychiatrist testified that the drug can prevent a person from appreciating the consequences of his actions.

The defense also contended that Koskovich's dysfunctional family life and drug addiction were mitigating factors in the crime. A slew of witnesses attested to the defendant's troubled childhood. "You need to know little more about the Koskovich family than the fact that Bertha Lippincott is assisting the state in the execution of her grandchild," Brause told the jury. "Is there evidence to show whether Mr. Koskovich had the ability to carry out a knowing and purposeful murder? . . . Only you and not the prosecutor can make the judgment."

Assistant prosecutor Briegel countered that all evidence of this terrible childhood had been provided by defense witnesses or the defendant himself. "Some of the mitigating factors carry the weight of grains of sand . . . compared to the total weight of the huge boulders that make up the aggravating factors in the prosecution case," he said in his closing argument.

The jury found Koskovich guilty. In capital cases, the jury must also determine whether or not to impose the death sentence. During the second phase of the trial, the defense and prosecution offer sentencing arguments. Koskovich had an unlikely ally—Loretta Giordano, the mother of Jeremy. Although devastated by Jeremy's death, she asked that the court spare the life of her son's killer. "Jeremy Giordano was so lucky to be loved by this family," defense attorney Brause said. "In reviewing Thomas Koskovich's life, the evidence shows that he did not have such a secure, loving home."

Before sending the jury off to deliberate, Judge Reginald Stanton informed them, "Even though Mrs. Giordano and her family may not support the death penalty, their response is not the end of the question. You must take into account the views of the larger society." Because of the heinous nature of the crime, no one was surprised that the jury voted for a death sentence.

In a controversial move, the judge imposed a five-year limit for the death sentence to be carried out. He noted that the average time awaiting execution is ten years, a wait that he felt was cruel. "It may be that we would be well advised to join most of the civilized countries of the world in abolishing the death penalty. But if we are to have a death penalty, then we should have the skill, the courage, and the decency to carry out the death sentences in a reasonably expeditious manner."*

Attorneys on both sides were equally baffled. "We don't exactly know what we think about it," Brause told reporters. "It cuts both ways. In Koskovich's case if the courts agree that the judge could do this, it could end up being a huge benefit because there's no way we could finish this in five years as the system stands now."

---

*The judge's stipulation was later overruled by the New Jersey Supreme Court.

With Koskovich's trial over, assistant prosecutor Michael Briegel focused his attention on trying Jayson Vreeland. To get a murder conviction, the prosecution needed to prove that Vreeland willingly and knowingly participated in the crime. Briegel used the defendant's own words, his taped confession, to show that the teenager was "equally responsible" for the murders.

Drugs, peer pressure, and Thomas Koskovich were to blame for the murder, defense attorney Paul Selitto insisted. "The main force behind this crime was Mr. Koskovich. I am asking you to view the evidence through the eyes of a seventeen-year-old, and to remember the days when you weren't as smart and mature as you are now . . . a time when peer pressure was paramount."

"We do not dispute the facts of this case, only the State's interpretation," Selitto said. "My client was duped. Mr. Vreeland had no idea that Mr. Koskovich would shoot anyone. Don't paint them both with the same brush."

The prosecutor reminded the jury that "Jayson Vreeland described in great detail about the planned, deliberate actions he and Thomas Koskovich undertook in the committing of these crimes. He knew full well what he was doing."

The jurors agreed and found Vreeland guilty. "I am not a murderer, I'm still a shy kid hoping to be understood," Vreeland said before sentencing. He addressed his victims' families. "I hope you can accept my apologies and grant me forgiveness . . . I know God has."

The judge, disgusted, retorted, "You're not the first defendant to walk into court with a Bible." She sentenced Vreeland to life in prison and tacked on an additional twenty years for aggravated manslaughter plus twenty-two more for robbery.

Thomas Koskovich appealed his conviction and in 2001 the New Jersey Supreme Court overturned his death sentence, ruling that the trial judge had committed technical errors in his instructions to the jury. Koskovich was retried and sentenced to life in prison.

twenty

LAW & ORDER: A young Jewish man flees to Israel to avoid a murder prosecution.

TRUE STORY: The Israeli government refused to extradite Samuel Sheinbein, an American teenager charged with murder in Maryland.

The murder of nineteen-year-old Alfredo "Freddy" Tello in September 1997 was one of the most gruesome crimes Montgomery County, Maryland, had ever seen. The killers didn't just cruelly end the young man's life, they mutilated and set fire to his body, leaving him in an abandoned garage in a nondescript suburb of the Aspen Hill area. Horrific as the murder was, though, it was the subsequent extradition hearing of one of the murderers, who had fled to Israel, and the ensuing legal wrangling among U.S. and Israeli politicians, investigators, lawyers, and judges that put the case in newspapers worldwide. The situation turned into such a legal circus, it prompted Montgomery County Executive Douglas M. Duncan to say that it was "something out of an episode of *Law & Order*."[1] And he didn't find it one bit entertaining.

It all began when Samuel Sheinbein decided to "practice" his murdering techniques on someone. One day, he expressed his intentions to his longtime friend Aaron Needle, who in turn suggested a specific victim. Sheinbein was a seventeen-year-old high school senior who drove a brand-new Firebird and had an odd obsession with locking people inside places like cars and rooms. Handy with tools, he once altered the lock on his bedroom door so that when it closed, it couldn't be opened from the inside. He did this, he told his friends, in preparation for the day when he would get a girl into his room. If she couldn't leave, it would be easier to rape her. In fact, there was one specific gal Sheinbein had in mind; only, she had no interest in the young psycho and was going out with someone else anyway. To remedy that situation, Sheinbein offered a school thug one thousand dollars to lure the boyfriend into his Firebird. Sheinbein would be waiting there for him, the car fitted with no-exit locks. From the beginning, this boyfriend was the real focus of Sheinbein's murderous fantasies; Tello was "practice."

Sheinbein and Needle, also a senior, went way back, friends since grammar school. Needle had a big fish tank at home and often hung out at Congressional Aquarium in town, where he met Freddy Tello, an employee at the aquarium supply store. Tello had recently dropped out of high school and moved from his mother's house into his own place. He was tall and slender, artistic, and spent his spare time deejaying, mixing, and writing rap songs. His high school art teachers were always impressed by his work, and Tello hoped to eventually pursue art as a career. Freddy was no angel. He had been pulled over that June for making a reckless turn with his car. The cop searched the car, found one hundred plastic sandwich bags and a Phillie Blunt cigar, and correctly surmised that it was drug paraphernalia. The teenager pled guilty and paid a one hundred dollar fine. Freddy might have been a little too comfortable on the "other side of the tracks," but all in all, he was just a young guy trying to figure himself out.

The fact that Tello could score pot any time probably had a lot to do with Needle's and Sheinbein's interest in him. The three soon began to hang out, driving around in Sheinbein's Firebird and smoking "blunts" in shopping center parking lots.

Needle also had his sights set on a certain girl, with whom he apparently stood no chance but pursued nonetheless. She actually ended up hanging out in the Firebird with the three guys one day. At one point, Needle and Tello got into an argument and Tello began punching Needle. Embarrassed and angered to be emasculated in front of the object of his puppy love, Needle harbored such a grudge against Tello that when Sheinbein mentioned one day that he'd like to murder someone, Needle said that someone should be Tello.

On September 16, Sheinbein and Needle picked up Tello from work. The three of them drove off and at some point before seven o'clock, Tello's new friends shocked him with a stun gun, then strangled, beat, and slashed him with a knife. In the Sheinbein family garage, the two severed Tello's arms at the elbows and legs at the knees.

The teenagers placed their victim into a garden cart, covered him with a blue tarp, and wheeled the cart down the suburban street and into the garage of a house for sale right around the corner. Inside the garage, they lit Tello's corpse on fire using propane cylinders. A few minutes later, they put out the fire, placed the remains in a garbage bag, and took off in the Firebird.

On September 19, a real estate agent selling an empty two-story brick home on the 14000 block of Breeze Hill Lane in Aspen Hill met a prospective buyer in front of the house. When they went inside they instantly smelled a powerful odor and followed it to the garage, where they found the remains of Freddy Tello, as well as a garden cart, a Makita power saw, propane cylinders, and a Home Depot sales receipt dated September 16. The would-be criminal masterminds couldn't have botched the murder more if they had tried. All the police had to do was show up.

After canvassing the neighborhood, cops quickly learned that residents had witnessed the boys pushing the cart up the street in the direction of the empty house. A search of the Sheinbein home produced an empty Makita power saw box. Then, the cops followed the trail of blood—literally. Drops of blood dotted the street from the Sheinbein garage and up a path leading to the vacant house.

After a little more investigating, detectives learned that Sam Sheinbein had called the son of the former owner of the vacant house on his cell phone. He was outside the house and asked how he could get inside.

Murderer Samuel Sheinbein fled to Israel to avoid murder charges in Maryland. Convicted in Israel, he received a considerably lighter sentence.
Photo courtesy of CNN

He told his friend that he had picked up a girl and needed someplace to bring her. The guy described where a spare key was hidden, and Sheinbein found it as they spoke.

With more physical and circumstantial evidence than investigators dare even dream of, the DA should have had a slam-dunk case. Unfortunately, Sam Sheinbein was better at manipulating legal systems and extradition treaties than he had been at covering his trail of blood. Perhaps the real credit, though, should go to the teen's father, Sol Sheinbein. When he learned that the police were looking for Sam, he drove his wife and son Robert to New York City, where the killers had fled. (Needle had already taken a train back to Maryland.) There he met Sam, who handed him a stun gun, sawed-off shotgun, and two letters—one of which was a notarized murder confession. Robert drove the Firebird back to Maryland and ditched it in a shopping center parking lot. Meanwhile, Sol took Sam to the airport and put him on a plane to Israel.

Sol was technically an Israeli citizen and carried an Israeli passport. Although Sol's mother lived in Israel, he hadn't been there since he emigrated to the United States at the age of six. Sol, a successful patent lawyer, later claimed that he had no idea that under Israeli law his own citizenship transferred to his son, and that Israeli law doesn't allow its citizens to be extradited for crimes committed abroad. In a strange twist of logic, the lawyer contended that he sent Sam to Israel because he feared that his son was going to commit suicide.

While the Sheinbein family attorney, Paul Stein, arranged with Israeli and American law enforcement to have Sam fly back to the United States and surrender, his older brother Robert flew to Israel to escort the murderer home. The brothers reportedly drank wine and entertained a prostitute in their hotel room the night before Sam was to return home. Then Sam overdosed on sleeping pills and was sent to Yitzhak Rabin Hospital in Tel Aviv, where he was committed for a week and put on suicide watch. It seemed that old Sol was wrong; people *can* try to kill themselves in Israel. Either that, or his son faked it to buy some time, which some investigators believed to be the case. Not a bad move given the fact that the Israeli legal system tends to go easier on those deemed mentally ill than the U.S. system does.

In fact, everything was going Sam Sheinbein's way. While Tello's mother, Eliette Ramos, was struggling to understand why her son was murdered, Sam Sheinbein, his family, and his lawyers were playing the legal system like a piano. A trial in Israel would be far more advantageous to the killer than one in the United States. For one thing, minors are not only exempt from execution in Israel, they're exempt from life in prison.

The only thing standing in Sheinbein's way was a treaty between Israel and America that allowed for the extradition of one another's citizens. U.S. officials, aware of the treaty, faxed an arrest warrant to Israel, along with enough evidence to convince Israeli officials to take the seventeen-year-old into custody. Sol Sheinbein quickly sold his house and took his family to Israel, where he and Robert were arrested for hampering an investigation. They were soon released, but their passports were seized.

Aaron Needle, meanwhile, was charged as an adult in Maryland for first-degree murder, a charge that carried the death penalty. He remained in custody at his own request. He didn't want to be out on the street in case Sheinbein did come home; he said he actually felt safer in jail. Needle further requested that if Sheinbein returned and was arrested, they be segregated from one another in jail. "[Aaron Needle] is afraid of Samuel Sheinbein and fears for his safety and his life if he is in the company or proximity of Samuel Sheinbein," said Michael

Statham, Needle's lawyer, at a pretrial hearing, as his client stared ex-
pressionlessly into space. When asked why his client would fear his best
friend, the lawyer answered, "Cain and Abel were brothers."[2] Needle
claimed Sheinbein was the one who killed Freddy Tello and that he was
innocent of the murder charges brought against him.

Initially, Israel had planned to send Samuel Sheinbein packing to the
United States, but the Sheinbein lawyers argued that the seventeen-year-
old was a citizen of Israel. Never mind the fact that he had never been
to Israel before now and didn't speak a word of Hebrew. He was a citizen simply because his father was. An extradition hearing was scheduled. Back home in Montgomery County, a grand jury indicted both
youths. The circus had officially come to town. The only thing missing
were elephants and dancing ponies.

To extradite or not to extradite? The answer to that question hinged
solely on the legitimacy of Sol Sheinbein's Israeli citizenship. Sol had
been born in British-run Palestine in 1944, before Israel became an in-
dependent state. He moved to the West with his family when he was six
years old, which meant he had lived in the nation of Israel for two
years, in effect making him a citizen of Israel. (Israel was granted na-
tionhood in 1948.)

The United States, however, argued that because the law granting
automatic Israeli citizenship to those born there wasn't passed until two
years after Sheinbein left for America, he was technically not a citizen
and, therefore, his son was nothing more than a murderer who had fled
the scene of the crime. Plus, they possessed documents showing that Sol
Sheinbein's mother had renounced her Israeli citizenship when she first
emigrated to Canada. U.S. prosecutors demanded Samuel Sheinbein's
return.

To Americans familiar with the case, the Sheinbein issue was turning into a travesty of justice. They wanted him back and behind bars for
the rest of his life. To make it clear that the United States meant business, Louisiana Senator Robert Livingston, who happened to be head
of the House Appropriations Committee, jumped into the ring. He

pointed out that Israel's yearly allowance was coming due and, perhaps, it might not be as high as it was the previous year; he floated numbers like $50 million around. In the language of diplomacy, it translated to, "Cough up Sheinbein, or choke on him." In addition, Livingston sent a letter to Secretary of State Madeleine Albright stating: "in the absence of a resolution [concerning Samuel Sheinbein], I intend to introduce the issues into consideration of the Foreign Operations spending bill." And—boom!—just like *that*, the Clinton administration and Israeli Prime Minister Binyamin Netanyahu took a keen interest in the kid from Aspen Hill.

The situation was this: President Clinton wanted to reenact the recently expired Middle East Peace Facilitation Act designed to help Yasser Arafat and the PLO end anti-Israeli terrorism. But it wasn't a done deal; he desperately needed Republican congressional support to get the act through. Clinton felt that if he pressured Israel to send Sheinbein home, the GOP would help him get the act restored.[3] It was a case of political horse trading at its finest.

Netanyahu was of the same mind as Clinton. Problem was, religious fundamentalists in the Israeli parliament weren't. They felt it was their duty to prevent the extradition of a Jew to a Gentile land. One member of parliament even said that if Israel had to cut all financial ties with the United States over the issue, so be it.

The political battle was waged, high-level officials in both countries holding closed-door meetings on the Sheinbein matter. At the end of October, Israel, under intense diplomatic pressure, once again changed position, announcing that the teen might be extradited; in order to reach a solution, the status of Sol Sheinbein's citizenship would need to be scrutinized more carefully.

Clearly, almost everyone *wanted* to send Samuel Sheinbein back to the United States, only they were caught up in a sticky web called "law."

In what had by now become an almost unrelated matter, Samuel Sheinbein's alibi in the Tello murder was brought to light. His brother Robert announced that Samuel had told him that the three teens had been talking in a parked car one day, when Sam flashed a wad of money. Tello, he said, whipped out a sawed-off shotgun and threatened to blow Sheinbein's head off if he didn't fork over the cash. Needle reacted by punching Tello, while Sheinbein reached in the back of the car, where he happened to find a telephone wire. He had had no choice but to strangle Tello with it. It was a clear-cut matter of self-defense.

When Sheinbein's cockamamie story surfaced, Needle tried to use it for his own defense. It proved what he had been saying all along, his lawyer argued: Sheinbein killed Tello, not Needle. But to no avail. No one took Sheinbein's story seriously, and Needle's murder trial would proceed as scheduled.

Proceedings dragged on. Sheinbein's lawyer in Israel, David Libai, was no slouch. He was Israel's former justice minister. American prosecutors doggedly pursued the extradition. In February 1998, a Jerusalem district judge involved in the extradition proceedings offered a suggestion he believed might make everyone happy. Sheinbein could return voluntarily to the United States to stand trial. If he were judged guilty, he would get a one-way ticket back to Israel to serve his sentence. Sheinbein jumped at the chance. And why not? Israeli prison conditions are far superior to those of the United States. But American prosecutors said no deal.

That spring, as Needle's trial was about to begin, his lawyer was still pursuing the Sheinbein confession angle, as well as arguing that Needle wasn't mentally fit to stand trial. He appeared devoid of emotion during his court appearances and displayed severe depression in his cell. Although he was on suicide watch, he hanged himself with a bedsheet in his cell on April 18, 1998.

After all the diplomatic threats, legal horse trading, and judgments against him, Sheinbein appealed his way to the Israeli Supreme Court.* The Supreme Court overturned by a vote of 3-2 the previous judgment against Sheinbein. It was final; Samuel Sheinbein would be tried in

---

*In one hearing, Sam Sheinbein's grandmother testified that she had renounced her Israeli citizenship only because her first husband, Sol's father, threatened to kill her if she didn't. Sol's father was murdered in the early eighties over a land dispute, rumored to have involved the Israeli mob.

Israel, as an Israeli. Although the United States and Israel had signed an extradition treaty, the court ruled, Israeli law took precedence.

Americans and Israelis were sickened by the decision, but none more than Eliette Ramos. "Freddy's death, the way he died, Sheinbein's escape: Layer after layer, my reality became more and more nightmarish,"[4] she wrote in a letter to the *Washington Post*. Legally, the Israeli Supreme Court defended its decision; personally, though, each judge expressed dismay at the decision. "One can wonder if there is any justification for protecting someone from extradition when that person is not a resident and has no connection with Israel,"[5] wrote one judge who ruled in Sheinbein's favor. Legally speaking, though, the extradition was a separate matter from the murder charges.

Only a few had the nerve to grandstand after the painful verdict. One Israeli government official couldn't help himself: "It's the kind of legalistic entanglement that a country like the United States should understand—a country where O. J. Simpson is released could understand a miscarriage of justice."[6]

Eventually, in August 1999, Samuel Sheinbein pled guilty and received a sentence of twenty-five years—which in the Israeli correctional system means that he'll probably be out on parole after fourteen years, when he's thirty-three years old. In addition, Israeli prisoners are also eligible for weekend paroles after one-fourth of their sentence is served. Plus, Sheinbein received credit for the two years he served during his extradition hearings. Not a bad deal for a merciless butcher.

The Israeli parliament (Knesset) immediately took steps to make sure such a travesty of justice doesn't happen again, passing a law requiring residency, not just citizenship, for protection against extradition.

As for Sol Sheinbein, he was charged with hindering an investigation and is a wanted man in the United States. He began practice as a patent lawyer soon after he set up shop in Israel. Sol's move to Israel, of course, protects him from the charges, but if he ever returns to the United States, he'll be arrested. Samuel, also, will be arrested for murder if he returns. Just as his son went shopping for legal and prison systems that suited him best, Sol Sheinbein chose a nation of convenience. Israel is his country now, and he has a passport to prove it.

In 2002, the Maryland Bar Association took away his license to practice law, and in 2005 the U.S. Patent and Trademark Office refused to do business with him. It was the best anyone could do.

PEN REGISTERS/TRAP AND TRACE

While the use of LUDs is commonplace in *Law & Order*, an investigation sometimes requires more direct methods. Two valuable investigation tools are pen registers, which decode the impulses of outgoing calls, and trap and trace devices, which identify incoming calls.

Police are authorized to obtain search warrants of people, premises, or vehicles. Only the DA or attorney general, or their assistants, however, can obtain one for pen registers or trap and trace devices. The application to the judge must contain such details as reasonable cause; nature of the information likely to be received and how it pertains to the investigation; identity of the person who leases the line, and that of the subject of the investigation; the phone number and physical location of the line; the specific period of time for which the device is to be used; and all past orders authorizing the use of pen register or trap and trace devices involving the person.

twenty-one

LAW & ORDER: A pit bull bred to be aggressive kills a woman and her dog in the park.

TRUE STORY: Diane Whipple, a popular lacrosse coach, was mauled to death by her neighbors' dogs in San Francisco.

The barking started around four o'clock. Seventy-eight-year-old Esther Birkmaier put down the book she was reading and listened. It wasn't unusual to hear barking; the neighborhood was home to dozens of dogs, as well as a boisterous group of sea lions that had commandeered nearby Pier 39. Their hoarse, throaty barking drew crowds of tourists and kept quite a few Pacific Heights residents awake at night. But this barking was different—angry, anxious, plaintive—and right outside Birkmaier's door. Something was wrong. Just then a woman cried out, "Help me! Help me!" Birkmaier rushed to her door and looked through the peephole. What she saw terrified her. One of her neighbors was lying on the hallway floor, a huge, dark dog was standing on top of her, a second dog was pulling at her clothing. She rushed to the phone and dialed 911.

"Yes, I'm just a wreck," Birkmaier told the dispatcher. "Please send the police . . . We have two dogs rampaging out in the hall up on the sixth floor and I think they have . . . their . . . even their owner cannot control them. They are huge."

"OK, the owner knows they are in the hallway?" the dispatcher asked.

"I think they're attacking the owner too, I reckon—she's screaming right now and I don't open the door because the dogs are huge . . . Please hurry!"

Birkmaier waited, silently willing help to arrive. The screaming had stopped, the barking had not. She returned to the peephole. Esther could no longer see her neighbor but she could hear her whimpering, moaning softly. Suddenly, something pounded on her door. Thud. Thud. Thud. The senior citizen jumped back in fear. It was the dogs—they were trying to knock down her door. Her hands shook as she phoned 911 a second time.

On Friday, January 26, 2001, Diane Whipple decided to leave work early. It had been a productive week for the popular St. Mary's College lacrosse coach. She was pleased with the progress her team was making. Practice had gone well, dissolving at the end into a lighthearted game of chase. The women's lacrosse team loved Whipple. She was smart, fun, and fair. A star athlete in her own right, thirty-three-year-old Diane had been winning sports awards and accolades since she was a kid.

With her golden hair, lithe build, and bright white smile, Whipple was the quintessential California girl, albeit with East Coast roots. Raised by her grandparents in Manhasset, an affluent Long Island suburb, the pretty blonde fell in love with sports at an early age. In high school, she helped lead her lacrosse team to the state championship. Her athletic prowess won her a lacrosse scholarship to Penn State, where she was affectionately dubbed the "Whip." There the undergrad trained hard and played even harder. Friends and family were thrilled but certainly not surprised when she was named All American Lacrosse Player and 1990's NCAA National Lacrosse Player of the Year.

After college, Whipple headed to San Diego to try out for the 1996 U.S. Olympic Track Team. She didn't make the cut, missing out by a narrow margin. Her Olympic dreams dashed, Diane was deeply disappointed. She picked herself up and recovered, always true to her motto, "Live life to its fullest." Besides, she was in love—with California and with an attractive Charles Schwab executive named Sharon Smith.

For Smith, the feeling was mutual. Whipple left San Diego and moved into Smith's apartment in the tony Pacific Heights section of San Francisco. Smith admired her lover's courage. Whipple was a fighter, a survivor, as evidenced by the battle she had waged and won against her own thyroid cancer. She was full of life and fearless too, on and off the playing field.

Except about the dogs. Not just any dogs, but "those dogs" as Whipple called them. They were two big, brutish creatures that hogged the elevator and menaced the tenants of her apartment building. The dogs' owners, an eccentric married couple who lived two doors down from the women, weren't much better; they seemed to take pleasure in the fear their pets inspired. The husband, a burly man with a walrus mustache actually appeared amused when one of his dogs bit Whipple's hand. Thankfully, the watch she was wearing received the brunt of the bite. The animal hadn't broken her skin but the bite left her hand red and swollen. She warned the man to control his dogs. He dismissed the attack as friendly canine play.

Not wanting to make trouble, Whipple went out of her way to avoid the animals and their owners, both of whom gave her the creeps. It wasn't easy though. The dogs seemed to be everywhere: in the hallway, the lobby, across the street, near the park, their powerful muscles rippling under taut skin, their strong jaws set in defiance. Their owners—"those people"—let them run wild. The knot in Diane's stomach grew tight every time she left her apartment. Safe at work, she would forget about the dogs for a while—until it was time to go home. Then, the knot would return.

After the bigger dog bit her, Whipple was more cautious than ever. She walked quickly but softly, trying to muffle her footsteps as she moved through the common areas in the building. She made Smith check the hallway before opening the door. A few times, she even hid behind her girlfriend on the way to the elevator.

As she left her job at St. Mary's College, the lacrosse coach wasn't thinking about the dogs. She was looking forward to the weekend. From her cell phone, she called Smith at work to persuade her to come home early. Diane told her she was going to make tacos for dinner. Before hanging up, they made plans to see a movie that evening.

Whipple steered her red Jeep Cherokee toward Pacific Heights. She sang along to the radio, the sunlight dancing across her golden hair.

Robert Noel and Marjorie Knoller lived two doors down from Diane Whipple and Sharon Smith. Attorneys both, the married couple practiced law out of their one-bedroom apartment. They kept to themselves, preferring not to socialize with the other tenants of 2398 Pacific Avenue.

The couple was considered odd but harmless. Much of their time was spent writing long rambling legal briefs, filing numerous lawsuits against their landlords (they sued over a broken showerhead), going to court, and making the trip to Pelican Bay State Prison where they had several clients. One of these clients was Paul Schneider.

A handsome, muscular blonde, Schneider was serving a life sentence for robbery and attempted murder. He also had ties to the Aryan Brotherhood, a white supremacist prison gang. Noel and Knoller were more than smitten with the inmate—they believed that they were connected to him on a psychic level. The often-frumpy Marjorie envisioned herself as their warrior queen, betrothed to both men. Soon they were referring to themselves as the "Triad" in the dozens of letters the threesome exchanged. Marked "confidential legal mail," these were no stodgy legal briefs. The letters detailed the couple's sexual fantasies and were often accompanied by nude photos of Marjorie. When Schneider told them he needed a favor, the couple was more than happy to oblige.

Schneider and fellow inmate Dale Brethches were running an illegal dog-breeding business from the prison. Their dogs were currently living with Janet Coumbs, a shy, single mother who was duped into raising the animals on her farm. Schneider was unhappy with Coumbs and wanted his attorneys to assume custody of the dogs. And so, in the spring of 2000, Noel and Knoller expanded their little family to include two large adult Presa Canario dogs, Bane and Hera.

Part Mastiff, part cattle dog, the Presa Canario is a heavy-boned canine with a massive, square shaped head, sturdy body, and short, coarse coat of fur. The breed hails from Spain's Canary Island where the animals guarded livestock and property. Unscrupulous owners trained the dogs to fight, pitting the animals against each other for sport.

Without proper training, the powerful Presa Canario can become aggressive and even dangerous to humans and other animals. In his book, *Pit Bulls and Tenacious Guard Dogs,* author Carl Semencic writes that the Presa Canario "will not hesitate to attack anyone whom it perceives as a threat to its family or home. Such an attack could only be a hopeless situation for any man involved."[1] It was the Presa Canario's capacity for violence that attracted Schneider. In fact, the inmate named his prize male stud "Bane"—bringer of death or ruin. Prison authorities would later allege that the dogs were being bred to guard methamphetamine labs for the Mexican Mafia.

Bane, the larger of the two dogs, weighed in at 130 pounds. He was an imposing creature with his massive chest and enormous head. Hera, the female, was slightly smaller and a few pounds lighter than Bane. Donald Martin, a veterinarian who examined the animals, found them to be aggressive and unsuited to city life. He worried that Noel and Knoller would be unable to control the dogs. He wrote to the couple:

> *I would be professionally amiss if I did not mention the following so you can be prepared. These dogs are huge, approximately weighing in the neighborhood of one hundred pounds each. They have had no training or discipline of any sort. They were a problem to even get to, let alone to vaccinate . . . these animals would be a liability in any household . . . The historic romance of the warrior dog sounds good but hardly fits into life today.*

His warning went unheeded. Under Noel and Knoller's care, the dogs grew stronger, bigger, and bolder, bolting out of the apartment whenever they got the chance. Previously, the dogs had lived on a farm. Life in the attorney's cramped, 800-square-foot apartment was markedly different. Restless, Bane and Hera sometimes paced back and forth for hours in the tiny one-bedroom, their thick nails click-clacking across the hardwood floor.

The couple took the dogs out for frequent walks around the neighborhood. At first, the dog-loving community welcomed the newcomers and their exotic-looking pets. But the Presa Canarios were unruly, defiant, and increasingly aggressive—barking and nipping escalated into bullying and biting. They quickly wore out their welcome. Unprovoked, Hera attacked a friendly three-legged shelty mix, puncturing the animal's skin with her teeth. Bane nearly severed Noel's finger when the attorney attempted to break up a dogfight his pet had provoked. A local dog trainer offered repeatedly to train the Presas but the couple turned him down. They also refused to muzzle Bane and Hera and, incredibly, continued to let the aggressive dogs run off-leash.

Paul Schneider received regular updates from the attorneys on the two Presas. Noel, apparently, was obsessed with the size of Bane's genitals. He called the dog a "ladies' man" and claimed that Bane got an erection the first time he met Knoller.

In another letter he brags about the dogs scaring a neighbor. "As soon as the door opens at 6, one of our newer female neighbors, a timorous little mousy blonde, who weighs less than Hera is met by the dynamic duo exiting and all most [sic] has a coronary." The neighbor is Diane Whipple.

Groceries in tow, Diane Whipple returned home from the supermarket a few minutes before four o'clock. Sharon would be home in an hour or so; Diane had just enough time to chop up all the ingredients and fill the taco shells she'd just bought. She took the elevator up to the sixth floor. The door slid open and the lacrosse coach breathed a sigh of relief: the hallway was empty. She fished inside her purse for her keys and made her way to her apartment. Home safe! Then she saw them. *Those* dogs and *that* woman. The trio was exiting the stairwell. The bigger dog spotted Whipple first. He jogged toward her, dragging his owner to her knees as the woman struggled to hold on to his leash. He was much too strong for her. The second dog followed along behind them, unleashed and barking.

Diane stood in the open doorway, frozen in fear. The bigger dog, the male, was the same one that had bitten her hand. He jumped at her, smashing his gigantic paws into her shoulders. The animal was a monster. Standing on his hind legs, his eyes—two big black, blank circles—were nearly level with hers. His owner yanked on the dog's leash. Distracted, the dog dropped back down to all fours. "Your dog jumped me!" Whipple said, shaking. The woman turned and headed to her own apartment. For a moment, it seemed as if they were retreating, the two dogs trotting off to the other end of the hallway, their frazzled owner scrambling after them.

Whipple reached for the groceries she had placed on the floor, ready to make a quick dash into her apartment. But the dogs had changed their minds. They turned and bounded toward her. The male, growling and baring his teeth, lunged at Whipple, knocking her to the ground. His enormous head was just inches from her face. The female was barking wildly. And then they were on her, at her, pinning her to the floor, clawing, shredding her clothes. At 110 pounds, the petite lacrosse coach was no match for the animals. Diane didn't stand a chance against what Noel had proudly described as "240 pounds of Presa."

The screaming had stopped. Esther Birkmaier waited inside her apartment. Minutes felt like hours and then she heard muffled footsteps and the crackle of walkie-talkies outside her door. One of the Presas was still in the hallway; it fled when the police arrived. The officers were unprepared for the horrific scene that awaited them at 2398 Pacific Avenue. Blood was everywhere—splashed against the doorway, soaked into the carpet, splattered across the walls in huge streaks and desperate handprints. Crushed groceries and bits and pieces of clothing covered the floor. The officers found Diane Whipple alone and lying facedown in the hallway, naked except for a single white sock. Her blonde hair, wet with her own blood, appeared black. Whipple, bleeding profusely, was trying to crawl to her apartment.

Marjorie, her face smeared with blood, stepped out into the hall to meet the officers. She was fine except for a small cut on her hand. Bane was in the bathroom, Hera, in the bedroom. The dogs were wild, throwing themselves against the locked doors. Yet to the officers, Knoller seemed calm, even nonchalant. The only emotion she expressed was annoyance—at their questions and at being inconvenienced by the police and animal control officers sent to collect the dogs. She never bothered to inquire about her neighbor's condition.

Diane was rushed to San Francisco General Hospital. She arrived in full cardiac arrest, her body covered in bite marks—seventy-seven in all—her jugular punctured. Surgeons worked to save her but it was too late. Diane Whipple was pronounced dead at 8:55 p.m.

The fatal mauling of Diane Whipple sent tremors through San Francisco, a city known for its devotion to dogs, a city named after the patron saint of animals. Bane was euthanized immediately after the attack. Hera's role in Whipple's death was unclear; the medical examiner had not been able to tie any of the bites to the female dog. She was held by animal control pending a dangerous-dog hearing. Noel and Knoller seemed distraught—not over Whipple's death but over the loss of their dogs. Noel broke the news to Schneider in a letter. "There is no way to ease into this. Bane is dead, as is our neighbor," he wrote. He told the inmate that he and Marjorie would fight tooth and nail to get Hera back, adding, "Neighbors be damned. If they don't like living in the building with [Hera], they can move."

While Hera languished in a holding pen awaiting her fate, her owners were busier than ever. They campaigned to get their remaining dog back, made television appearances, wrote letters—and became proud parents. Three days after Diane's death, the couple legally adopted Schneider. They also went on the offensive, blaming the pretty lacrosse coach for causing her own death. On *Good Morning America*, Knoller denied she bore any responsibility for her dogs' actions. When host Elizabeth Vargas referred to the mauling as an "attack," Knoller corrected, "I wouldn't say it was an attack, and I did everything that was humanly possible to avoid the incident."

As Vargas looked on incredulously, Knoller continued, "Ms. Whipple had ample opportunity to, to move into her apartment . . . It took me over a minute restraining him from my apartment down to the time that

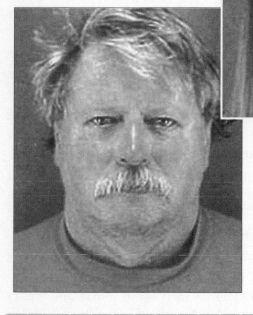

Unrepentant Marjorie Knoller, owner of the pit bull that killed Diane Whipple. "I wouldn't say it was an attack," she rationalized in defense of her dog during a *Good Morning America* interview. *San Francisco Police Dept*

Robert Noel, Knoller's husband and co-owner of the killer pitbull. "Neigbors be damned. If they don't like living in the building with [our dog], they can move," he once said. *San Francisco Police Dept*

he jumped up and put paws on either side of her. She was in her apartment. She could have just slammed the door shut. I would have."[2]

Then, in a rambling, nineteen-page letter he sent to District Attorney Terence Hallinan, Noel suggested that Whipple may have been wearing perfume that antagonized his dogs. Or, since she was an athlete, perhaps she was using steroids—steroids that may have sent Bane into a frenzy. The medical examiner would disprove both claims.

The couple showed no compassion or remorse over their neighbor's death. Their behavior further inflamed San Franciscans who were already demanding justice for Diane Whipple. DA Terrence Hallinan sent the case to a grand jury. Eager to tell their side of the story, Noel and Knoller insisted on testifying. Knoller shocked the court when she flippantly said that Bane responded to Whipple as if she were "a bitch in heat." Appalled by the couple's self-serving, callous testimony, the grand jury indicted both for involuntary manslaughter, and Marjorie for second-degree murder. "If they had behaved differently, it would have been different," Hallinan told the *San Francisco Chronicle.* "It wouldn't have been murder, that's for sure. We went into that grand jury thinking we had a manslaughter and vicious dog case. The difference was they went into the grand jury and testified."[3]

As lawyers, the couple should have known better than to talk to the press about the case. The prosecutors would use the defendants' own words, immortalized in print and on video, against them in court. Because of intense pretrial publicity in San Francisco, Judge James Warren granted a change of venue. On February 19, 2002, Noel and Knoller stood trial in a Los Angeles courtroom. Lead prosecutor James Hammer had been deeply affected by Diane Whipple's death. Throughout the trial he carried her championship ring in his pocket. In his opening statement, Hammer described the horrific way Whipple was killed and showed jurors a series of gruesome photographs of her many injuries. He also cited the defendants' outrageous conduct before and after Diane's death.

A parade of prosecution witnesses testified about Bane's and Hera's aggressive behavior. Jurors learned that Bane had twice bitten a blind woman and her guide dog, lunged at a young boy and a pregnant woman, and that both dogs had terrorized the neighbors and mail carriers. One witness who had encountered Knoller and Bane in the park testified that Knoller told her, "Please leash your dogs. You don't know how serious this is. This dog has been abused. He'll kill your dogs." Janet Coumbs, the dogs' first caretaker, testified that she told Marjorie that Hera had killed sheep, chickens, and her pet cat. Coumbs claimed she warned Knoller that Hera was dangerous and should be put down.

"Diane Whipple was not the first victim of these dogs—she was the last victim of these dogs," Hammer told the jury. The defendants "knew with their own eyes what these dogs could do. They read about it, they heard about it. They willfully ignored it, arrogantly."

Not surprisingly, the defense saw things differently. They claimed that their clients didn't know that their loving pets were capable of such violence. Outside of court, Marjorie's attorney, Nelda Ruiz, accused the district attorney's office of trying to "curry favor with the homosexual community." Trying her first murder case, Ruiz was nothing if not energetic. In court, she cried, shouted, flailed her arms around, kicked the jury box, and, in a particularly memorable moment, got down on all fours and crawled around on the floor reenacting the attack. "It would be helpful for the decorum of the court if you would stay on two feet instead of four," Judge Warren told her.

Ruiz did her best to rehabilitate her client's image. She cast Knoller as a tragic hero who tried to save Whipple's life—valiantly throwing herself on top of her neighbor to protect her from a frenzied Bane. Knoller "risked her life trying to save Ms. Whipple," from the "jaws of this berserk beast," Ruiz told the jury.

Noel's attorney, Bruce Hotchkiss, was the polar opposite of Ruiz. A quiet, reserved man, Hotchkiss skipped the theatrics, and wisely kept his client off the stand. Marjorie, however, testified in her own defense. She wept and said she was traumatized. It was too little, too late. "It's offensive to call yourself a hero when you abandoned a woman to die and you never called 911," Hammer said in closing.

The jury agreed. After deliberating for eleven hours, they found Marjorie Knoller guilty of second-degree murder and involuntary manslaughter, and Robert Noel of manslaughter (prosecutors had not charged Noel with murder because he was out of town at the time of the attack). Additionally, they were both found guilty of keeping a mischievous animal.

Knoller was the first person to be convicted of murder in a dog mauling case in California. The distinction would be short-lived. After calling Marjorie a liar, Judge Warren overturned her murder conviction. According to the judge, the prosecution failed to prove Knoller knew her dogs would kill Diane Whipple that day. There was no implied malice, a requirement for a murder conviction, he explained. "I cannot say, as a matter of law, that her conduct was such that she subjectively knew on Jan. 26 that a human being was likely to die," Warren said. "In the eyes of the people, both defendants are guilty of murder. In the eyes of the law, they are not." He then sentenced the "most despised couple in the city" to four years each for involuntary manslaughter.

The prosecution appealed the decision and in 2005, the appellate court reinstated Knoller's second-degree murder conviction. "The prosecution only had to prove that Knoller knew that, by taking Bane outside of her apartment without a muzzle, she was endangering the life of another," the appellate court ruled. "The key to the issue is her conscious disregard for the life of another person."

Noel and Knoller served their sentences and were released on parole. They have yet to apologize to Diane Whipple's friends and family.

JUDGMENT NOTWITHSTANDING THE VERDICT

The Sixth Amendment grants every American accused of a crime the right to a trial by an "impartial jury." It doesn't state, however, that the jury's verdict is necessarily the final word on the subject. If a trial judge deems the jury's verdict in direct opposition of the law, he or she can overturn it in favor of the losing party. It's called Judgment Notwithstanding the Verdict, or JNOV (*judgment non obstante veredicto*), and in criminal cases it applies only to guilty verdicts; judges can't overturn not-guilty verdicts.

In one episode of *Law & Order*, Judge William Wright (Ron McLarty) barks that he's entering a not-guilty verdict the moment after the jury foreman reads "guilty." While a judge technically has the power to do this, the protocol isn't quite that simple. As in life, you don't get what you don't ask for. In order for a judge to bypass the jury's verdict, a motion must be filed with the court requesting the JNOV after the trial and within a set time frame.

twenty-two

LAW & ORDER: A fire in a Dominican nightclub leaves dozens of patrons dead.

TRUE STORY: Cuban boatlift refugee Julio Gonzalez committed the worst mass murder in American history when he set fire to the Happy Land nightclub in the Bronx, killing eighty-seven people.

The music was pumping and the young people danced without a care in the world. Here in the East Tremont section of the Bronx, poverty was a way of life for the many Central and South American immigrants who had arrived in recent years. In many ways, life was better than it had been in their homelands, but for most of them the American dream was an elusive goal that might never be attained. Right now, though, on the second-tier dance floor, grooving to the reggae beat of Coco Tea, speaking in their native tongues, the outside world seemed very far away, and they were happy; they felt at home. Even though Ruben Valladarez was situated in the back of the room, he was in the middle of it all. The club's resident DJ, he provided the music that was right now unifying sixty-odd people into a single pulsing, gyrating mass of bodies.

Then he heard it: "Fire!" a voice screamed. He looked up and saw one of the club's doormen on the dance floor frantically shouting. Smoke was billowing up the stairs. Some people were paralyzed by confusion and fear; others instinctively searched through the dense crowd for friends and family. Pandemonium was instantaneous. Without hesitation, Valladarez pulled the plug on the music, turned on the lights, and yelled into his microphone, "Everybody get out! I've got a fire!" He ran to the front of the room, grabbed a friend, and said, "We have to get out, man."[1] They ran down the smoke-choked stairs next to the DJ booth. "Mama!" a voice yelled from somewhere in the smoke. A light-bulb popped. The club's one and only exit on the ground floor was engulfed in fire. No one knew what to do. Some people had found another door and were desperately pushing against it, but it was locked. The one window leading to the street had bars over it.

Valladarez thought of his wife and two-year-old daughter and decided to take his chances, running through the flames in the direction of the front door. Within seconds Valladarez emerged from the flames onto the street, where EMTs had just arrived. He fell to the ground and someone doused him with water.[2] Though burned beyond recognition, he would at least live to tell the tale, along with five others, including his friend. Everyone else inside the Happy Land Social Club during the early hours of March 25, 1990, was killed.

As eighty-seven lives were being snuffed out by fire, smoke, and toxic gasses, Julio Gonzalez was walking away from Happy Land. An alert passerby might have noticed an odor of gasoline coming from Gonzalez, but would have probably assumed he was coming home from a job at a twenty-four-hour service station.

The fact was, though, that Gonzalez had no job. Six weeks earlier, he had been laid off from his job at a lamp warehouse in Long Island City, Queens, and had resorted to panhandling and squeegeeing car windows. Meanwhile, his girlfriend of eight years, Lydia Feliciano, had recently dumped him, forcing Gonzalez to move out of her two-bed-room apartment and into a ten-by-ten rented room. Gonzalez, who spoke only broken English, was going nowhere fast. His only connection to anything remotely stable was his ex-girlfriend.

Earlier that night, he had gone to Happy Land, where Feliciano worked as a ticket- and coat-checker. Gonzalez disapproved of the job, though he never articulated exactly why. Was it because Happy Land was an illegal social club? Did he fear for her safety because of the late

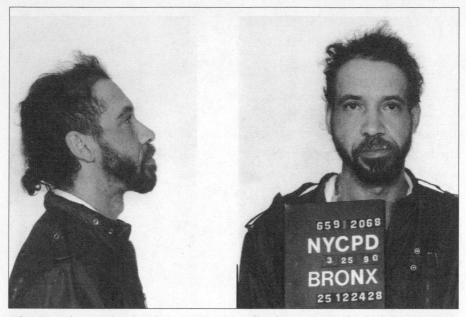

Julio Gonzales murdered eighty-seven people when he set the Happy Land Social Club ablaze in March 1990. It was the worst mass murder in New York history. *NYCPD/ Bronx*

hours she worked? Was he just jealous because Feliciano had a social life that didn't include him?

Whatever the reason, Gonzalez had entered the club at about 2:30 a.m. and approached Feliciano. Gonzalez was generally a quiet guy who preferred staying at home and taking care of Feliciano's kids over dancing and drinking through all hours of the night. Places like Happy Land weren't where he chose to spend much time. Seeing him there must have surprised Feliciano, which Gonzalez was banking on. "You see, I'm here like the police," he said with a cocky smile. "They come to a place unannounced." He then told Feliciano that he loved her and wanted her back. Feliciano made it clear that she was moving on without him. She had broken up with him in the first place because she suspected he had been trying to hook up with her niece, who happened to be in the club now. Visibly angry, Gonzalez walked upstairs.

A bouncer, who had witnessed the short exchange, made sure to keep an eye on Gonzalez. Just as the bouncer knew he would, Gonzalez

Gonzalez's fit of jealousy resulted in New York City's deadliest blaze since the Triangle Shirtwaist Factory fire, which killed 146 young factory workers. Ironically, it occurred on the same day as the Happy Land fire in 1911. *Photo courtesy SteveSpak.com*

eventually came back downstairs and started arguing with Feliciano again. The bouncer told him to leave. "I know you have a boyfriend," he told Feliciano on his way out, adding cryptically, "It doesn't matter. You and I until death." He told the bouncer that he'd be back and that he was going to shut the club down. As a bouncer of an illegal social club, he had heard it all before—and from tougher characters than the diminutive Gonzalez. But on this particular night, Gonzalez was deadly serious.

Gonzalez walked straight to an Amoco gas station, stopping only to pick up an empty plastic oil jug lying on the street. He told the attendant that he needed a dollar's worth of gas. The attendant, suspicious, hesitated, but Gonzalez told him his car had died up the road and that he needed the gas to get it started again. With the jug nearly full, he went back to Happy Land, where he poured a trail of gasoline from the front door to the street. He stepped back, lit two matches, and tossed them onto the wet sidewalk. The gas flared up at his feet and made a beeline for the club. Within seconds, Happy Land was in flames.

Someone called the fire department, and the trucks arrived within three minutes—but for most people it was about three minutes too late. Now it was a matter of putting the flames out, not saving lives.

Built in 1921, the building wasn't much more than a tinder box, a disaster waiting to happen. The second level had been added illegally, and although a low-grade sprinkler system had been installed in 1961, it wasn't in working condition by 1971. The building was inspected by city officials in 1981 and found to lack virtually every permit, license, and safety system required by a commercial building. Combined with the complete lack of fire prevention and safety systems, the relatively small room, low ceilings, toxins from burning wood, linoleum, and plastic, and "flashover"—the production of lung-searing gasses up to 1,800°F added up to a nearly 100 percent death rate.[3]

The only ones who survived were those lucky enough to get out of the building within the first few moments. Among the survivors was Lydia Feliciano, who, because she worked there, knew about a door in the back of the building. She and Elena Colon, the owner's wife, forced open a grate covering it and ran to safety. Afraid that Gonzalez would be outside waiting for her, she jumped into the first cab that came around the corner and took off.

As Feliciano sped off, at least one of her coworkers, Minerva Laguna, a bartender, remained inside, attempting to help patrons to safety. She didn't make it out of the building.

Veteran New York City firefighters, EMTs, and cops had seen it all. At least they thought they had. But when first respondents entered the Happy Land Social Club after the flames were put out, the scene was so ghastly many of their lives would change on the spot. The fire was so powerful that it had instantly sucked all oxygen out of the air; many people suffocated within seconds. And because firefighters had extinguished the flames so quickly, the macabre scene inside Happy Land was frozen in time. "Some [people] looked like they were sleeping," one shaken firefighter said. "Some looked horrified. Some looked like they were in shock. There were people holding hands. There were some people who looked like they were trying to commiserate and hug each other."[4]

Some people still sat at the bar, glasses in hand and feet wrapped around the bar stool legs. The club's manager lay dead with a fire

Only four people in the building
escaped with their lives,
including Gonzalez's girlfriend,
the target of his fury.
Photo courtesy SteveSpak.com

extinguisher in his hands; he had died seconds before he could pull the pin. Nineteen bodies were found on the ground floor. Upstairs, the dance floor was a mass open grave: sixty-eight people who had gone out for a night of music and fun had suffocated on the spot.

As respondents began the grim task of removing the bodies from the Happy Land Social Club, the perpetrator was lying on the floor at the foot of a friend's bed screaming, crying, and confessing that he had set a fire and that people must have died. Whether the tears expressed remorse or fear of the law is a mystery, but after a few minutes of venting, Gonzalez went to his tiny room in the same building.

Police didn't need to search long for the suspect. Witnesses outside Happy Land identified Gonzalez as the killer. Police arrived at his room that afternoon unannounced and found him there sleeping. His shoes reeked of gasoline. As they were arresting him, Gonzalez said, "I got angry. The devil got into me."[5] He blithely admitted to everything.

"It was like he was being picked up for a traffic warrant," said one baffled police officer. "It was nothing."[6]

Gonzalez, a Cuban immigrant, had come to America in 1980, when Fidel Castro decided to send Cubans he didn't want to the United States in what is known as the Mariel Boat Lift (made famous in popular culture by the Al Pacino movie *Scarface*). This little joke on Castro's part resulted in a flood of criminals and mental patients on U.S. shores. Ironically, Gonzalez had received a free trip to the States with 125,000 of his compatriots by *pretending* he was a criminal; now he had perpetrated the worst mass murder in American history.

Residents who hadn't been awoken by the sirens, or who had been working a night shift, were shocked that morning at the unspeakable sight of shroud-covered bodies lining the sidewalk of the once unremarkable city street. Across the street from the illegal social club, at P.S. 67, the Red Cross and city agencies set up a body-identification center. Hundreds of neighborhood residents stood on line to view photos of bodies, hoping beyond hope that their loved ones happened to have spent the night at a friend's house without calling, or committed some other family infraction that in normal circumstances would be grounds for an argument.

The line of people stretched around the block. People would exit from the building after identifying a child, sibling, parent, or friend—screaming, crying, falling to the ground. Those still on line tried to brace themselves for the same news they knew their grief-stricken neighbors had just heard. The morning dragged. Some stood on that line for over four hours.

Victims of Julio Gonzalez's evil tantrum included one woman's teenage daughter, brother, and four cousins; another woman's three brothers; one girl's uncle; another girls' friend; five Roosevelt High School students; seven members of another family; a single mother of five children under ten years old; a father of three whose wife was pregnant with their fourth.[7] These only account for a small percentage of the victims. In all, Gonzalez created sixty widows and 106 orphans,[8] and ruined the lives of countless others.

Firefighters outside the Happy Land
nightclub in East Tremont, Bronx,
during the early hours of March 25,
1990. Eighty-seven people perished
in a blaze set by Julio Gonzalez.
Photo courtesy SteveSpak.com

A pall was cast over the Bronx neighborhood for years to come. One father who had no idea his son was in the club had come outside to see what the sirens were all about, thinking he was just another spectator.[9] His life would never be the same. The owner of a deli in the neighborhood sold bagels every morning to two girls on their way to Roosevelt. He didn't know their names, but after the fire he never saw them again. Maybe they had simply found another place to get breakfast. And maybe not. He'd never know.[10]

The funerals went on for days, the residents of East Tremont in a perpetual state of mourning. Some funeral homes were so overcrowded, they had to borrow space from other buildings in the neighborhood. Neighborhood residents stood on lines in the streets once again, this time to close the door on the lives of their loved ones. The grim sight of funeral-goers funneling through velvet ropes into neighborhood buildings was a constant sight in the days following the Happy Land fire. When they weren't silently thinking about the deceased or discussing their lives in hushed tones with friends, they were expressing their anger and rage at the man who put them there.

Julio Gonzalez was indicted on 178 counts of murder, attempted murder, assault, and arson. All added up, New York City Assistant District Attorney Eric Warner pointed out, the sentences for all charges would equal over two thousand years. The trial began on July 18, 1991. On the way to and from the court, Gonzalez was surrounded by cops to protect him from a city that despised him.

The prosecution didn't have to prove Gonzalez lit the fire. Eyewitnesses had seen him commit the atrocity, and Gonzalez had confessed to the crime both to arresting officers and on videotape while in custody. But if Gonzalez didn't get the maximum, or at least close to it, it would be considered a failure. Bronx DA Robert T. Johnson put all his eggs in one basket: "The maximum of 25 years to life doesn't nearly reach the level of premeditation in this crime," he told reporters.[11] In his opening statement at the trial. Johnson read the name of each victim. It took about ten minutes.

Defense attorney Richard Berne predictably argued that Gonzalez was "insane" when he burned down the social club. He also maintained that Gonzalez was, to put it plainly, kind of dumb and didn't fully understand the consequences of pouring gas in the doorway of a building and lighting it up. His inability to reason, Berne maintained, was the result of a headfirst spill he took on his bicycle when he was eight years old.

Berne also claimed that Gonzalez suffered from a number of mental disorders, and he put a psychologist on the stand to bolster the argument. Dr. Roy Aranda, an adjunct psychology professor at Hofstra University, testified that Gonzalez had suffered from a "psychotic episode" on the night in question. Getting kicked out of the bar put Gonzalez into a sort of trance; he heard voices telling him to pour the gas and light it.[12]

According to Aranda, Gonzalez had a litany of problems, including "mild schizoid tendencies . . . narcissism, grandiosity, instability in relationships, alcohol abuse, erratic behavior and lack of remorse when, in an example [Aranda] cited, Mr. Gonzalez ran red lights." He also traveled to Cuba to interview Gonzalez's family; some of the members seemed a little crazy, leading the psychologist to speculate that Gonzalez inherited his craziness.[13]

This was the best the defense could do. The courtroom was, of course, packed with the victims' family and friends, who displayed incredible restraint as they quietly listened to all this. As the trial wound down, the judge commended the audience for their patience.

Six weeks after the trial began, the jury retired to the deliberation room. Four hours later, they entered the courtroom, and the foreman spent five minutes reading the word "guilty" 176 times. The spectators released a unified cry of triumph. Brief as the elation may have been—they would each have to begin a new version of their lives now—it was a much-needed release. Gonzalez got the maximum: twenty-five years to life.

In the hallway outside the courtroom, one woman, whose daughter had been murdered by Gonzalez, threw her hands up in the air and exclaimed, "Now I know a God exists!"[14]

FIRE CODES

At the time of the Happy Land fire, three entities were responsible for issues regarding permit and safety violations: The NYPD, the FDNY, and the NYC Buildings Department. All three had previously looked into the Happy Land Social Club location, and all three had created paper trails charting the landlord's numerous violations. But that's all. There was no official coordination among the three entities and, when it came down to it, they had no "teeth." All they could do was chart the violations and offer warnings to the landlord. If the landlord didn't comply, the city could take him or her to court. The appeals process alone could drag out a case for years, and if the landlord had a good lawyer, he or she could stall the process even longer. These cases were nearly impossible to prosecute. Besides, an investigation after the fire revealed that about one hundred illegal social clubs existed in city-owned buildings, making New York City the biggest landlord of illegal social clubs.

twenty-three

LAW & ORDER: Shoddy forensic science leads a homicide to be wrongly classified as a suicide.

TRUE STORY: Oklahoma City police chemist Joyce Gilchrist's faulty forensic work sent innocent men and women to prison—and may have cost one man his life.

Forensic chemist Joyce Gilchrist had a way with numbers, figures, fingerprints, DNA. She made the evidence work, tweaked it until it was just right. Crimes were like puzzles, and there in the police lab Gilchrist worked to make the pieces all fit. The cops called her "Black Magic," because, in the words of an angry defense attorney, she was "able to do things with evidence that nobody else was able to do."

In reality, magic had nothing to do with the fact that so many perps found themselves behind bars after Gilchrist got through with their cases. As a forensic chemist working for the police, Gilchrist had people's lives in her hands, and she didn't always use that power wisely. No one knows this better than Jim Fowler. He didn't know Gilchrist personally, but their lives kept intersecting. In the summer of 1985, Fowler's son was accused of a triple homicide. Three months later, Fowler's mother was murdered in her home. Neither case was related. Gilchrist testified as a prosecution witness at both trials. Jim Fowler was in the unique position of having been on both sides of the fence, or rather, courtroom. Gilchrist helped send his son and his mother's killer to death row. It gets stranger still—Gilchrist was instrumental in winning a rape conviction against a close friend of the Fowler family.

During her twenty-one years with the Oklahoma police lab, Joyce Gilchrist worked on more than three thousand cases. In addition to collecting and analyzing crime scene evidence, her job involved testifying at criminal trials. She was a dream witness for the prosecution. She was attractive, well-dressed, and knew how to make complicated science accessible to a jury. Gilchrist testified in twenty-three capital cases that resulted in convictions.

District Attorney Bob Macy could always count on Joyce Gilchrist to come through in a pinch. He was fond of the chemist. And why shouldn't he have been? Gilchrist worked hard and went the extra mile. As Macy saw it, Joyce was one of the good guys, one of the prosecution team. Nicknamed "Cowboy Bob" for his love of roping cattle, Macy was tough on crime and proud of his record. Over the course of his twenty-year tenure as DA, Macy sent seventy-three people to death row, more than any other active district attorney in the country. Oklahomans had elected Macy five times.

But some legal professionals believed his judgment was often clouded by his stubborn determination to win cases. In 2001, the plaintiff in a civil suit brought against the district attorney alleged that Macy had "fostered an environment within his office wherein questionable prosecutorial tactics, including reliance on unfounded forensic analysis, were routinely used to secure convictions."

Joyce Gilchrist seemed to enjoy working with the prosecutor's office. Trouble with this of course is that scientists are supposed to remain impartial. The practice of putting forensic labs under the supervision of police departments is inherently flawed. It creates a dangerous environment, one in which scientists may feel pressured to deliver results favorable to the police and prosecution. In an interview on *60 Minutes II*, Gilchrist's former supervisor and former Oklahoma police chief Dave McBride told host Dan Rather, "I think Joyce Gilchrist may have fallen

Mark and Jim Fowler. Mark was sent to death row largely due to the work of Joyce Gilchrist, a forensic chemist whose lab techniques and court testimonies have been questioned by everyone from defense lawyers to her own colleagues. *The Fowler Family*

into an internal feeling that she was on the police team, [that] she was on the prosecution team, I mean, what scientists should always feel like is they are on the side of science."[1]

While Gilchrist was scoring home runs for the team, rumors about her competency and integrity were swirling. The defense attorney who called her a "sorcerer" in court wasn't the only one who questioned the chemist's lab results. For years, colleagues had been accusing Gilchrist of shoddy work; a few even lodged formal complaints against her. She was disciplined by one professional forensics association for violating its code of ethics and expelled from another for giving court testimony not supported by scientific facts. In spite of this, Gilchrist was enjoying a successful career. She was promoted to lab supervisor, named employee of the year, and received a commendation for her work on the Jeff Pierce trial.

The Fowler family got along well with Jeff Pierce. He was a good guy and had been the best man at Jim Fowler's daughter's wedding. Not long after that happy event, Pierce was charged with raping and robbing an Oklahoma City woman in her home. He had been seen working with a landscaping crew in the area when the crime occurred. Pierce was interviewed by police and asked to provide a hair sample. He readily agreed; he was innocent and had nothing to hide. And then the lab results came back. Although the victim failed to identify Pierce, the tests *had* identified him as her rapist. Pierce was floored. At his trial, Joyce Gilchrist, who had analyzed the evidence, testified that his hair was microscopically identical to hairs taken from the crime scene. Pierce, who had a new wife, two-year-old twin sons—and a solid alibi—was found guilty and sentenced to sixty-five years in prison.

Science had branded him a rapist and a liar. Pierce said he was innocent, but that was not surprising. In prison, 95 percent of the inmates will tell you they're innocent. So when he protested, no one paid much attention. Pierce severed all ties with his family. He did not want them to spend their holidays and weekends in a prison waiting room. At his insistence, his wife Kathy divorced him and she raised the boys out of state.

Jeff Pierce languished in prison for fifteen long years before DNA tests exonerated him. The results were matched to another man, a convicted felon who, coincidentally, was serving time at the same prison. Pierce was released, sent home to Kathy and the twin boys he never got to know. It was difficult for him to adjust. He had been away so long and had lost so much. Pierce sued Joyce Gilchrist and Bob Macy in civil court. His complaint alleged that they "engaged in a pervasive pattern of railroading defendants through the Oklahoma courts and into extended prison sentences." Further, their "behavior reflects a pattern and practice of the OCPD (Oklahoma Police Department) and the district attorney's office in securing convictions on the basis of falsified or misleading evidence." If Pierce had been wrongly convicted, could there be others? "I'm just the one who opened the door," he told *Time* magazine. "There will be a lot more coming out behind me."[2]

Jeff Pierce would hardly consider himself lucky. After all, he had lost fifteen years. Mark Fowler lost much more. Based largely on Gilchrist's

Mark Fowler spent fifteen years on death row before being executed by lethal injection in 2001.
The Fowler Family

testimony, Jim Fowler's son was sentenced to death and executed in 2001. A former altar boy and the nephew of a Catholic priest, Mark was a big, happy kid until his late teens. When his mother died of cancer, Mark fell apart. He started doing drugs and hanging out with a bad crowd. Mark was nineteen when he met Billy Ray Fox at a party. Four days later, he agreed to help Fox rob an IGA supermarket. Fox, a strutting, bantam man easily manipulated the much larger but slightly goofy, genial Mark. Fox said he had an inside contact at the market who agreed to hand them over the money from the till. The men would divide the loot three ways. Whether this contact existed is unknown. What is known is that Fox had been fired from IGA and harbored a serious grudge. As Mark told it, Fox took the employees into the back room while Mark waited up front as a lookout. Soon, Mark heard shots ring out. Panicked, he fled the store and waited in the pickup truck for Fox.

Billy Ray Fox went home and told his roommates that he had murdered the three market employees. "I killed two of them. Then I killed the third one. I hit him over the head with a gun," he said.[3] The roommate turned him in. Once in custody, Fox quickly changed his story and pointed the finger at Mark Fowler. Both men were charged with robbery and the murders of IGA employees Rick Cast, John Barrier, and Chumpon Chaowasin.

District Attorney Bob Macy was uninterested in making a deal with the defendants. Mark Fowler, who denied taking part in the murders, would have pleaded guilty to the robbery and accepted the long prison sentence. Instead, Macy pushed for the death penalty for both men. He also fought the defense motions to sever the trials. Fox and Fowler were tried together. Mark admitted his part in the robbery but swore he had not harmed anyone. Testifying for the prosecution, Joyce Gilchrist told jurors that hairs found on the murder weapon, a shotgun, belonged to Mark Fowler. She said the evidence proved both Fowler and Fox had been in "close violent contact" with the victims. A defense expert refuted Gilchrist's testimony. He had found that it was impossible to positively match the hair to Fowler. Gilchrist, it appears, was the more persuasive witness. The defendants were found guilty and sentenced to death.

Mark Fowler swore he was guilty only of the robbery, that and very poor judgment. He made his final confession just before his execution. He was sorry for many things, but his conscience was clear. He was not a murderer. Mark Fowler and Billy Ray Fox were executed days apart from each other in 2001.

Joyce Gilchrist had given the jury the impression that the hair analysis was nearly foolproof. In reality, hair analysis was notoriously unreliable. Consider Jeff Pierce. "Conventional hair analysis, based on looking at one strand of hair under microscope and comparing it to another, is subjective junk science," contended Barry Scheck and Peter Neufield, co-founders of Project Innocence, a legal foundation that works to free the wrongly convicted through DNA testing. "Hair experts have never been able to agree on consistent criteria for 'associating' a suspect with an unknown hair, nor have they produced persuasive data showing the probative value of these 'associations' . . . Among the first 74 prisoners exonerated by DNA testing over the past decade, 26 were implicated, in part, by hair analysis."[4]

. . .

Jim Fowler had always supported capital punishment—until he watched, helpless, as his son was put to death by lethal injection. Fowler and his second wife, Ann, had a change of heart after Mark's death. They began to speak out against the death penalty. Jim Fowler decided to ask the court to spare the life of the man accused of killing his mother. Robert Miller was charged with the rape and murder of Anna Laura "Goldie" Fowler and a neighbor, Zelma Cutler. Miller insisted he was innocent. The police thought otherwise and shared their opinions with Joyce Gilchrist. She understood how important it was for the county to get a conviction.

At Miller's trial, Joyce Gilchrist testified that hairs found at both crime scenes belonged to the defendant. Miller's defense attorney asked the state to send the evidence out for DNA testing but DA Bob Macy claimed the tests were too expensive (more expensive than a man's life?). The prosecution relied instead on far less reliable hair sample matches. Gilchrist left the jury with the impression that hair analysis was an accurate science. Miller was sentenced to death. While Miller was incarcerated, more elderly women were attacked and raped in Goldie Fowler's neighborhood. Except for the fact that these women survived, the crimes were identical to those Miller had been convicted of committing.

For ten years, Goldie Fowler's son Jim struggled with his feelings about Miller. As a Catholic, Jim Fowler believed it was wrong to wish for the death of the man who had raped and killed his mother. But as a human, it was hard not to. And then came the shocker. Miller, the man who had haunted Fowler's dreams for a decade, was innocent. Miller sat on death row for seven years before DNA tests cleared him of the crimes and identified Ronnie Lott as the perpetrator—a man Gilchrist had, years earlier, excluded as a suspect. Jim Fowler felt dizzy. Especially when he considered the fact that Miller had been sentenced to death. Gilchrist was wrong about Jeff Pierce, wrong about Robert Miller. Was she wrong about Mark Fowler?

Jim Fowler believed Mark was guilty of robbery but not murder. He also believed that his son deserved to be punished for his crimes, but not executed. "Mark was not a violent person. He could be dumb about things and he didn't make the right decisions," he said. As for the triple homicide, Jim and Ann Fowler insist, "Our son did not do this."

For Robert Miller's attorney, Garvin Isaacs, "The saddest part . . . is that all these innocent people have gone to prison. I think there's a high degree of possibility that some of those people who were executed were innocent." Joyce Gilchrist "was not inept. She was mean. She deliberately convicted innocent people," Isaacs said.[5]

Behind the scenes, Joyce Gilchrist's detractors were becoming more vocal. In 1999, a federal appeals judge accused the forensic chemist of giving testimony that was "without question untrue," and "terribly misleading, if not false." Her testimony in a rape case had been "entirely unsupported by the evidence," he wrote in his ruling. Furthermore, she had held back crucial evidence from the defense. Gilchrist's supervisors sat up and took notice.

After the judge's ruling was released, things began to unravel for the police lab's 1985 employee of the year. Gilchrist now found herself at the other end of the microscope, the subject of three separate investigations. She was being scrutinized, her work reexamined, her every move analyzed. A preliminary investigation conducted by the FBI turned up a series of glaring inconsistencies and mistakes in her analysis of crime scene evidence, analysis that according to the report, "went beyond the acceptable limits of forensic science." Gilchrist had routinely made hair and blood sample matches that other chemists had deemed unmatchable. She had withheld evidence from defense teams—a clear violation of the constitutional right to due process.

In a confidential memo sent to the police chief, Gilchrist's supervisor accused her of gross misconduct. An internal investigation into her work had turned up numerous transgressions. Aside from mismanaging the forensics lab, the memo stated that there was "compelling circumstantial evidence" that Gilchrist had "either intentionally lost or destroyed" crime scene hairs used in a capital murder trial to prevent the defense from having it retested. Additionally, the chemist was found to have doctored her case notes from the same trial, erasing and writing over notes that definitely excluded the defendant as a suspect. The defendant was given a death sentence.

"It's very obvious that she was not an arbiter of fact," Jim Bednar, a former prosecutor who heads up the Oklahoma Indigent Defense System, told reporters. "If she was, this wouldn't have happened. They [police and prosecutors] basically had an advocate and not a scientist in Joyce Gilchrist. That's tragic."[6]

Joyce Gilchrist was reassigned to the equine lab (a demoralizing demotion for a woman who had considered herself part of the prosecutor's team), before being fired in 2001. The fall from grace was swift and painful. "The criticism of her around here is second only to that of Timothy McVeigh," Gilchrist's attorney Melvin Hall told *Time*.[7] In the wake of the growing scandal, district attorney Bob Macy resigned. Gilchrist was left to fend for herself. For her part, Gilchrist stands by her work. "They're keying in on the negative and not looking at the good work I did," she said. "I worked hard, long and consistently on every case. I always based my opinion on scientific findings . . . I feel comfortable with the conclusions I drew."[8]

THE "SQUEEZE"

Say Detective Briscoe approaches a drug dealer who he just *knows* has information valuable to his case. The scene will usually play out like this: Briscoe asks a question, and the dealer plays dumb, so Briscoe comes up with an excuse to frisk the dealer. He finds a bag of cocaine and says something to his partner like, "What do you know? Our friend here was just about to powder his nose." The cuffs come out. The dealer gets the message and spills his guts. It's called the squeeze, and it's illegal.

According to procedure, the detectives are supposed to arrest the person on the spot and bring him to a DA, who will work out a plea-for-information deal. Only the DA's office has the authority to put the squeeze on.

Oklahoma public defender David Autry disagrees. Autry, who was instrumental in getting Jeff Pierce released, is one of Gilchrist's more vocal critics. He has described her as "an incompetent, malicious pseudo-scientist who's done everything she could in every trial to help the prosecution get a conviction."[9]

The Oklahoma legislature has set aside $750,000 in state funds to go toward the review of Gilchrist's cases. As of this writing, no charges have been brought against her. It's worth noting that Gilchrist never testified for the defense in a case. She was a prosecutor's dream come true. She was also a defendant's worst nightmare.

twenty-four

LAW & ORDER: An unbalanced young man with a grudge against women goes on a shooting spree in Central Park.

TRUE STORY: Misogynist Marc Lépine, armed with a semiautomatic rifle, killed fourteen women in an antifeminist tear through a Canadian engineering school.

When the Canadian Armed Forces told Marc Lépine they didn't want him in their ranks, the young man was confused. He considered himself an ideal soldier. His uncle, who had trained with the vaunted Green Berets and served as a Canadian Forces paratrooper, had taught him at an early age how to handle a rifle. Lépine would amaze his friends by knocking pigeons right out of the air with his BB gun.[1] And not only was he a crack shot, he possessed a keen knowledge of war, too, gleaned mainly from his obsession with combat magazines and war movies. He was an electronics buff, which surely should have helped him get into the service. In Lépine's mind, he was a perfect fit. So what was the problem? According to the Canadian Armed Forces, the problem was the young man's obvious personality disorder. Lépine didn't buy it. The *real* reason was women.

Marc Lépine had convinced himself that women—especially feminists— were responsible for his near-complete failure in life. At the age of twenty-five, he had accomplished very little. An unemployed hospital worker who hoped to someday attend Montreal's prestigious engineering school, Ècole Poytechnique, Lépine shared a five-room apartment with a male friend and spent most of his time watching war movies, dabbling in electronics, and dreaming of being a great engineer. He was a generally quiet, introverted man who attracted attention to himself only when he cranked rock music, which annoyed his neighbors. Lépine did like women enough to want to date them, but the relationships never lasted. These periods would be followed by reclusiveness, sulkiness, self-absorption, and—one can deduce given his subsequent actions—seething anger.

Feminists, Lépine believed, were ruining the world—and they were surely ruining his life. Women weren't just rivals when it came to things like military service or engineering school placements, they were taking over everything, every aspect of life. Like all misogynists, Lépine was quick to point out his belief that feminist hate men, yet failed to recognize his own hatred for women. But he revealed how deeply his pent-up hatred ran when he entered the Ècole Polytechnique on December 6, 1989, dressed in combat gear and armed to the teeth.

As the students in Room 303 of the Ècole Polytechnique were taking an oral exam to finish up the semester and soon begin a much-needed winter vacation, Lépine entered the building. It was about 4:30 p.m. He walked upstairs and into Room 303. Two students were standing in front of the room and sixteen were seated. Lépine, holding his Mini-14 "varmint" rifle, a .223-caliber semiautomatic largely favored by small-game hunters and ranchers, told the men to get on one side of the room, women on the other. "The women here are a bunch of fucking feminists! I hate feminists!" he shouted. Everyone froze. Some of the students thought the bizarre scene was all a joke. Lépine told the males to leave the room. No one moved, so Lépine fired two warning shots into the ceiling to show he was deadly serious. The men fled. One of the females remaining in the room attempted to talk to Lépine and calm him down. He shot her. Then he unloaded on everyone in the room, murdering seven unarmed people.

Lépine left the room and walked through the building's hallways, firing at every woman he saw, and any men that might be foolish enough to challenge him. Students scattered, either fleeing the building or running to warn friends. Many, whether in classrooms, lounges, or the cafeteria, assumed the warnings were pranks—until they heard gunshots popping down the hallway.

Someone called the police. Another pulled the fire alarm. Terrified students knew nothing except that someone was shooting a gun in the building; the shots sometimes sounded close, sometimes distant. In the meandering, echoing hallways of the school, they couldn't tell whether the gunman was coming closer to them or moving farther away. All they could do was attempt to get out of eye-shot if he entered their area and hope for the best. The few who dared to try to find an escape route would turn a corner and see blood on the floor, not knowing which way to run. For almost a half hour, the Ècole Polytechnique was an enormous deadly maze.

The executioner shouted "I want the women," as he took pot shots at people in the cafeteria. He stalked the halls and shot and killed a nursing student, who happened to be waiting for a friend. He murdered another student at point-blank range. Then another. He shot numerous others who, luckily, escaped with their lives. Lépine then went back upstairs and into Room 311 where another oral exam had been in session. There he shot and wounded a woman giving a presentation, then shot and killed three others as they tried to run. As the professor took cover under his desk, Lépine sat next to the wounded woman, pulled out a knife, and stabbed her in the heart, killing her—his fourteenth and final murder victim. Then he sat on the podium, placed the barrel of his Mini-14 under his chin, said, "Oh, shit," and blew his own head off.

In total, Lépine shot twenty-seven people, killing fourteen women: Geneviève Bergeron, Nathalie Croteau, Hélène Colgan, Barbara Daigneault, Anne-Marie Edward, Maud Haviernick, Barbara Maria Klueznick, Maryse Laganière, Maryse Leclair, Anne-Marie Lemay, Sonia Pelletier, Michèle Richard, Annie St-Arneault, and Annie Turcotte. Thirteen others—almost all women—were injured.

In the months following, the death toll climbed even higher. Nearly a year later, a male Ècole Polytechnique student who was present in one of the classrooms, unable to cope with the fact that he did nothing to stop Lépine, committed suicide. Both his parents followed suit, killing themselves ten months later. And Lépine's sister shortly after the murders developed a drug problem. She OD'd and died at twenty-eight years old.[2]

. . .

Marc Lépine's rampage was the worst mass murder in Canadian history and shook the entire nation to the core. With a dead perpetrator on their hands, the police had nothing to solve. The people of Montreal, however, along with all Canadian citizens, had an important mystery to solve: How in the world could this have happened? The question inevitably led to two main issues: violence against women and gun control. Just as Marc Lépine came out of nowhere, these subjects were suddenly being hotly debated in mainstream dialog.

Numerous feminists used Lépine's actions as a springboard to shed light on a subject all but ignored in mainstream dialog: violence against women. Lépine had written a three-page suicide note, in which he vented his fury with feminists. He began by oddly apologizing for any spelling mistakes, as he had had only fifteen minutes in which to write the screed. He then stated that his actions were purely "political" in nature and not based on the fact that his life was a shambles. After boasting that he did well in school even though he didn't study, that he was "rational and erudite," he pointed his finger at feminists, who "always have a talent for enraging me." After an antifeminist tirade and an apology for such a short note, Lépine wrote the list of nineteen women he wanted to kill. (One name on the note was Maryse Leclair, daughter of the Montreal Police Department's chief spokesman Pierre Leclair. It turned out that she was one of the victims, and her father, who arrived on the scene as a cop, left as a grieving father.)

Mainstream newspapers passed Lépine off as a nut, a crackpot, a freak of nature. The crime defied explanation. The inner workings of this madman's brain could never be understood. Many feminists had a different view of the matter. Lépine's actions were not a surprise at all, but rather one more instance of male brutality against women.

This stance was, of course, countered with hysterical defensiveness from male advocacy groups: Blatant male bashing! They say we're monsters! The feminist message is clear: Men are scum! In stunningly shameless self-victimization, one thin-skinned male talk show host reported said, "I've come to think of December sixth as Men are Monsters Day."

In a Canadian Broadcasting Corporation (CBC) article, columnist Judy Rebick pointed out that most feminists weren't claiming that Lepine was an extreme version of most men, but that his actions were an extreme version of *abusive* men, and that abuse is a widespread problem. She summed up the feminist argument: "[T]he Montreal Massacre was an extreme example of the violence women face every day from abusive men. Most men are not abusive but too many are. Statistics Canada tells us that three out of ten women have been physically or sexually assaulted by their spouse or ex-spouse. One out of four have [sic] experienced sexual assault, half by the age of eighteen."[3]

Two other writers pointed out that no one would question the political motivations of someone who ransacked a synagogue or beat a black man in the streets of a white neighborhood. Those instances would clearly be seen as extreme acts of anti-Semitism and racism, and no one would bat an eye if the perpetrators were referred to as anti-Semites and racists. Why, then, the confusion over Marc Lépine, feminists were asking? Just as anti-Semitism and racism are considered societal problems, which are embodied by vicious acts against members of certain groups, misogyny, too, is a societal problem, embodied by the Montreal Massacre.[4]

The other side didn't take these views lying down. In a *Newsmagazine* article titled "Feminism's 'Grotesque' Celebration," the author took offense to a sculptor's text accompanying a work largely inspired by the Lépine killings—in particular, her use of the phrase "societal war on women." This attitude, the article asserts, conveniently leaves men in the dust. Statistics show that males are murdered at a much higher rate than women.[5] What the author forgets to mention is that males usually do the murdering, too.

Since the murders, some male advocacy websites have posted opinions that the "liberal" press unfairly labeled Lépine a misogonyst. One article contended that he was really just anti*feminist*, and went to great lengths to defend Lépine from accusations that he hated women in general, and even claims that the killer "was not only not sexist, as the media stated—he was actually fighting sexism."[6] Yet, witness after witness said that Lépine shouted, "Give me the women!" Women, not feminists. Either Lépine hated women in general, or his political views weren't quite as nuanced as the writer implies. To most Canadians in the weeks and months following Lépine's bloodbath, syntax didn't really matter, anyway.

Feminism wasn't the only social issue to surface in the mainstream as a result of Lépine's slaughter. Canadians, it was believed up until now, didn't have problems with guns. The problem was with those crazies down south, in the United States. Gun violence statistics from the other side of the border made those of Canada seem negligible. But would it last? Was the violence spreading north? Would Canada's streets soon resemble those of the violent cities in the Heartland and beyond? Gun control activists primed themselves for a major offensive.

Gun control advocates immediately called for stricter nationwide firearms regulations. Lépine had not had the slightest problem purchasing the semiautomatic weapons. "He didn't appear to be any crazier than anyone else," said the gun salesman who had sold Lépine his Mini-14.[7] (Compare this to one of Lépine's neighbor's comments after the shooting: "I had nothing against [Lépine], but the way he was looking at everyone with big eyes! He was crazy."[8]) Until now, Canada had lax gun laws—and a relatively low murder rate. In 1988, 575 people were murdered in Canada; the United States had over 20,000 murders (and only ten times the population). Gun advocates argued that they didn't want to be another United States.

Canada's politicians carefully navigated the subject, making no promises in the beginning of the controversy. But by 1995, gun regulators' voices grew louder and they got their way. In the end, Canada ended up passing strict, sweeping laws requiring every gun owner to register his or her firearm on a national registry. And the best thing about it was, the government said, the program would cost only $1.3 million. A decade later, the bill had reached $640 million, and it was still rising. Plus, upward of 90 percent of the records contain inaccuracies. And little had seemingly changed in terms of crime: 1995 saw 176 murders with guns; 2001, 171, and the numbers for each year between were about the same.[9]

For the families of the murdered women, Marc Lépine's hateful actions changed their lives forever. For the rest of the world, they showed that hatred and violence is alive and well—everywhere.

twenty-five

LAW & ORDER: A witness to a robbery turns out to be a fugitive running from a twenty-year-old murder conviction.

TRUE STORY: Sixties radical Ira "Unicorn" Einhorn fled the country after police discovered his girlfriend's badly decomposed body inside a trunk in his closet.

The courtroom was packed. It was like a Who's Who in Philadelphia as the city's most prominent and wealthiest citizens gathered to show their local counterculture hippie guru some serious brotherly love. One by one, these shining sons and daughters and captains of industry rose to attest to the impeccable character and unmistakable brilliance of Ira Einhorn. It was an amazing sight, so many well-dressed, elegant Philadelphians gathering together in support of a slovenly, egocentric, fat, bearded hippie with bad B.O. Yes, Ira stank, "like a hoagie with onions all the time,"[1] a friend said. But, his intellect and superior being put him above such mortal trifles as bathing.

And so, the crème de la crème of the City of Brotherly Love came together to see Ira vindicated. He said he was innocent, wrongly accused, and they believed him. Einhorn promised to explain it all at his trial, explain how the mummified body of his beautiful honey-blonde girlfriend wound up in *his* steamer trunk in *his* closet, in *his* apartment. He insisted he was being framed by the system, by the government, by the "man"—that mysterious mythical fat cat who gets his kicks by keeping the enlightened little guys down.

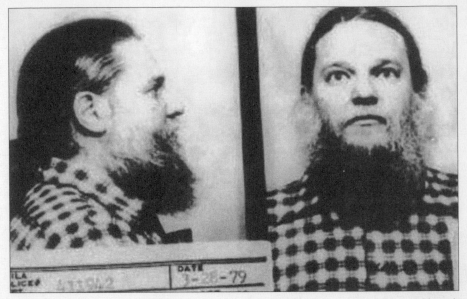

Ira Einhorn, the pseudo-intellectual Philadelphia hippie who murdered his girlfriend, Holly Maddux, and stored her corpse in his closet. *Philadelphia Police Department*

Just about everyone in Philly was looking forward to Einhorn's murder trial, which promised to be the event of the season. Free on bail paid by a wealthy benefactor, Ira continued living in the Race Street apartment where his dead lover had been found. Apparently, all that brotherly love wasn't enough to persuade Ira to show up in court. Days before his trial, the "innocent" victim of the system jumped bail and fled town.

From the start, Ira Einhorn's mother knew he was destined for great things. Ira, a bright boy with even brighter blue eyes, grew up believing that he was special, better than the other little boys. He projected an air of supreme confidence even as a child. Ira was a voracious reader and read up on dozens of subjects. He loved to talk, about everything he read and learned, and more so about himself. By the time he got to college, he'd developed an unshakeable superman complex. Early on, he earned a reputation as an iconoclast. Ira was curious, sharp, and questioned

everything, a habit that drove some of his professors crazy. College chum
Michael Hoffman told author Steven Levy that Einhorn would "tell people
the books that they needed to read, the thinkers they needed to think
about, the ideas that they had to come in contact with. He was a sort of
a cultural Bolshevik in that way."[2]

In some ways, Ira was ahead of his time. His ideas were radical for
the fifties and he had little use for rules and regulations. It wasn't long
before he realized he was ill-suited to the structured college routine of
classes, cramming, and set curriculums. Ira believed education should
be fluid, free-floating, and unfettered by things like schedules and grades.
In the midsixties, academia would adopt a similar school of thinking
about education (at least for a time). But in the fifties, such ideas were
met with derision. As a student, Ira felt stifled.

"Ira Einhorn had been preparing for the sixties long before the
coalescing forces of rebellion, drugs, liberation, and baby-boom power
reached critical mass," Steven Levy explains in his book *The Unicorn's
Secret*.[3] But there was a darker, more sinister side to Ira. He was controlling and seemed to need to dominate the women in his life. "To beat
a woman—what a joy," Einhorn once scribbled in his journal. He was
prone to violence toward his girlfriends, attacking two women who
dared to break up with him in college. "Violence," Einhorn wrote,
"always marks the end of a relationship."

In 1966 Einhorn traveled to Berkeley, California. He was in awe of
the thriving counterculture movement that had commandeered Haight-
Ashbury. Compared to this scene and the one sprawling into the streets
of New York City, Philadelphia was completely square. Einhorn returned home and happily threw himself into his new role: Philly's resident hippie guru. Spreading the message of peace, love, and LSD, Ira
became a local celebrity. He was a walking contradiction, espousing
peace and love, protesting the war, but privately battering his lovers.
His views on the fairer sex were far less egalitarian than he pretended.
Physically, Ira was a mess. He was overweight, out of shape, and was
legendary for his poor hygiene. Einhorn rarely bathed and his body
odor often entered the room before him, and lingered long after he
had gone.

Einhorn was hired to teach classes at the University of Pennsylvania's Free University, an experimental program designed to meet the needs of the new turned-on and tuned-in generation. Ira, whose last name is German for "one horn," took to calling himself "The Unicorn." Students were both repelled and fascinated by this highly unorthodox professor who discussed sex and drugs in the classroom and invited them back to his apartment for a party. One female student made a quick retreat when the professor stripped naked and began to dance. No matter to Ira, he had plenty of other fans and many lovers. However, Ira Einhorn's biggest fan was Ira Einhorn. "I feel no desire to be anything but Ira—fully realized in whatever manner possible," he said.[4]

By the seventies, Ira was firmly entrenched as Philadelphia's counterculture expert. As the flower power movement wilted, Ira shifted his attention to the New Age movement. He could frequently be overheard spewing rhetoric about a psychic world order, mind control, transcendental meditation, the paranormal, and other exotic topics. The Unicorn insisted the world was on the verge of a major transformation. He was busy as ever, hobnobbing with an ever-evolving circle that included physicists, psychics (Uri Geller being the most prominent), economists, bigwigs from the phone and gas companies, and bored socialites looking to be entertained. Einhorn ran for mayor, a bid made more for publicity than actual victory. He ran as a "planetary enzyme," and told reporters that he wasn't interested in taking office if he won.

Hoping to find new ways to market products and services to the younger generation, the city's business elite turned to Ira for insight. And suddenly, the anti-establishment guru was working for the establishment. It was certainly a hypocritical position for the Unicorn to take but he didn't seem to notice or care. If Philadelphia's power brokers wanted to wine and dine him, that was just fine with Ira. "People give me money just for being Ira," he bragged.[5] He was enjoying a free meal, one of many, at La Terrese bistro when he first laid eyes on Holly Maddux.

Helen "Holly" Maddux was an elegant, stately young girl who resembled nothing so much as a prima ballerina. Her sister compared her fragile beauty to that of actress Michelle Pfeiffer. Holly was one of five children born to Fred and Elizabeth Maddux. Growing up in Tyler, Texas, Holly found her views on life and politics often differed from the accepted, conservative party line. Still, she flourished academically and didn't seem to mind being the odd one out. She spent a lot of time by herself, reading, thinking, and drawing.

Young Holly was an enigma, an icy beauty who earned top grades and surprised everyone when she tried out for the cheerleading squad. It seemed somehow beneath the girl who eschewed most mainstream pursuits and graduated at the top of her class. But Holly was like that. Just when you thought you had her figured out, she would turn around and do something completely unexpected. Small town life stifled her and after graduation she eagerly departed for Bryn Mawr. In Texas, Holly had been something of a rebel, but compared to the girls at the exclusive Pennsylvania liberal arts college, she was conservative, shy, a good girl with Southern manners and a Texas twang.

Once again, Holly felt out of place. She withdrew from her classmates, spending time in her room with the pet squirrel she'd brought with her from Texas. Holly didn't want for dates though. She was much sought after by boys from the neighboring colleges.

Gifted and bright, Holly was also unsure of what she wanted to do with her life. After graduation, she set off to Europe and later Israel, where she traveled alone and fell in and out of love. Holly had no trouble meeting men. Her only trouble was with commitment. As soon as a lover became too serious or pressed for a commitment, Holly would take off or take up with someone else. She left one lover for another that she met while working on a kibbutz in Israel. It was the seventies and such sexual abandon was common. Holly was a liberated woman, free to do as she pleased. That would all change when she met Ira Einhorn in the fall of 1972.

Holly moved into Ira's shabby apartment at 3411 Race Street in the Powelton Village section of Philadelphia. Their relationship was rocky, and over the next few years, they would break up and make up several times. Holly was a quiet beauty; Ira was a beast of a man with terrible table manners and a tremendous ego. But unlike the fairy tale, no amount of kindness would ever turn this beast into a prince. There would be no happy ending to their story. Ira constantly put her down. He had a double standard: Holly was to remain loyal to him but he was free to carry on with other women. He flaunted his affairs and chastised Holly when she complained about his promiscuity. Once, he left her at a party and went home with another woman.

Friends recall Einhorn verbally abusing Holly and treating her like a servant. The bright Bryn Mawr alum faded into the background whenever Ira was present. Systematically, he chipped away at her self-confidence. Ira was the star, the dynamo in the relationship, and often, the bully. Holly was fragile, diffident, and life revolved around Ira and his needs. Her family witnessed this first-hand when she brought her new boyfriend home. Ira behaved like a boor, eating with his hands and scratching all through dinner. He picked fights with her conservative father and bossed Holly around. She wanted to show Ira her baby photos but he was uninterested, demanding that she brush his hair instead. The visit was a disaster and the couple left days earlier than planned. The Madduxes were worried about Holly, who seemed to be under the spell of the Rasputin-like Einhorn.

For five years, Holly lived in Ira Einhorn's shadow. In the summer of 1977, she finally summoned up the courage to leave him. This time she was serious. She had met someone new and they really hit it off. They were even planning to go away together. Her new boyfriend was named Saul and she was staying at his place in New York City when Ira phoned and demanded that she return at once to the Race Street apartment; if she didn't he would throw all her things out in the street. Ira was enraged, screaming and cursing at her. Holly was unable to placate him so she called some mutual friends and asked that they try to calm him down. They were unsuccessful. "I just have to go down [to Philadelphia] and get Ira off the wall," she told Saul before rushing back to Philadelphia to retrieve her clothes and family keepsakes. She promised to be back in time for the boat trip they had planned.

· · ·

Helen "Holly" Maddux, an intelligent, artistic young woman, who entered into an abusive relationship with Ira Einhorn. When she finally summoned the courage to leave him, Einhorn murdered her.
Photo courtesy of CNN

It wasn't like Holly to forget birthdays. The Madduxes began to worry when weeks and family birthdays passed without a word from her. Elizabeth Maddux phoned the Race Street apartment looking for her daughter. Ira answered and matter-of-factly informed her that Holly had left for the food co-op one day and never returned. His explanation didn't make sense but he abruptly ended the conversation before Elizabeth could question him further. A second call Elizabeth made a few days later proved equally fruitless. When pressed, an annoyed Ira told her that Holly had recently called to say she was dropping out for a while and wanted to be left alone. He also told Elizabeth he was too busy to talk to her and hung up.

The Madduxes weren't the only ones who had not heard from Holly. She had not contacted any of her friends or her new boyfriend. She seemed to have vanished into thin air. The Philadelphia Police Department, contacted by the Madduxes, hadn't turned up any leads. Desperate, Holly's parents hired two private investigators to look for their daughter. Bob Stevens and J. R. Pearce, both retired FBI men, criss-crossed the country interviewing people who knew Holly. All roads led back to Ira Einhorn. Nearly everyone they spoke to described

Ira as nonviolent. But Ira's story was full of holes and the investigators began to suspect foul play. It was clear that Ira knew much more than he was telling them—and that much of what he did tell them was false. To top it off, he was adamantly refusing to cooperate with their investigation.

Pearce learned that former tenants of 3411 Race Street had complained to the landlord about a sickening smell and putrid brown liquid oozing through their closet ceiling. The tenants cleaned, deodorized, and painted, yet the odor remained and the disgusting goo continued to seep through the ceiling. The landlord sent for a repairman but the man living on the second floor—one Ira Einhorn—refused to let him enter his apartment. Another former tenant recalled hearing a "blood-curdling" scream coming from Einhorn's place around the time Holly went missing.

Stevens and Pearce handed this information over to the Philadelphia Police Department. On March 28, 1978, detectives arrived at Ira's apartment with a warrant to search for evidence relating to Holly's disappearance. Einhorn, who had been sleeping when they knocked on the door, begrudgingly let the men in. Their search led them to a closet where they found several boxes marked "Maddux" and a green suitcase that held Holly's social security card and driver's license. A large steamer trunk took up most of the closet space. Homicide Detective Michael Chitwood opened the trunk and discovered a mummified body buried under a sea of styrofoam peanuts—and crumpled newspapers from September 15, 1977.

Chitwood turned to Einhorn and told him, "We found the body. It looks like Holly's body."

Unmoved, Ira responded, "You found what you found."

Chitwood asked him, "Do you want to tell me about it?"[6]

Ira refused. He was arrested and taken to the police station.

The medical examiner determined that Holly had died as a result of craniocerebral injuries. She had been struck about the head numerous times with a blunt object. Her severely decomposed body weighed just thirty-seven pounds. For eighteen months Ira Einhorn had gone about his business, all the while Holly Maddux had been decomposing in a trunk in his closet.

Ira was charged with first-degree murder. He was represented by Arlen Specter, the future U.S. Senator from Pennsylvania. At a bail hearing, Specter called on Ira's many friends to testify to his character. The judge, clearly swayed by the praise offered by Philly's shining stars, granted Einhorn's bail request. Bail was set at $40,000, of which a paltry $4,000 was required to spring Ira from jail. A wealthy friend, one of many, paid the bail.

In a letter sent out to his friends and fans, the Unicorn said he was "sick to heart" over the "interruption of work" that he "slowly and patiently created over a period of many years." He continued, "The psychological shock of such an abrupt transition has left me dazed and totally without a context. I feel as if I have lost my home planet. It would be so easy to give up or disappear. Yet I know that I must not desert at such a critical time, for the transformation is accelerating rapidly and must be understood if we are to survive."[7] Ira goes on to ask for financial support to fund his legal defense.

Released on bail, an indignant Ira went on the offensive. He told the *Inquirer*, "I have been outspoken all my life but I have never been violent . . . I want to be very direct about this. *I did not kill whoever was supposed to be in there*. I am not a killer. I do not know if a body got in there—if it was a body."[8] The coroner had, by this time, identified the corpse as Holly.

Ira spun a fantastic tale about spies and the cold war and Tesla mind-control technology. He claimed that the CIA and/or the KGB killed Holly to silence and discredit him because he had information that posed a threat to the government. The KGB in particular was out to get him. Why these agencies would murder Holly and not Ira was a mystery the Unicorn never explained.

Throughout the investigation and discovery of Holly's body, Ira had been concerned with one thing: Ira. He never expressed sorrow or grief over Holly's death. In fact, he barely mentioned her name. George Keegan, a friend of Einhorn's, said that after the arrest, "People who would once come up and hug Ira crossed the street and averted their eyes . . . He looked at me and said, 'I'm not going to be able to be Ira Einhorn now.' And I realized he was a selfish, arrogant bastard."[9]

Ira said that he would be vindicated at his trial. He promised to expose the CIA/KGB frame-up. But on the eve of his murder trail in 1981, Ira Einhorn jumped bail and fled the country. He moved around Europe, staying for a time in Ireland until authorities tracked him there. At the time, the United States did not have an extradition treaty with Ireland and Irish officers were unable to arrest Einhorn. The Unicorn slipped away, one step ahead of the American detectives who doggedly pursued him. "It's not like on TV where you just pick up the phone, call Interpol and they're there in two hours. With the red tape, it takes forever to make something happen," FBI agent Richard DiBenedetto told *Time* magazine.[10] DiBenedetto would spend nearly two decades hunting Einhorn.

In 1993, Philadelphia District Attorney Lynne Abraham took advantage of a new state law that allowed trials to be held in absentia when the defendant was missing on his own accord. After a two-week-long jury trial, Einhorn was convicted of first-degree murder in absentia. The defendant was still on the lam in Europe. In all, Einhorn would spend seventeen years eluding capture. He got married and moved to the south of France. For a fugitive, he had a pretty nice life, funded largely by an American socialite admirer and the wealthy parents of his Swedish wife, Annika Flodin. Neighbors in the picturesque French village knew the couple as the Mallons. On June 13, 1997, Einhorn's past finally caught up with him. He told the French gendarmes that arrested him that they had the wrong man. But fingerprints don't lie and Eugene Mallon's prints proved he was really Ira Einhorn.

Back home, the Maddux family and Pennsylvania authorities—especially DiBenedetto—rejoiced at the news of Einhorn's arrest. However, the news soon turned out to be bittersweet. France refused to extradite Einhorn on the grounds that his in-absentia murder conviction violated his civil rights. According to French law, a defendant tried in absentia is automatically entitled to a new trial when he or she is located, or as in Einhorn's case, apprehended. France also objected to America's use of capital punishment—a moot point in Einhorn's case as Pennsylvanian prosecutors agreed not to seek a death sentence against him. Many French citizens seized the moment to protest what they viewed as American barbarism. Einhorn's French lawyer Dominique Tricaud declared that the Einhorn affair was the perfect opportunity for the French to "give the United States a lesson in human rights."[11] While the issue was hotly debated, Ira remained free and became a cause célèbre in France. He posed naked in his garden for a magazine and was interviewed on French television. The mayor of Champagne-Mouton where Einhorn was living, told the press, "Me, I believe in the innocence of this man, who doesn't look like a killer. We'd love to keep him. He lives here in peace."[12]

It took four years of legal wrangling before Ira was extradited to Pennsylvania. To appease the French authorities, Pennsylvania passed a bill—nicknamed the "Einhorn Law"—granting defendants convicted in absentia the right to request a new trial. Einhorn was sent home. In September 2002, he was retried for the murder of Holly Maddux. When you took away all the exotic trimmings, the fancy friends, the charming village in France, the esoteric mumblings, it was a simple case with one of the oldest motives known to humankind: jealousy. Holly was leaving Ira Einhorn for another man. Einhorn was jealous of the new beau but more so of the new Holly. She had threatened to leave him before, and had even done so for short periods, but she had always wavered and come back to him. This time was different. Ira knew it. Holly knew it. He refused to let her go and so he killed her and kept her locked inside a trunk in his closet. Her spirit was gone but her body remained, his possession. No one left Ira Einhorn, at least not without a fight.

Rita and Judy, the two young women who dated Ira in college found this out for themselves. He nearly choked one of them to death when she tried to break up with him. The woman actually lost consciousness. His second college sweetheart wound up in the emergency room after she told Ira their relationship was over. Enraged, Ira had smashed a Coke bottle over the woman's head. Afterward, Ira wrote a

The fugitive in cuffs after decades on the run. Clean-shaven with short hair, Einhorn retains the sadly narcissistic views of his hippie youth. "Even on the stand, it was like he thought he was God," one juror said. *Photo courtesy of CNN*

poem about it: "Suddenly it happens. Bottle in hand I strike away at the head. In such violence there may be freedom." Neither woman pressed charges against Einhorn. Both were grateful to have escaped with their lives. Holly was not so lucky.

At trial, prosecutor Joel Rosen disputed the defense's characterization of Ira as a peace-loving, nonviolent man. He used Ira's own words to hang him, a poetic justice that was probably not lost on the man who once dreamed of becoming a famous writer. Excerpts from Ira's college diaries included the following:

> *Sadism—sounds nice—run it over your tongue—contemplate with joy the pains of others as you expire with an excruciating satisfaction. Project outward the vision of inward darkness. Let no cesspool of inner meaning be concealed. Reveal the filth that you are. Know the animal is always there . . . Beauty and innocence must be violated for they can't be possessed. The sacred mystery of another must be preserved—only death can do that.*[13]

> *To kill what you love when you can't have it seems so natural that strangling Rita last night seemed so right.*[14]

*There is a good chance I will attempt to kill Judy tomorrow—
the rational awareness of this fact brings stark terror into my
heart but it must be faced if I wish to go on—I must not allow
myself to deviate from the self-knowledge which is in the process
of being uncovered![15]*

At one point, Einhorn actually objected—not to the diary excerpts themselves but because he felt the prosecutor wasn't reading them with the right inflection. Rosen handed them to Ira, who read them to the court himself. Einhorn told them they were taking his words out of context. "It's literature. It's metaphorical," he said.

Former friends of the defendant testified that they had seen Holly with bruises and that Einhorn had treated her badly. A college friend told the court that Einhorn was inspired by the life and work of Marquis de Sade, the infamous writer who heralded the pleasures of sado-masochism. The friend testified that Ira informed him that violence was the "base of all human interaction." Other prosecution witnesses included a bookseller who testified that Einhorn was interested in buying a book about mummification, a do-it-yourself guide with information on herbs and chemicals. Two women told the court that Ira had asked them to help him dump a trunk in the river "because it was filled with secret Russian papers."

Defense attorney William T. Cannon told the court that Einhorn had fled the country not because he was guilty but because he was convinced he was being railroaded and would not get a fair trial. Who killed Holly? That, declared Cannon, was the $64,000 question. Ira was innocent. What's more, if he had killed Holly, he surely would have gotten rid of her body, wouldn't he have? "One of the things that attracted Holly to Ira was his great mind," Cannon said. "Not a mind stupid enough to keep a body in his closet." He also told the jury that just because Holly's body was found in Ira's apartment "doesn't mean at all that Ira Einhorn was responsible for her murder."

Ira Einhorn was the last to testify. There was no way any defense lawyer was going to convince him to remain silent. The Unicorn took the stand in his defense, babbling on and on about mind control, secret government experiments, psychic warfare, Tesla, and other mumbo-jumbo. The judge told the overly verbose defendant to stick to the facts of the case. Einhorn, slimmer and gray-haired, but with the same shocking bright blue eyes, insisted Holly was killed by CIA agents in an attempt to frame him. He was a threat to the CIA because he had uncovered top secret information on mind-control experiments the agency was conducting. He also told the jury that he had a "Virgo Moon."

It took the jury two hours to find Einhorn guilty of first-degree murder. A juror later told reporters that the defendant "had a warped mind," and "even on the stand, it was like he thought he was God." Judge William J. Mazzolla didn't mince words in his assessment of the defendant, whom he described as a "pseudo-classicist," and "an intellectual dilettante who preyed on the uninitiated, uninformed, unsuspecting, and inexperienced." District Attorney Lynne Abraham summed it up best: "Ira Einhorn and his Virgo Moon are toast." The Unicorn was sentenced to life without the possibility of parole.

endnotes

ONE

[1] Gary Cartwright, *Texas Monthly*, "Durst Case Scenarios," February 2002.

[2] Ibid.

[3] Ibid.

[4] Ibid.

[5] Ibid.

[6] Matt Bierbeck, *A Deadly Secret: The Strange Disappearance of Kathie Durst* (New York: Berkley Books, 2003), 92.

[7] Charles V. Bagli, *New York Times*, "Investigators in Two Other Cases Await Verdict in Durst Trial," Metropolitan Desk, November 7, 2003.

[8] Charles V. Bagli and Kevin Flynn, *New York Times*, "Man Is Accused of Murder, but Not the Long-Suspected One," Metropolitan Desk, October 12, 2001.

[9] Bill Hewitt, et al., *People*, "Heir of Mystery," November 5, 2001.

[10] *Court TV Online* Chat, "Juror 12," http://www.courttv.com/talk/chat_transcripts/2003/1112durst=lovell.htmlith.

[11] Corey Kilgannon, *New York Times*, "Jeanine Pirro's Pursuit," Westchester Weekly Desk, February 3, 2004.

Additional sources include court documents, trial transcripts, and personal interviews conducted by the authors.

TWO

[1] Jim Schaeffer, Nancy Jeffrey, and Robert Musial, *Detroit Free Press*, "Soldier Comes Home to His Death," March 19, 1991, A1.

[2] Ibid.

[3] Gareth G. Davis and David B. Muhlhausen, "Young African-American Males: Continuing Victims of High Homicide Rates in Urban Communities," May 2, 2000, 4.

[4] Associated Press, "Wife's Kin Arrested in GI's Killing," *Syracuse Herald-Journal*, March 26, 1991, A6.

[5] T. Mathews and P. Annin, *Newsweek*, "A Widow in a Deadly Web," April 8, 1991, 34.

[6] Associated Press, "Divorce, Death Greet Soldier," *The Post-Standard*, March 27, 1991, A6.

[7] Jim Schaeffer, *Detroit Free Press*, "Boast May be Riggs' Downfall," November 19, 1993, A1.

[8] Ibid.

[9] Joe Swickard, *Detroit Free Press*, "On Tape, Riggs Tells How Plot Unfolded," May 28, 1994, 3A.

[10] Ibid.

[11] Joe Swickard, *Detroit Free Press*, "Riggs Wanted Witness Eliminated, Video Shows," June 1, 1994, 3B.

[12] Jeffrey S. Ghannam, *Detroit Free Press*, "Jurors Say Tapes Sealed the Verdict," June 9, 1994, A1.

[13] Ibid.

THREE

[1] David F. White, *New York Times*, "Unlikely Figures in Murder Case," July 9, 1977.

[2] William Gaylin, *The Killing of Bonnie Garland* (New York: Penguin, 1995), 78–79.

[3] Ibid., 122.

[4] Jesse Kornbluth, *New York Times*, "A Fatal Romance at Yale," May 7, 1978, SM12.

[5] Joseph Sobran, *The Daily Herald*, "Why Does Public Put Up with Insanity Plea?" June 1, 1982, section 1, 6.

Additional sources include Richard Herrin's confession to Coxsackie police and court documents.

FOUR

1 *Court TV*, "Sideline Rage or Self-Defense?", www.courttv.com, December 31, 2001.

2 *Court TV*, "Fatal Injuries Describe in Words, Photos," Harriet Ryan, www.courttv.com, January 4, 2002.

3 *CBS News*, "Six to Ten for Hockey Dad," www.cbsnews.com, January 25, 2002.

4 *Court TV*, "Sideline Rage or Self-Defense?", www.courttv.com, December 31, 2001.

5 Court TV, "Jury Convicts Hockey Dad of Sideline Rage," Harriet Ryan, www.courttv.com, January 11, 2002.

6 *The Providence Journal*, "Hockey Dad Gets Six Years in Jail," Michael Corkery, January 25, 2002.

7 Ibid.

8 *Commonwealth vs. Junta* (Appeals Court Decision), Properties of the Social Law Library, © 1999–2006, www.sociallaw.com.

Additonal sources include the transcript of Thomas Junta's confession to Reading police and the prosecution's Statement of the Case, both of which can be found on www.courttv.com

FIVE

1 *Crime Library Online*, Crimelibrary.com.

2 Bruce Jackson, *Buffalo Report*, "Jack Henry Abbott, 58," Buffaloreport.com, March 1, 2002.

3 Ibid.

4 Jack Henry Abbott, *In the Belly of the Beast* (New York: Knopf, 1991).

5 Terrence Des Pres, *New York Times*, review of *In the Belly of the Beast*, July 19, 1981.

6 Ibid.

7 *Crime Library Online*, Crimelibrary.com.

8 Ibid.

9 Ibid.

SIX

1 *Court TV's Crime Library*, "A Cry in the Night: The Kitty Genovese Murder," Courtroom Television Network LLC. www.courttv.com.

2 Ibid.

³ Martin Gansberg, *New York Times*, "Thirty-seven Who Saw Murder Didn't Call the Police," March 27, 1964, 1.

⁴ Jim Rasenberger, *New York Times*, "Kitty, Forty Years Later," February 8, 2004, sec. 14, 1.

⁵ Martin Gansberg, *New York Times*, "Lindsay, Recalling the Genovese Murder, Deplores Apathy," October 13, 1965, 35.

⁶ For what is perhaps the most in-depth account of the Kitty Genovese murder and subsequent controversy, see www.oldkewgardens.com, which contains a number of *New York Times* articles about the murder, plus such documents as Winston Moseley's confession transcript, trial testimony transcripts, various legal briefs, photos and commentary of the site's creator, a longtime Kew Gardens resident. The website was invaluable to authors researching this case.

⁷ "Kitty Genovese," www.oldkewgardens.com.

⁸ Ibid.

⁹ Maurice Carroll, *New York Times*, "Genovese Slayer Yields Gun, Gives Up," March 22, 1968.

¹⁰ Ibid.

¹¹ Ibid.

¹² Ibid.

¹³ Winston Moseley, *New York Times*, "Today I'm a Man Who Wants to Be an Asset," April 16, 1977, 15.

¹⁴ *Court TV's Crime Library*, "A Cry in the Night: The Kitty Genovese Murder," Courtroom Television Network LLC. www.courttv.com.

¹⁵ Joe Sexton, *New York Times*, "Reviving Kitty Genovese Case, and Its Passions," July 25, 1995, B4.

SEVEN

¹ Blake Morrison, *As If* (New York: Picador, 1997), 54.

² David James Smith and Donald I. Fine, *Beyond All Reason* (New York: Penguin, 1995), 80.

³ Morrison, 111.

⁴ Ibid., 103.

⁵ Ibid., 139.

⁶ Ibid., 136.

⁷ Ibid., 137.

⁸ Smith, 216.

⁹ Ibid., 215.

¹⁰ Ibid., 217.

[11] Libby Brooks, *Guardian*, "I Don't Doubt They'd Have Been Ripped to Shreds," February 6, 2003.

Additional sources include court transcripts and the article "The Death of James Bulger," by Shirley Lynn Scott available at www.crimelibrary.com.

EIGHT

[1] Joseph Berger, *New York Times*, "A Family Must Deal with the Murders of the Couple Who Shaped Their Lives," June 24, 1994, B5.

[2] Ibid.

[3] Marjorie Rosen and Lorna Grisby, *People*, "The Blackout," July 11, 1994.

[4] The twelve steps are listed on Alcoholics Anonymous's website, www.alcoholics-anonymous.org.

[5] *Cox v. Miller*, 2nd Circuit Court of Appeals Decision, retrieved from www.law.com, July 17, 2002.

[6] Marjorie Rosen and Lorna Grisby, *People*, "The Blackout," July 11, 1994.

[7] Joseph Berger, *New York Times*, "Jurors Tell of Friction in Murder Mistrial," June 30, 1994, B7.

[8] Joseph Berger, *New York Times*, "Mistrial Declared in Case of Suspect in 2 Murders," June 29, 1994, B5.

[9] *Cox v. Miller*, 2nd Circuit Court of Appeals Decision, retrieved from www.law.com, July 17, 2002.

[10] David Goldnamn, *Biography*, "AA vs. DA: The Case of Paul Cox," March 2003, 21.

NINE

[1] Edwin Miller, *Seventeen*, "Rebecca Schaeffer: A Breath of Fresh Air," May 1987.

[2] M. Tharp, *U.S. News & World*, "In the Mind of a Stalker," February 17, 1992.

[3] Ibid.

[4] Katherine Ramsland, Court TV Crime Library, "It Takes A Star," crimelibrary.com/criminology2/stalkers.

Additional sources include trial transcripts, Robert John Bardo's police confession and psychiatric evaluation.

TEN

[1] Court of Appeals of New York, People of the State of New York v. Bernhard Goetz, July 8, 1986, http://web.lexis-nexis.com.

[2] Brian Kates, *New York Daily News*, "The Subway Vigilante," December 26, 2004.

[3] Norimitsu Onishi, *New York Times*, "Court Case Nudges Goetz Out of Co-coon," December 31, 1995, 27.

[4] Brian Kates, *New York Daily News*, "The Subway Vigilante," December 26, 2004.

[5] Stanley Crouch, *New York Magazine*, "The Joy of Goetz," March 7, 2003.

ELEVEN

[1] Kathy Walt, *Houston Chronicle*, "Execution May Haunt Texas," December 14, 1997.

[2] *Larry King Live*, broadcast on CNN, January 15, 1998.

[3] Beverly Lowry, *Crossed Over: A Murder, A Memoir* (New York: Random House, 2002).

[4] ABC News, interview with Dean Reynolds, February 2, 1998.

[5] Tucker Carlson, *Talk Magazine*, "Devil May Care," September 1999, 106.

TWELVE

[1] Crystal Nix, *New York Times*, "Slain Woman Found in Park," August 27, 1986, B1.

[2] Timothy Clifford and T. J. Collins, *Newsday*, "Cops Describe 'Cracking' Chambers," June 17, 1987, 19.

[3] Mike McAlary and Marianne Arneberg, *Newsday*, "Suspect: Death Was Accident During Sexual Tryst in Park," August 28, 1986, 3.

[4] Samuel Freedman, *New York Times*, "Sexual Politics and a Slaying," December 4, 1986, A1.

[5] Quote taken from Helen Benedict, *Virgin or Vamp?: How the Press Covers Sex Crimes* (New York: Oxford University Press), 179. (Benedict provides a valuable, in-depth "reading" of the media's coverage of Chambers's trial; in it, she interviews reporters after the fact, most of whom admit their coverage was salacious at the very least.)

[6] Kirk Johnson, *New York Times*, "Chambers, with Jury at Impasse, Admits First-Degree Manslaughter," March 26, 1988, 1.

[7] Bob Liff, et al., *Newsday*, "Leaving Home for a Number and Cell," March 27, 1988, 2.

THIRTEEN

[1] Brian T. Meehan, *Sunday Oregonian*, "An Oregon Century: The Promise of Eden," December 19, 1999, A14.

² Elinor Langer, *A Hundred Little Hitlers* (Metropolitan Books, 2003), 42.

³ Anti-Defamation League (ADL). Law enforcement report: "Extremism in America: Tom Metzger/White Aryan Resistance," www.adl.org/.

⁴ Ibid.

⁵ Ibid.

⁶ Langer, 228.

⁷ Ibid., 250.

⁸ Ibid., 250.

⁹ David S. Jackson, *Time*, "Skinhead Against Skinhead," August 8, 1993, 40.

¹⁰ "The High Price of Hate," *New York Times*, Jason Berry, March 21, 1993, 27.

¹¹ Langer, 344.

¹² Ibid., 345.

FOURTEEN

¹ All information about the lives of Candace Newmaker and her blood relatives comes from Carla Crowder's and Peggy Lowe's in-depth *Rocky Mountain News* article, "Her Name Was Candace," October 29, 2000.

² Ibid.

³ Pat Crossman, LCSW, *Skeptic Report*, "The Etiology of a Social Epidemic," www.skepticreport.com, September 2004.

⁴ Ibid.

⁵ Christopher Caldwell, *The Weekly Standard*, "Death by Therapy," May 28, 2001. (According to this article, Foster Cline ended his practice in 1988 "after a gutsy 11-year-old ran away following a [rage reduction] session and described to authorities the abuse she had been made to undergo. Cline settled in court with the state of Colorado and moved to Idaho.")

⁶ Evergreen Consultants in Human Behavior, Attachment Therapy Program, www.attachmenttherapy.com.

⁷ Crowder and Lowe, "Her Name Was Candace."

⁸ Crossman, LCSW, "The Etiology of a Social Epidemic."

⁹ The rebirthing scene was pieced together through segments of the videotape transcript published in numerous sources.

¹⁰ Crowder and Lowe, "Her Name was Candace."

¹¹ Peggy Lowe, *Rocky Mountain News*, "Therapist Denies Risking Candace's Life," April 20, 2001.

¹² Ibid.

¹³ Christopher Caldwell, *The Weekly Standard*, "Death by Therapy," May 28, 2001.

Additional sources include "Attachment Therapy: A Treatment without Empirical

Support" by Jean Mercer, published in *The Scientific Review of Mental Health Practice*, Winter 2002; "The Etiology of a Social Epidemic" by Pat Crossman, published by the *Skeptic Report*, September 2004 Evergreen Consultants' website attachmenttherapy.org; and the ATTACh (sic) website www.attach.org.

FIFTEEN

[1] John Marzulli, *New York Daily News*, "I'm No Hood, Rao's Slaying Suspect Says," January 3, 2004.

Additional sources include: court and police documents. The following articles were also used as source materials:

Steve Fishman, *New York Metro*, "Louie Lump Lump's Bad Night at Rao's" January 19, 2004.

Frank Pellegrino, *Rao's Cookbook* (New York: Random House, 1998).

Gerald Meyer, "Italian Harlem: America's Largest and Most Italian Little Italy," 2004, located at www.mibarrio.org/italian_harlem.htm.

SIXTEEN

[1] Jacinthia Jones, *Naples Daily News*, "Leaders Were Trying to Heal Boy Who Died During Prayer Service, Pastor Says," August 23, 2003.

[2] Ibid.

[3] Ibid.

[4] Ibid.

[5] Monica Davey, *Charlotte Observer*, "Exorcism Sparks Death Debate," August 29, 2003.

[6] Ibid.

[7] John Biemer and James Janega, *Chicago Tribune*, "Church 'Healing' Is Ruled Homicide," August 26, 2003.

[8] Jones, "Leaders Were Trying to Heal Boy."

SEVENTEEN

[1] *Holland Michigan Sentinel*, "Girl Missing 70 Days; Find Body," December 4, 1969.

[2] *San Jose Mercury News*, "Murder Hunt in San Mateo," December 3, 1969.

[3] Harry Maclean, *Once Upon a Time* (New York: HarperCollins, 1993), 219.

[4] American Psychological Association, *"Questions and Answers about Memories of Childhood Abuse,"* 1995. Available online at www.apa.org.

[5] Maclean, *Once Upon a Time*, 439.

EIGHTEEN

[1] Dick Lehr and Gerard O'Neill, *Black Mass: The True Story of an Unholy Alliance Between the FBI and the Irish Mob* (New York: Perennial 2000), 162–63.
[2] Ibid.
[3] Dick Lehr and Shelly Murphy, *Boston Globe*, "Agent, Mobster Forge a Pact on Old Southie Ties," July 19, 1998.
[4] Ibid.
[5] Lehr and O'Neill, *Black Mass*, 167–68.
[6] Lehr and O'Neill, *Black Mass*, 84–87.
[7] T. J. English, *Paddy Whacked: The Untold Story of the Irish American Gangster* (New York: Reagan Books, 2005), 414–22.
[8] Ibid.
[9] Shelley Murphy, *Boston Globe*, "Cases Disappear as FBI Looks Away," July 22, 1998.

NINETEEN

Sources instrumental to the writing of this chapter include court documents, trial transcripts, the defendants' police confessions, and interviews constructed by the authors. The following articles were also used as source material:

New York Times, "Judge Overruled on Limit in Pizza Delivery Murder," Metro News Brief, June 18, 1999, B4.

New York Times, "Second Gunman in Pizza Delivery Slayings Sentenced to Fifty-one Years," East Coast Late Edition, February 26, 2000, B4.

New York Times, "Victim's Kin Favor Sparing Killer's Life in Pizza Case," East Coast Late Edition, May 6, 1999, B5.

New York Times, "Confession Allowed in Trial on Killing of Pizza Deliverers," East Coast Late Edition, August 18, 1999, B5.

Andy Newman, *New York Times*, "Lawyers Question Dealine on Killer's Death," May 9, 1999.

John Cichowski, *The Record (Bergen County, NJ)*, "Jury Attempts to Enter the Mind of a Killer," November 27, 2002, A4.

John Chichowski, *The Record (Bergen County, NJ)*, "Addition to Painkillers Blamed for Pizza Delivery Ambush," November 19, 2002, A3.

John Chichowski, *The Record (Bergen County, NJ)*, "Peer Pressure Cited in Sussex Killings," December 7, 1999, L1.

TWENTY

[1] Melinda Henneberger, *New York Times*, "Israel Refuses to Extradite a Murder Suspect," October 1, 1997, A12.

[2] Steve Vogel and Barton Gellman, *Washington Post*, "Access to Crime Scene Sought," September 27, 1997, H1.

[3] Steve Vogel and Karl Vick, *Washington Post*, "One Suspect in MD Slaying Shuns Robbery Defense," October 3, 1997, D2.

[4] Ramos, *Washington Post*, "My Son, Alfredo Tello," April 14, 1999, B8.

[5] Laura Blumenfeld and Katherine Shaver, *Washington Post*, "Sheinbein Can't Be Extradited," February 26, 1999, A1.

[6] Ibid.

TWENTY-ONE

[1] Carl Semencic, *Pit Bulls and Tenacious Guard Dogs*, (Thomasson Grant & Howell, Charlottesville, VA 1991).

[2] *Good Morning America*, ABC News Broadcast February 8, 2001.

[3] Marianne Costantinou, *San Francisco Chronicle*, "Bad Company," June 10, 2001.

Additional sources include official court documents and trial transcripts.

TWENTY-TWO

[1] Associated Press, *New York Times*, "Club Survivor Recalls Dash Into Flames," April 7, 1990, p. 29.

[2] Ibid.

[3] Thomas P. Mulligan, *Fire Engineering*, "Happy Land Fire: Have We Learned the Lessons?", August 2001.

[4] Ralph Blumenthal, *New York Times*, "Death in Minutes," March 26, 1990, A1.

[5] Ed Magnuson, *Time*, "The Devil Made Him Do It," April 19, 1990.

[6] Blumenthal, "Death in Minutes," A1.

[7] James Barron, *New York Times*, "The Living Search the Faces of the Dead," March 26, 1990, A1.

[8] Evelyn Nieves, *New York Times*, "Bronx Man Is Guilty in Fire That Killed 87," August 20, 1991, A1.

[9] *New York Times*, "Seven Victims: Their Stories, Struggles and Dreams of Better Lives," March 29, 1990, B4.

[10] James Barron, *New York Times*, "Grief Deepens as Horror of the Disaster Sinks In," March 27, 1990, B3.

[11] Ralph Blumenthal, *New York Times*, "Portrait Emerges of Suspect in Social Club Blaze," March 27, 1990, A1.

[12] Robert Tomasson, *New York Times*, "Psychologist Calls Bronx Fire a Psychotic Episode," August 7, 1991, B3.

[13] Ibid.

[14] Evelyn Nieves, *New York Times*, "Refugee Found Guilty of Killing Eighty-Seven in Bronx Happy Land Fire," August 20, 1991, A1.

TWENTY-THREE

[1] *60 Minutes II*, CBS, "Under the Microscope", broadcast July 24, 2002.

[2] Belinda Luscombe, *Time*, "When the Evidence Lies," May 21, 2001.

[3] Mark Fuhrman, *Death and Justice: An Expose of Oklahoma's Death Row Machine*, (New York: HarperCollins, 2003), 140.

[4] Barry Scheck and Peter Neufeld, *New York Times*, "Junk Science, Junk Evidence," May 11, 2001, A35.

[5] Deborah Hastings, Associated Press, "Questionable Evidence Handling Haunts Oklahoma Man," October 6, 2004.

[6] Arnold Hamilton, *Dallas Morning News*, "Chemist's Errors Stir Fear: Were Innocent Executed?" October 22, 2001, A1.

[7] Luscombe, "When the Evidence Lies."

[8] Ibid.

[9] Bill Hewitt, et al., *People*, "Shadow of A Doubt, May 28, 2001.

Additional sources include court transcripts, documents, and personal interviews conducted by the authors.

TWENTY-FOUR

[1] *Chicago Tribune*, "Montreal Killer Excelled in Hunting," December 10, 1989, 26.

[2] Anthony Wilson-Smith, *Maclean's*, "A Stain That Will Not Fade," December 6, 1999.

[3] Judy Rebick, *CBC News*, "It Is About Violence Against Women," www.cbc.ca.

[4] Jane Caputi and Diana E. H. Russell, "Femicide" (an extended version of an article appearing in *Ms.* magazine, Sept./Oct. 1990), www.dianarussell.com.

[5] Les Sillars, *Newsmagazine*, "Feminism's 'Grotesque' Celebration," December 19, 1994.

6 See the article "Media Censors Extremist Protest against Media Censorship," by Peter Douglas Zohrab and posted on various websites, including www.mensactivism.org.

7 Christopher Daly, *Washington Post*, "Montreal Women's Slayer Identified," December 9, 1989, A1.

8 *Los Angeles Times*, "Montreal Looks within Itself in Wake of Mass Killing Violence."

9 Barry Brown, *Chicago Tribune*, "Canada Debates Woeful Gun Registry," December 20, 2002, 24.

TWENTY-FIVE

1 Steve Lopez, *Time*, "The Search for the Unicorn," September 29, 1997.

2 Steve Levy, *The Unicorn's Secret* (New York: Prentice Hall Press, 1988), 42.

3 Ibid., 70.

4 Ibid., 28.

5 Suzanne Sataline, *Christian Science Monitor*, "In Philadelphia, A Strange Return of the 1970s," October 17, 2002.

6 Levy, *The Unicorn's Secret*, 14.

7 Ibid., 244.

8 Ibid., 18.

9 Lopez, "The Search for the Unicorn."

10 Ibid.

11 Ibid.

12 Craig R. Whitney, *New York Times*, "France Grants Extradition in 1977 Killing," February 19, 1999, National Desk.

13 Levy, *The Unicorn's Secret*, 280.

14 Ibid., 282.

15 Ibid., 286.